THE EVERYTHING®
Get Ready
for Baby Book

Dear Reader,

When I had my first child, Lilly Eleni, in 1992, no one told me what a wonderful journey lay ahead. Sure, there were lots of birthing stories from other moms and unsolicited advice from complete strangers, many of whom asked to touch my stomach like I was a good-luck Buddha. But with all the advice and books out there on the topic of pregnancy, nothing seemed to directly address what was really happening: I was becoming part of a larger circle, a conduit through which the past, present, and future would converge into one beautiful little life.

Flash forward fourteen years, and I now literally see the fruits of my labors: two wonderfully talented daughters, Lilly and Madelyn, as well as two sweet children, Zoe and Simon, whom we adopted from China. Now the circle is complete—at least until they grow older and start expanding it themselves.

Our purpose as parents is to continue the legacy of life, to give more than what we alone can leave behind, to keep history moving forward with a new life and a renewed sense of hope for a brighter future. It's also to help our children learn how to love themselves and exceed even their own dreams of what is possible.

Of course, while babies are a gift of the future, they are also a continuance of the past. They contain in them a thousand specks of ancestors, from red, curly hair and freckles to deep brown eyes and black hair. They may have Daddy's eyes, but they will pass along all of our stories, traditions, and songs, building a bridge for all other family members to cross and transcend time.

The Everything® Get Ready for Baby Book, now in its second, updated edition, offers you hundreds of thought-provoking tips and guidance to help you on this new life journey as a creator of the future. It's filled with useful information, fun facts, and unusual ideas for celebrating your role in the "Great Circle of Life."

Enjoy this special time as you anticipate your baby's arrival!

Katina Z. Jones

Welcome to The EVERYTHING® Series!

These handy, accessible books give you all you need to tackle a difficult project, gain a new hobby, comprehend a fascinating topic, prepare for an exam, or even brush up on something you learned back in school but have since forgotten.

You can read an *Everything*® book from cover to cover or just pick out the information you want from our four useful boxes: e-questions, e-facts, e-alerts, e-ssentials. We give you everything you need to know on the subject, but throw in a lot of fun stuff along the way, too.

We now have more than 400 *Everything*® books in print, spanning such wide-ranging categories as weddings, pregnancy, cooking, music instruction, foreign language, crafts, pets, New Age, and so much more. When you're done reading them all, you can finally say you know *Everything*®!

E-QUESTION
Answers to common questions

E-FACT
Important snippets of information

E-ALERT!
Urgent warnings

E-SSENTIAL
Quick handy tips

Editorial

Director of Innovation: Paula Munier

Editorial Director: Laura M. Daly

Executive Editor, Series Books: Brielle K. Matson

Associate Copy Chief: Sheila Zwiebel

Acquisitions Editor: Lisa Laing

Associate Development Editor: Elizabeth Kassab

Production Editor: Casey Ebert

Production

Director of Manufacturing: Susan Beale

Production Project Manager: Michelle Roy Kelly

Prepress: Erick DaCosta, Matt LeBlanc

Design Manager: Heather Blank

Interior Layout: Heather Barrett, Brewster Brownville, Colleen Cunningham

Visit the entire Everything® Series at *www.everything.com*

THE EVERYTHING®

GET READY FOR BABY BOOK

2nd Edition

From preparing the nest and choosing a name
to playtime ideas and daycare—all you need
to prepare for your bundle of joy

Katina Z. Jones

Technical Review by Vincent Iannelli, M.D.

Avon, Massachusetts

For my own "circle of life": My parents (all four of them!); dear friend, Mary Lund; wonderful husband John; and our four beautiful children, Lilly Eleni, Madelyn Dela, Zoe Quan Yin, and Simon Fu Xing. Where would I be without all of you to keep things moving forward every time I take on another book project? You mean the world to me—and you make it all so worth it in the end.

An Everything® Series Book.
Everything® and everything.com® are registered trademarks of F+W Publications, Inc.

Published by Adams Media, an F+W Publications Company
57 Littlefield Street, Avon, MA 02322 U.S.A.
www.adamsmedia.com

ISBN-10: 1-59869-402-2
ISBN-13: 978-1-59869-402-4

Printed in the United States of America.

J   I   H   G   F   E   D   C   B   A

Library of Congress Cataloging-in-Publication Data
Jones, Katina Z.
The everything get ready for baby book / Katina Z. Jones, with Vincent Iannelli. – 2nd ed.
p.   cm.
ISBN-13: 978-1-59869-402-4 (pbk.)
ISBN-10: 1-59869-402-2 (pbk.)
1. Pregnancy—Popular works. 2. Childbirth–Popular works. I. Iannelli, Vincent. II. Title.
III. Title: Get ready for baby book.
RG525.J677 2007
618.2–dc22

2007015891

Please consult your doctor on any and all issues regarding your pregnancy. Although these may be good general pregnancy tips, every pregnancy is different, and each deserves the attention of a doctor or health care provider.

This publication is designed to provide accurate and authoritative information with regard to the subject matter covered. It is sold with the understanding that the publisher is not engaged in rendering legal, accounting, or other professional advice. If legal advice or other expert assistance is required, the services of a competent professional person should be sought.

—From a *Declaration of Principles* jointly adopted by a Committee of the
American Bar Association and a Committee of Publishers and Associations

Many of the designations used by manufacturers and sellers to distinguish their products are claimed as trademarks. Where those designations appear in this book and Adams Media was aware of a trademark claim, the designations have been printed with initial capital letters.

This book is available at quantity discounts for bulk purchases.
For information, please call 1-800-289-0963.

Contents

Acknowledgments

Special thanks to Dr. Vincent Iannelli; writer/researcher and new mom Emily Resmer; editor Kerry Smith of Adams Media; and, as always, Frank Weimann of The Literary Group International. Also, thanks to my good friends and fellow writers Kathy Baker and Elaine DeRosa, for their love and support in the last decade.

Top Ten Things Expectant Parents Need to Know

1. Your lives are about to change forever.

2. Your body is not yours alone anymore—you're sharing it with your baby.

3. Having a good birth plan in place early on will help you both deal with everything that will happen to you later.

4. Preparing your baby's "nest" will require more time and energy than you think.

5. Choosing baby's name can become quite a politically charged experience.

6. It's important to have good working relationships—and open communication—with both your obstetrician and baby's pediatrician.

7. Dad can—and definitely should—be very involved throughout the process of having and raising baby.

8. In the end, the baby really is the only one who knows when birth will actually happen.

9. You'll forget the pain of labor, but never the joy of the birth experience.

10. From this moment on, you'll find it hard to imagine you ever had a life before baby!

Introduction

▶ FROM THE MOMENT the pregnancy test showed a positive result, your mind became a whirlwind of thoughts and emotions: Will it be a boy or a girl—or twins? How will your body—and emotions—change over the next nine months? Will you be able to handle labor and delivery? Will you be able to be the kind of parent you always dreamed of being? When will you go back to work—or should you just stay home?

In the rush of excitement and anticipation surrounding the "big day," it's not uncommon to have all kinds of thoughts, hopes, dreams, and worries constantly swirling around in your head. But perhaps the most burning question during the seemingly long nine months you're given to prepare for the birth of your baby is this: How will you *ever* be ready for this entirely new experience?

You'll need to decide how you want to chronicle this experience—whom to tell and when to tell them. You'll choose how you want your birthing experience to be by creating a sensible birth plan. You'll want to pick out wall paint and baby furniture, as well as stock the changing table with the right supplies, blankets, and clothes—and, of course, you'll want to figure out how to take baby's "show" on the road without hassle, too! With such a multitude of details, it's easy to see how a tiny little person can create an overwhelming experience for all of the adults in its young life. If only your baby could know what a stir he or she is already causing!

Thankfully, you've got lots of time in the months ahead to prepare yourself, as well as the rest of your family, for the new limb on the family tree. Not only will you find time to take better care of yourself, you'll also discover that there's a wealth of information available to help support you through every step of this amazing process. You'll get tons of great advice from everyone in your close circle of family and friends—and maybe lots of unsolicited advice from complete strangers. Your medical or birthing team will also be there to support you as each month of your pregnancy progresses.

Over the next eight to nine months, as you get ready for your baby, you'll join forces with an exciting and informative network of people. Ideas will abound on everything from what to name your baby and what to expect during labor to how to decorate the nursery and how to bond with your baby.

This second edition of *The Everything® Get Ready for Baby Book* offers you the guidance, insight, and advice you'll need in the days and months to come—with lots of updated information and tips on everything from how to keep a pregnancy journal and take good care of yourself to bonding with your baby, daycare options, and choosing a pediatrician. Of course, there's also helpful information for dads, too!

Whether you're ever completely ready for this exciting change in your life, you'll appreciate the hundreds of tried-and-true answers to your most pressing questions as they unfold in the pages ahead. You'll learn how to prepare not just the baby's room, but also your mind and body, for this precious little life that's about to join yours forever. Even though right now it may seem like nine months is too long a wait, when D-day arrives and you're finally holding your baby in your arms, you'll be grateful for the months of preparation that made your transition to parenthood as seamless as possible.

So, take a nice, deep breath. Relax, prop up your feet, and know that now is definitely the time to get ready for baby—because later on, you'll be too tired to do anything else but love this incredible little being that's magically transformed your life!

Chapter 1

Your Baby's Future . . . and Past

Whether this is your first or fourth baby, or simply the baby you've always dreamed of having one day, the child you are carrying at this moment has now become yet another link between the past and the future of all mankind. This blessed child will carry forward many centuries of combined learning experiences, and will add to a vast universe of collective thought. That's quite an incredible birthright. And you thought your pregnancy was just about you!

You're Pregnant! Now What?

You feel a little out of sorts. Your period is more than a week late, and you've been extra sleepy, too. Perhaps you've even felt a little bit nauseous in the morning. "Could I be pregnant?" you wonder. So, you buy a home pregnancy test—and voila, the stick turns pink!

Maybe this is the happiest moment of your life, and this is the "good news" you've always wanted to receive. Or perhaps it has come at a time that is completely unexpected, and you're feeling the rush of a thousand worries. Either way, everything you thought you would feel at this moment is swirling around you in one moment of time that is changing your life forever: You are pregnant!

Tick, Tock . . . Set the Countdown Clock!

Once your doctor confirms your pregnancy, you'll likely receive a due date, and then the countdown begins. While nine months sounds like a long time to get ready for your baby's arrival, you'll be surprised at how quickly the time passes by. In just three trimesters, you'll have so many decisions to make—everything from what to name the baby and where to give birth to how, when, and with whom you'll share the baby. You might even need to make some decisions regarding how or when you'll return to work once the baby is born.

There are lots of practical concerns as well. For instance, where in your home will you make room for baby—and how exactly will you decorate the baby's room? How will you go about baby-proofing your home, and what changes will you and your husband or partner need to make to your lifestyle in order to be the best parents?

With all of these kinds of decisions to make, it's really a good thing that the pregnancy will last nine months—you'll definitely need every bit of that time to get ready!

Make a To-Do List

Once you settle down from your state of euphoria, it's time to start thinking about what you need to do next. Sit down, grab a pen, and start making a to-do list—chances are, once you start telling everyone the good news, you'll be too excited to stay focused on your next steps! To really stay on top of things, make several lists, including Appointments, Calls to Make, Budget Issues, Insurance Policy Review, and Parental Leave Policy Review. Some newly expectant moms even keep a journal with tabs for each of these items so that they can keep a running record of information throughout their pregnancies. This is one of the best ways to stay organized, and it's something you can carry with you to your doctor's office.

E-SSENTIAL

Be sure to schedule your first appointment with your obstetrician as soon as possible. That way, you can be sure to get a good start on prenatal vitamins—and you can get answers to any questions about what lies ahead in the months leading up to your baby's birth. Come prepared with your list, and take lots of notes.

Take Care of Baby

Naturally, you'll want to be sure that you're doing everything possible to ensure the healthy development of your baby—starting with making your first doctor's appointment. At (or even before) your first office visit, your doctor will likely tell you to start taking prenatal vitamins immediately. This you will do to help meet the extra nutritional requirements necessary for a healthy pregnancy; also, the folic acid in each vitamin will go a long way toward helping to prevent spina bifida. If you're taking any medications, ask your doctor which are safe to continue taking and which you'll need to either discontinue or modify until after baby's arrival. Don't make any assumptions, especially if this is your first-ever pregnancy.

Take Care of Yourself

One of the items on your to-do list should be a visit to the dentist. Many experts believe that gum disease, if left untreated, can lead to preterm labor—and a premature baby. Another way to take better care of yourself throughout the next nine months is to quit smoking, since cigarette smoke contains carcinogens that not only harm you, but also your unborn baby. While you're in a quitting mode, try to quit or at least limit caffeine and alcohol as well. On a healthier note, now is the time to be good to yourself—take more naps, improve your eating habits, and get some moderate exercise. After all, you're growing a new life—and you'll want to set the best examples possible later on for baby!

Start Spreadin' the News!

In the first few days after you learn that you're pregnant, you may be so excited about the news that you want to shout it from rooftops—or tell everyone you see. However, it's often best to wait at least until your pregnancy is confirmed by your doctor. Some expectant moms choose to wait even longer due to previous miscarriages or disappointments. Other moms-to-be choose not to reveal their pregnancies until after the third month simply out of superstition.

Since your doctor and the baby's father are the only other people on the planet besides you who know that you're pregnant in the early days of your first trimester, there's nothing wrong with basking in the glow of your wonderful little secret until you feel ready to announce your good news to the rest of the world. Maybe you can go away for the weekend to celebrate something only the two of you know—or perhaps you can spend some time together making a list of the people in your inner circle who you feel should be told the news in the next day, week, or month. Whatever you choose to do, remember that all of the decisions from this point on are for the two of you to make together—and that includes whom to tell and when to tell them. Savor each moment that you can—you'll be glad you did so later.

Fun Ways to Share the News

While you can always go the traditional route and simply call everyone on your speed dial to share the news of your impending arrival, it's also fun to share the news in more creative ways. For instance, you might invite all of the new grandparents to dinner at your house, then serve a baby-themed cake for dessert as a surprise. Or create a montage of your own baby photos and print them as a greeting card with a message like, "Guess whose baby . . . is having a baby!" Be creative, and you'll have a memorable keepsake of your early pregnancy days.

Revisiting Your Family Tree

As soon as you're ready to spread the news to your extended family, it's time to start thinking about your baby's connections to everyone on the family tree. If you don't already have your family history documented, now is a terrific time to start. It can be as simple as entering birth, marriage, and death data into a genealogy software program and printing up the results—or it can be as detailed and visually interesting as a family history scrapbook, complete with photos, letters, and any other items of historical significance.

E-SSENTIAL

Working on your family tree will not only provide you with important health information, it can also be a great way for you and your partner to learn even more about one another. You'll never have a better excuse to deep dive into each other's family history—and finally answer questions like, "Where'd you get those beautiful eyes?"

Recording your family history is not only an interesting way for you to pass some time in the early months of pregnancy; it's something that could also be of vital importance to your baby later in life. Keeping a "family archive" can be a meaningful way of sharing information with your child when he or she is older and becomes curious. As an added bonus, your child will be far ahead of the game for those family tree projects they'll face in elementary school—which, believe it or not, is just a few short years away from now!

Keeping Your Family History Alive

Where do you begin when you want to start compiling your family history? The best place to start is with your oldest living relatives. Ask them for any details, anecdotes, or stories that might provide a good starting point for your family history research. In most cases, they'll be thrilled you asked, and more than happy to help with your project.

Once you have some preliminary information, you can get moving on rounding up the more archival items such as:

- ✓ Letters from grandparents telling about their own childhoods, how they met, and what you and your husband were like as babies.
- ✓ Pictures from everyone in the family, including group shots from family reunions.
- ✓ Any mementos from great moments in the family history, including, for example, a baseball Grandpa caught at a major league baseball game or a celebrity photo autographed expressly for Grandma—or anything that other members in the family might like to preserve for future generations.
- ✓ A family tree that shows where the family came from and how they got to where they are now (include tombstone rubbings, if you can get them).
- ✓ Newspaper clippings relating to family "passages"—births, deaths, graduations, and so on.

Choosing a Display Method

After you've begun to collect some items of significance, you'll need to find a special place in which to keep these family memories archived for later reference. You may use a two-drawer file cabinet in the beginning, and then transfer the items to a more permanent scrapbook or memory box once you've determined how to best display all of the items. Or perhaps you'll want to scan in images of each item and burn them onto CDs for easy electronic reference. Whatever method you choose to display your family history, remember that this project is a work in progress—most likely, you'll be making updates or additions to your family history project for the rest of your life, passing it on to your children and hopefully on for generations to come.

Find Family Online

There are many genealogy sites on the Web. Many are dedicated to specific surnames. Use a search engine and keywords like "Smith family genealogy" to find one that may contain items of significance to you and your family. If you can't find one that pertains to your family surname, or aren't sure how or where to look for more options, consider joining a genealogy group at your local library to learn how to locate all of the information you'll need.

E-FACT

The National Archives (*www.archives.gov*) is an excellent government resource for beginning genealogists, with military, immigration/ naturalization, land, and census records dating back as far as 1790. There's even helpful information on how to get started on your search, as well as links to other helpful sites.

Create a Family Medical History Record

Now is also a good time to take a good look at your family's medical history. Let your doctor know as soon as you can about any medical conditions that could be hereditary. Create a family medical record that you can update and use in the future as well. Having a good running record of medical conditions and treatment will help both your obstetrician and pediatrician stay informed—and increase the quality of care your family receives both now and in the future. For instance, a family history of food allergies or an allergic type illness such as hay fever, eczema, or asthma, is important to know about so that you can avoid common allergens while you're pregnant or breastfeeding.

Babies in Your Family History

By now, you've probably heard lots of family stories about what life was like when you were a baby. But what about when your parents were young—or when their parents were little ones? Are there any family traditions you may be expected to carry on, such as using Grandma's christening gown, or an antique bassinette?

When you share the news about your baby's impending arrival, don't be surprised if your relatives start offering you lots of items long considered to be part of your family's history. Sometimes they'll offer to lend you actual pieces of furniture such as an antique crib or high chair, while other times it could be clothing or perhaps a baby ring that once belonged to your great-grandmother. Just be sure that any of these family heirlooms is actually safe to use with baby today. In cases where safety cannot be guaranteed, you can still find a way to include such items, even if it's only for decorative purposes.

Keeping Family Stories Alive

Of all traditions to pass from generation to generation, the most powerful are stories. Over the next nine months, many of your closest relatives—and perhaps some you never knew you had—may tell you fascinating details about your baby's heritage, and about the small things that, over many generations in your family, have come to mean so much more. That's a family treasure definitely worth passing on to a new generation. You may decide to capture these stories in print form by writing them down, or in audio form by creating mp3 files or podcasts, or simply by pasting photos with captions in a scrapbook. Whatever you do, remember that it's your responsibility to keep the stories moving forward into the future—in whatever way best suits you!

E-ALERT!

When considering which family traditions you most want to honor or keep, don't forget to include some from both sides of your family. If your family is a culturally or religiously blended one, it's important to blend the traditions as well—so try to take at least one from each.

A Place for Family Photos

It's easier than ever to preserve heirloom family portraits for future genera-tions (like the one growing inside you at this moment!). You can even use easy online tools like SnapFish (*www.snapfish.com*) to share photos in a slideshow format—narrated by you! You can even add photos you've taken of other fam-ily heirlooms, places of interest, and historic timelines that will add color, inter-est, and a larger perspective of your family's place in the world over time.

Still, if you prefer a lower-tech option, you can take old photos to a pho-tography studio for restoration. However you decide to preserve the images of your ancestors, remember that these are the faces you'll be looking after baby arrives—you'll want to find as many family resemblances as possible then!

Myriad Myths and Timeless Tips

When you first hear the news that you're pregnant, it's easy for you to get caught up in all of the things that will happen in the future. At times through-out the process, you might feel alone. But remember, you are one of millions of women who've given birth over thousands of years. In this way, you will benefit from all of the lessons learned over a continuum of time. It shouldn't come as a surprise, then, that so many of our best modern ideas regarding the comfort and safety of both mother and child have their roots in ancient belief systems.

E-ALERT!

Even today, giving birth in a chair may be the most comfortable posi-tion. Back in biblical times, women knelt or stood beside chairs for support during labor. Today, some women sit backward on a chair so that their partners can rub their backs and relieve some of the pain.

Early American Myths

In early American life, doulas (women helpers, not quite midwives, based on ancient Greek practices) were far more common than doctors. Physicians were called on only when there were problems with the birth or in high-risk situations. Typically, older, wiser women attended births, since they had the knowledge and hands-on experience. More and more women are using doulas today for the same reason; it's a comfort to have another woman in the room that has been through the experience.

Myths from Other Lands

Africans believed that a pregnant woman was holy and to be exalted for bringing a new life into the world. This belief is still prevalent in South African culture today, as in many other cultures (whose people bring gifts to the new mother in honor of her life-giving ability).

Europeans made the first obstetric birthing chair in the mid-1500s. It had a back, and the bottom could be removed to accommodate the birth. This design is similar to the birthing chair of today, although more Europeans use these uniquely designed chairs than do Americans. Birthing chairs are most prevalent in Scandinavia; these countries place a high value on a birthing mother's comfort.

E-FACT

The ancient Chinese relied on a birth calendar to predict the sex of their babies, and many expectant parents still use this method today. It's supposedly 90 percent accurate; however, it's for your entertainment and not to be entirely relied upon as an accurate predictor of your baby's sex.

Make Some New Traditions

Regardless of your ethnicity, heritage, or spirituality, there are some traditions you may want to create all on your own. For instance, if you haven't been as close as you would like to be with your parents, siblings, or other members of your family, perhaps the occasion of your pregnancy is a good opportunity to reconnect. Perhaps you can host Sunday dinners at your home, or take turns visiting and sharing family stories. If you live far away, it can be a good time to start e-mailing more often, sharing everything from how you're feeling to images from your most recent ultrasound.

Heal Family Rifts

Sometimes news of a pregnancy is just what's needed to bring estranged relatives back together, united in a common cause that's bigger than any disagreement or misunderstanding that might have gotten out of hand months or even years ago. Often, babies bring with them good news, peaceful feelings, and even hope for the future—all necessary ingredients for healing family troubles. Of course, for deeper troubles or more seriously dysfunctional family issues, it's best to consult with a counselor or clergy to work things out; healing major rifts is way too much expectation to put on a new baby.

Reach a New Understanding

Likewise, the prospect of a new baby may cause you to reexamine your relationship with your own parents, healing any issues you may have with them and bringing you to a new understanding of their motivations as parents when you were growing up. In other words, now that you're a parent-to-be, you might finally understand why your own parents said and did some of the things they did during your childhood, and that can take you to a very good place mentally and spiritually.

Open Yourself to the Possibilities

You're creating a whole new life on the planet, and that calls for you to open yourself up to fantastic new opportunities. Pregnancy does more than change your life. It also changes all of your important relationships, allowing you a new and special opportunity to heal, to grow, and to move forward toward a greater sense of unity and connection to all mankind. In this new phase of your life, you have become part of a world that is much bigger than you ever imagined. Welcome aboard!

Chapter 2

Journaling: Pregnancy in Your Own Words

Whether it's your first, second, or fifth baby, you have within you a unique being with a distinct personality and its own set of hopes and dreams. But what are your own hopes and dreams during your pregnancy? One of the blessings of pregnancy is that you have plenty of time to think, to dream, and to adjust to the idea of becoming a new mother. You've probably noticed a flood of emotions, worries, and thoughts about the impending birth; it may seem like you're spending too much time thinking about something that's still so far away.

A Million Little Thoughts

You can't stop thinking about this incredible little life inside of you: What will she be like? Will the baby look more like you or your partner? Will it be healthy? Questions like these will fill your mind from time to time during this nine-month odyssey.

The best part about having plenty of time before baby comes is that you also have plenty of time to record your thoughts. A few years from now, when your new baby enters toddlerhood, you can pull out these notes for those inquiring eyes asking you to "tell me about the day I was born"—a moment that most assuredly will come.

E-SSENTIAL

Whether you choose to create a pregnancy journal, time capsule, collage, book, or any other kind of memento to mark your baby's important passage into your lives, this keepsake will become a treasure for many years to come. It's worth the time and effort to make it as complete a history of "time before baby" as possible!

One Month

You're elated to discover you're pregnant! There's a lot for you to tell others in your life; for example, how you found out you were pregnant, when the baby is due, and some of the names you have thought about. It's all a big ball of emotions for you this month. In fact, there's so much to think about, you hardly know where to start. Of course, physically, you're probably feeling a little tired and possibly even queasy, since morning sickness begins right away with some women.

Tiny Developments

This month, baby is the tiniest little blip on an ultrasound machine, at this point, something that looks more like a jellybean than a baby. But so much is happening with baby, it's astounding. He has a head, a mouth, and eyes; arms and legs are beginning to develop; and a crude digestive system is already in place. Three-quarters of the way through this month, the baby's heart will begin beating, although it is still fairly tubelike rather than fully developed. Baby weighs less than an ounce now and isn't even an inch long. Here's what you might cover in your baby journal this month:

✓ What you were feeling this month
✓ How you told the baby's father the news
✓ When you told other people and who you told
✓ What the first trip to the doctor was like
✓ The best part of knowing you were pregnant

Two Months

You may be more tired now than you were during the first month, and the morning sickness could also be more pronounced. Then again, you could be having a great time and not have either of these problems. Every woman is different, and so is every pregnancy. Some women have to stop wearing their pre-pregnancy clothes at this point, although looser fitting garments can often go the distance.

E-ALERT!

You may develop cravings for unusual combinations of food and may avoid some foods that you previously enjoyed, since they make you nauseous. Emotionally, you might be worried about the baby's development—everything is so unknown at this point that it's hard for mothers-to-be to relax and enjoy this part of the process.

The Cutest Little Baby Face

What's happening with baby? Now baby's face is becoming a little more developed, as are buds for fingers and toes. Elbows and knees are beginning to show, too. All of the baby's major organs are present, though they are not fully developed. Baby is still less than an ounce in weight and is a little longer than an inch in length. But don't worry—greater growth spurts are only one month away! Here's what you might write about this month:

✓ What you were feeling this month
✓ Foods you could tolerate
✓ Foods you absolutely could not be anywhere near
✓ What the doctor said at this month's checkup

Three Months

Remember the emotional mood swings of premenstrual syndrome—the ones you thought were gone, at least for nine months? Well, you may have a relapse this month, as hormones rush through your body at warp speed. It might make you a little irritable, a little restless—and if you've had the other major discomforts of pregnancy, you might even be a little teary-eyed at times.

E-SSENTIAL

You should be feeling much better now. Though you may still be a little tired at times, the good news is, by the end of the third month, morning sickness should have subsided for you. However, trips to the bathroom will still be fairly frequent, as increased pressure on your bladder can make you need to go more often.

A More Human Form

Baby, of course, has graduated to a new classification: that of fetus. From this point on, more humanlike features begin to appear. Legs begin to kick, arms to flutter. Baby is having a great time, with plenty of room in which to begin moving around. Teeth and genitals have begun to form. At this point, it's definitely a girl or a boy—though your doctor may not be able to tell yet without an amniocentesis. One thing is for sure: The baby is comfy in its own tiny bubble inside you, and it continues to thrive and grow. Here are some thoughts on what to write in your journal this month:

✓ What you remember thinking as your body changed
✓ Things you said to your baby
✓ Special things you did for your baby this month (i.e., bought crib or baby clothes)
✓ What the doctor said at this month's checkup

Write a "Dear Baby" Letter

Write your baby a letter telling her what you looked forward to most after learning you were pregnant. Were you excited, nervous, or giddy? What kinds of thoughts ran through your mind? Whom did you think the baby would look most like? What other thoughts consumed you when you learned you had this precious little one growing inside you?

Here's an example of a letter you can write to baby:

Dear Baby,

You are my precious little one, even though you are not even born today. I feel such an incredible connection to you! When I first found out that I was carrying you, I was so happy—and so surprised. It wasn't always easy, though. I was sick a lot in the beginning, and you were a feisty little thing, twisting and turning so that we were never really sure which way was up. But you should know that you have been loved since the day you were created, and we promise to love you forever. Thank you for coming into our lives!

Love, Mommy

Four Months

Congratulations! You're now in the second trimester of your pregnancy. You're nearly halfway there, and yet there is the growing frustration that this is taking too long. Impatience may rule the day, but there is still much work to be done. If the morning sickness is truly gone, you should eat better this month and your weight should begin to reflect this. Also, you look every bit as pregnant as you feel. If you're taking your prenatal vitamins, your energy level may seem to pick up this month.

Movin' and Groovin'

What's happening with baby? Movement! Now you know you're really pregnant, because you can feel the tiny kicks the baby is making. This is called quickening, and it will get stronger over the next few weeks, although no one else will be able to detect it except you. Baby weighs about five ounces and can be as long as seven or eight inches. This month, you might write in your journal about:

✓ The first movements you felt with your baby
✓ How much better you were feeling this month
✓ What the doctor said at this month's checkup

Five Months

With all of the increasing pressure you're likely to be feeling this month, it's no wonder that you'll have bowel troubles. Thankfully, there isn't much other discomfort—and the things that are slightly uncomfortable can be easily dealt with (i.e., drink more water if you're constipated). This month is, at least for some women, the highlight of pregnancy: You're showing, but you're not so big that you're uncomfortable; you're glowing but not tired looking. It's a beautiful in-between time, so enjoy!

Rapid Growth Stage

What's happening with baby? In the fifth month, the baby develops the "vernix," a waxy white substance that will protect its tender skin; also, some hair follicles begin to fill. You will provide the necessary ingredients (vitamins and minerals) to nourish the baby from this point on, and baby will grow rapidly. In fact, he may reach the one-pound mark and will grow to between eight and ten inches—and that's a milestone worth mentioning in this month's journal entry, along with:

- ✓ What you were feeling this month
- ✓ Some interesting things that happened to both of you this month
- ✓ Stories your own mother shared with you about her pregnancy
- ✓ What the doctor said at this month's checkup

Six Months

About now, you're beginning to feel used to this pregnancy thing. You probably have your new, slightly larger wardrobe hanging in the closet and have gotten over the fact that you won't wear your favorite jeans again until sometime next year. You may experience some swelling in your legs, feet, or hands. Try to elevate your feet when you can; sleeping on your side with a pillow between your knees may become your new favorite sleeping position from now until delivery.

E-ALERT!

Watch out for stretch marks, which can begin to appear this month. As soon as you start seeing them, apply some cocoa butter or stretch mark cream (available at most drugstores) twice daily to avoid major wrinkles as your tummy expands. If you apply regularly, your skin should be able to retain its elasticity without any worries!

A Growing Person

This month, baby is becoming more of a person than ever, with eyes that open and close, ears that hear, and the ability to suck its thumb. This, of course, leads to hiccups, which you'll notice mostly by the rapid, repetitive movements you feel in your lower abdomen. At the end of this month, your precious cargo may be one and a half pounds and measure up to thirteen inches in length. Your journal entry may be longer this month as well, since you'll want to write about:

✓ What you were feeling this month
✓ Funny dreams you had this month
✓ New foods you ate
✓ Fun things you and baby did together this month
✓ What the doctor said at this month's checkup—and what the ultrasound showed

Moms in Dreamland

The baby was born, and as I held it in my arms, it began speaking to me.

I went to the doctor, and he told me that I wasn't really pregnant . . . that it was really just the flu.

The baby's head was coming out, and in this otherwise beautiful moment, I looked down in horror to see that it was not a baby at all, but a monster.

Are these experiences real? Of course not. Do they seem real to the pregnant woman who is dreaming them? You bet. Many an expectant mother has awakened in a cold sweat, shaking with fear and wondering just what made her dream such awful or strange things.

Strange, or even disturbing, dreams are not uncommon during pregnancy. In fact, nearly every mother will tell you she has had at least one dream that made her worry. Some tell their partners; others tell their doctors; but the response is likely to be the same: "Don't worry about it. It was only a dream." These words are easily said, but anxious mothers-to-be do not so easily heed them.

So, what do these dreams mean? Should they be totally ignored, or do they really have meaning? Actually, they do have a meaning, and it's usually tied to your fears or anxieties about the baby's welfare or your own ability to be a good mother. Mind you, this does not mean that you are a sick, paranoid individual or that you really aren't cut out for the mothering thing. What it does mean is that you may have some underlying fears or doubts about motherhood; the dreams may be nature's way of encouraging you to give these worries a little more thought.

E-QUESTION

What can you do to overcome any fears you are having?
Talk to other mothers and ask them to share their experiences with you. You might be surprised to find that they, too, worried about whether they might make good mothers. If you don't know any other moms to talk with (or that you feel comfortable enough to talk with), talk with your husband or obstetrician about your dreams. Getting to the heart of your fears as early as possible will help you conquer pregnancy nightmares and leave you feeling better about the new role you are about to take on.

Seven Months

Can it really be that you are now in the last trimester of your pregnancy? Sometimes an ultrasound will give you a clear picture of the baby's sex. Do you want to know, or do you want to be surprised? You and your partner should discuss things like this during the seventh month; it is hoped that you'll both agree on what you do and don't want to know at this stage of the pregnancy.

Someone's Listening . . .

As for baby, he or she is moving much more intensely than you know; baby's lungs are more developed, and much movement can be attributed to increased breathing capacity. Be careful what you say from this month on, since baby can hear sounds outside of its tiny bubble. The skin is red and appears wrinkled; it's just getting ready for deposits of baby fat to begin. Baby is now about fifteen inches long and can weigh nearly two full pounds. In this month's journal, celebrate entering your third trimester by writing about:

✔ What you were thinking or feeling this month
✔ Funny dreams you had
✔ Songs you listened to this month (babies do remember!)

✓ Exciting things the two of you did together
✓ What the doctor said at this month's checkup

E-FACT

If you've got leg cramps, try drinking more milk from this point on. Calcium can help prevent cramping. You should also exercise and stay off your feet as much as you can this month; kick your feet up (as far as you can!) and take a well-deserved break.

Eight Months

Do you find yourself gasping for air sometimes? It could be that the baby is taking up some of your breathing space. Check with your doctor if you're worried. Even though the baby could be in ideal birth position, the blessed event is still at least one month away. Your back may be feeling the strain, too, as the baby grows and presses against your spinal column. Try to get as many back rubs as you can from your partner; they can really help minimize your discomfort. Wind down your workload if possible so that you can get the rest you'll need for next month's "Big Event."

Presenting . . . Baby!

What's happening with baby? The baby should be in a "presenting" position now, with head down. Not all babies do this, however, and some who decide to stay breeched at this point have good reason for doing so (i.e., the cord is around its neck or a limb). Discuss with your doctor the pros and cons of turning a breech baby now; many doctors do not want to take the risk of hurting you or the baby and may recommend a Cesarean section to lessen the dangers. Baby can be sixteen to eighteen inches long and weigh about three and a half to five pounds. Here's what you might write about in this month's journal entry:

✓ What you were feeling this month
✓ Dreams you had this month that worried you or made you laugh

✓ Fun things you did together (i.e., baby showers, room preparation, etc.)
✓ Childbirth classes and how they went
✓ What the doctor said at this month's checkup

Nine Months

You have finally made it this far. Can it be that in a few short weeks you'll be holding in your arms the little one you've been talking to and dreaming about all this time? This final month of pregnancy will undoubtedly leave you breathless—perhaps both literally and figuratively!

Gearing Up for Birth

This is the final stage of growth for the baby; most of its major organs are fully developed by now, except for the brain, which is now experiencing its largest growth spurt. The skin is smooth, and the skull will be soft and flexible enough to mold its way down the birth canal when labor approaches. As the baby begins its descent into the pelvis in preparation for birth, it continues to gain weight and muscle strength. Your baby may be eighteen or more inches long and could weigh between five and a half and eight pounds. In your final month of rest and relaxation before baby's arrival, you might write about:

✓ What you were feeling as delivery day approached
✓ Things people said about baby in the last few days before the birth
✓ What you thought about most this month
✓ The doctor's predictions in the last few weeks

The "Big Day" and What Happened

This is the part of your journal that is guaranteed to be dog-eared and worn out before any other. Children are fascinated by the birth process and, more specifically, the way that they came into the world. Try to jot down your responses to these items as soon as you can, so as not to forget the tiny details of this momentous occasion. If you don't feel like writing, ask your partner to do it for you as the two of you talk it through.

- ✓ How you noticed labor was beginning
- ✓ How baby's father reacted to everything that happened
- ✓ What you were feeling and thinking as labor progressed (if you remember!)
- ✓ Where (and how) your baby was born (i.e., at home, in the hospital, or with a doula)
- ✓ Details you want baby to know about his or her birth
- ✓ How you told the world the news of your baby's birth

E-ALERT!

Don't forget to pack your journal with you for the trip to the hospital. When you're not resting or caring for your newborn, you might want to jot down a few thoughts—to capture them while they're still fresh. You might even consider bringing a small voice recorder so that you can dictate now and transcribe your notes later.

Remember, there are lots of ways to capture the emotional impact of the big day. While a journal is most accessible, you may also choose to chronicle the magical event of your child's birth with a video diary (vlog) or even an audio recording. It's all up to you!

Precious Moments

Every moment leading up to (and, truthfully, beyond) your baby's birth is precious. Years from now, you'll both enjoy talking about the events surrounding baby's grand entrance to the world. Even though you may not always feel like writing in your journal, you'll be thankful you did so. Once your child starts growing, and life brings you countless more memories, you'll find it more challenging than ever to remember all of the tiny details about baby's prebirth development. When it all becomes a faded memory in your mind, you'll take great comfort in knowing that the ink in your journal is as fresh as ever—and baby's memories are timelessly preserved.

Chapter 3

Taking Care for Two

Here's the scoop: Your body isn't yours alone anymore. Now you've got another person growing inside of you—and this tiny life depends on getting its nourishment and growth support from everything you put into your body, as well as from everything you do to keep it healthy and well. That's why diet and exercise are so critical. Your doctor will tell you exactly how much exercise you can (or should) do throughout your pregnancy, but you can start right now with healthier eating habits!

Healthy Eating During Pregnancy

Eating for one is sometimes challenging enough, with all of the tasty temptations currently offered. Here are some general guidelines that will help you make smart choices when it comes to your food intake.

Take the prenatal vitamins your doctor has prescribed. They contain all of the supplements you'll need during the pregnancy—and then some. Folic acid, now a mainstay in prenatal vitamins, has been shown to combat spina bifida, a disease affecting the baby's central nervous system.

However, don't rely solely on your prenatal vitamins to carry you through your entire pregnancy. You'll still need to eat well-balanced meals, since the vitamins are only a supplement to regular eating. Of course, many foods already contain the vitamins you need—the prenatal vitamins are simply extra protection for you and baby.

E-ALERT!

While fish can be full of nutrients, it can also have contaminants like mercury, which can affect baby's brain development and nervous system. FDA guidelines for pregnant and prepregnant women state that no more than twelve ounces of low-mercury fish should be consumed weekly. Limit high-mercury fish consumption to three six-ounce servings a month—and avoid highest mercury fish (king mackerel, shark, swordfish, and tilefish) completely.

Follow the Food Pyramid

Remember the food groups you learned about in grade school? Never have you needed them more than when your body is developing a healthy baby. Eat foods from each of the food groups every day. You'll need at least four servings of protein foods (such as meat, cheese, eggs, milk, beans, and tofu); at least one vitamin C–filled food (including fruits and vegetables such as grapefruit, oranges, mangoes, papaya, cantaloupe, strawberries, cabbage, cauliflower, and spinach); two or three green leafy vegetables or yellow fruits or vegetables (such as peaches, raw carrots, broccoli, lettuce, spinach, and yams); four to five servings per day of breads, cereals, and grains (such as whole wheat bread, rice, grain cereal, wheat germ, and pasta). Snack on grapes, apples, nuts, and granola when you can; these foods are easy to pack and carry with you even if you're on the road or at work.

E-FACT

Folic acid is an important ingredient in prenatal vitamins recommended by your doctor because it is proven to help prevent neural tube defects in babies. Most of these kinds of defects can be avoided by proper daily amounts of folate in the mother's diet. On their own, most women simply do not consume enough to make a positive difference.

Consume More Calories

You'll need to consume a lot more calories than you used to—but only the good kind, so lay off the chocolate mousse! Also, simply eating more food than you usually do is not going to cut it; your body needs to have calories with high value—not the empty calories found in cakes, cookies, and pies. You don't have to gain a lot of weight to have a baby, and many doctors prefer that you eat better and weigh less rather than eat everything in sight and weigh more. Most women gain between twenty-five and thirty pounds during pregnancy. You need only an additional 300 to 500 calories per day for the baby's development. (But see your doctor for advice concerning your own individual requirements, as you may have underlying issues or health problems that require different plans of action.)

E-QUESTION

What if eating seems to make me sick?
If you are experiencing lots of morning sickness to the extent that nothing seems to stay down, call your doctor to see whether there's a medical solution that will enable you to eat better. Antinausea medications, or simply trying smaller amounts of bland foods at different times of the day, may help.

Drink Plenty of Fluids

You'll need to keep your body hydrated and refreshed, especially with water and milk. Water will flush out any impurities in your system and keep you hydrated. This is particularly important in early pregnancy, when your body is at work cleansing its system in preparation for building a new life. Especially in the last trimester, your milk (or soymilk) intake should be three to four glasses per day; this helps your body build calcium levels sufficient for strengthening the baby's bones—with the added benefit of warding off those miserable leg cramps you might be getting. In fact, the leg cramps are nature's way of telling you to consume more calcium. (This also means you should limit the amount of caffeine you consume, since caffeine is notorious for depleting calcium levels in women.)

Have a Snack or Two . . . but Not Three

Small, healthy snacks such as wheat or saltine crackers, granola bars, cheese sticks, oatmeal cookies, raisins, or fruit can help keep your stomach focused on processing food versus creating more nauseating acids. It's a good idea to eat small, high-protein snacks throughout the day even when you're not pregnant, since this is a good way to curb hunger and avoid excess binging. If you eat too much at one time while you're pregnant, your stomach will have a more difficult time processing all that food at once, which could lead to diarrhea, nausea, or even vomiting. If it's still early in your pregnancy and you're having morning sickness, avoid the more acidic fruits, as they tend to upset the stomach.

E-ALERT!

If you're not getting enough iron, your doctor may put you on supplements. If this happens, be sure to take only what the doctor prescribes, since too much iron can damage a developing fetus.

Keep a Food Diary

To stay on top of how much and how well you're eating, one of the best things you can do is keep a food diary. This will not only help you record the number of calories you're consuming, it will also provide a clearer picture of your eating habits, helping you learn where you can improve in order to provide the best "room service" for your growing baby. Share your food diary with your health care provider at your monthly appointments, and ask for suggestions or ideas for improvement. For instance, your doctor may recommend restricting certain foods, such as peanuts and peanut butter, if food allergies run in your family. Even if you don't have a particular allergy, your baby might have inherited one from someone else on your family tree!

E-SSENTIAL

Your food selection is not as limited as you may think—you'll still have choices! For example, a Mexican meal consisting of refried beans (protein), avocados and salsa (fruit and vegetable), low-fat sour cream (protein), and flour tortillas (bread) offers a tasty and fairly nutritious meal.

Getting Enough Exercise

If you've been in great shape all of your life, and exercise regularly, you'll have no problem staying in shape throughout and even after your pregnancy. However, if you're like most people, you'll need to take extra care to manage your body during your pregnancy—and long after the baby's born. All pregnant women, especially those in high-risk pregnancies and those who were inactive prior to pregnancy, should speak with their physician about exercise options.

The best forms of exercise are the ones that work your entire body, like swimming, walking, or cycling (as long as you can do it comfortably). More extreme forms of exercise (like racquetball, marathon running, and gymnastics) should be avoided. Low-impact exercise that requires moderate exertion is probably best. Walking, swimming, dancing, and cycling seem to be comfortable and enjoyable activities for most pregnant women. Your best bet is to choose a form of exercise that's not only comfortable, but also less likely to injure either you or the baby.

Start Slowly, Warm Up, and Cool Down

When you embark on a new exercise regimen, start slowly and work up to a more intense workout. For example, if you're walking, start out with a slow fifteen-minute stroll and work up to a faster thirty- to forty-five-minute walk. Do warm-up stretches before exercising, and cool down when you're done. Remember to stay well hydrated before, during, and after exercise—especially since you'll need to keep both you and baby replenished.

E-FACT

A pair of good walking or running shoes is an exercise essential, especially due to the fluctuations in weight that will take place over the next several months of your pregnancy. Since your feet may grow in addition to your belly, you may need to purchase a size larger for better fit and comfort.

Why Exercise During Pregnancy?

Whether you're pregnant or not, exercise is one of the best things you can do for your physical and emotional health. The American College of Obstetricians and Gynecologists (ACOG) recommends pregnant women without health problems or pregnancy complications exercise moderately for thirty minutes or more on most, if not all, days of the week. Exercise helps keep the heart, bones, and mind healthy. Staying active also seems to give some special added paybacks for pregnant women.

Here are some really good reasons to get regular exercise during pregnancy:

- ✓ It can ease and prevent aches and pains of pregnancy including constipation, varicose veins, backaches, and exhaustion.
- ✓ Active women seem to be better prepared for labor and delivery and recover more quickly.
- ✓ Exercise may lower the risk of high blood pressure and diabetes during pregnancy.
- ✓ Fit women have an easier time getting back to a healthy weight after delivery.
- ✓ Regular exercise may improve sleep during pregnancy.
- ✓ Staying active can protect your emotional health. Pregnant women who exercise seem to have better self-esteem and a lower risk of depression and anxiety.

Exercise may not be safe for all pregnant women, but for most healthy moms-to-be who do not have any pregnancy-related problems, it's a safe and valuable habit. Regardless, your doctor or midwife will be able to suggest a fitness plan that's safe for you. Getting a doctor's advice is important for women who exercised before their pregnancy as well as for those who'd like to start a fitness routine.

General Guidelines for Healthy Workouts

According to ACOG, many different types of exercise can be safe for most pregnant women. They recommend following these guidelines when choosing a pregnancy exercise plan:

- ✓ Avoid activities in which you can get hit in the abdomen, such as kickboxing, soccer, basketball, or ice hockey.
- ✓ Steer clear of activities in which you can fall, such as horseback riding, downhill skiing, and gymnastics.
- ✓ Do not scuba dive during pregnancy. Scuba diving can create gas bubbles in your baby's blood that can cause many health problems.

E-ALERT!

Stop exercising and call your doctor as soon as possible if you experience dizziness, headache, chest pain, calf pain or swelling, abdominal pain, blurred vision, fluid leaking from the vagina, vaginal bleeding, decreased fetal movement, or contractions.

Remember to follow these tips to have safe and healthy workouts:

✓ When you exercise, start slowly, progress gradually, and cool down slowly.

✓ You should be able to talk while exercising. If not, you may be exercising too intensely.

✓ Take frequent breaks.

✓ Don't exercise on your back after the first trimester. This can put too much pressure on an important vein and limit blood flow to the baby.

✓ Avoid jerky, bouncing, and high-impact movements. Connective tissues stretch much more easily during pregnancy. So these types of movements put you at risk of joint injury.

✓ Don't exercise at high altitudes (more than 6,000 feet). It can prevent your baby from getting enough oxygen.

✓ Make sure you drink lots of fluids before, during, and after exercising.

✓ Do not work out in extreme heat or humidity.

✓ If you feel uncomfortable, short of breath, or tired, take a break and take it easier when you resume exercise.

Exercises for Labor and Delivery

Pelvic floor muscle exercises, or Kegel exercises, can help prepare your body for delivery. The pelvic floor muscles support the rectum, vagina, and urethra in the pelvis. Strengthening these muscles by doing Kegel exercises may help you have an easier birth. They will also help you avoid leaking urine during and after pregnancy.

Pelvic muscles are the same ones used to stop the flow of urine. Still, it can be hard to find the right muscles to squeeze. You can be sure you are exercising the right muscles if when you squeeze them you stop urinating. Or you can put a finger into the vagina and squeeze. If you feel pressure around the finger, you've found the pelvic floor muscles.

Kegel Exercises

Kegel exercises are easy to do. Simply tighten your pelvic floor muscles for five to ten seconds, then relax for five seconds. Repeat this exercise three times a day, ten to twenty times each repetition. You can do Kegel exercises standing, sitting, or lying down—and no one has to know about it but you.

Hormones and Emotions

One minute you're laughing hysterically . . . and the next, you're crying a river of tears. What is going on? you wonder (and your partner probably does, too). The sharp hormonal fluctuations necessary to help develop the baby are kicking your emotions all over the map—and the discomfort of an expanding belly just seems to add to the misery.

With all that's going on, it's important to realize that all of this will eventually pass. Mood swings are, quite thankfully, temporary as the body adjusts to its changes. Crying jags are normal, as are worries about your baby's development and the impending birth experience. Your partner should read some materials about changes in mood so that he better understands what's going on—and doesn't add to the stress by reacting emotionally.

Try to Minimize Stress

Since your body is already under a lot of stress, it only makes sense that your emotional life may be impacted as well. Still, you should do everything possible to minimize stress, since it can negatively impact your baby's development and potentially even cause a miscarriage.

Several studies show that there's a correlation between high stress levels or marital discord and postpartum depression. Keep it cool and you'll be thankful long after the baby's born! Also, increased stress hormones have been linked to preterm labor and low birth weight—more good reasons to take better care throughout your pregnancy.

There are many ways to help keep stress levels to a minimum. Practicing good stress-management techniques such as prayer, meditation, breathing and relaxation exercises, and even visualization, can help you achieve and maintain a sense of emotional equilibrium. Not only that, but they have the added bonus of being able to help you get through labor as well!

E-ALERT!

If you seem to feel more depressed than usual, ask your doctor if there's any medication you can take to help. Women who are more prone to depression in their prepregnancy lives can experience recurrence during and after pregnancy. Don't be afraid to speak up!

Getting Enough Rest

Sleep is the body's way of restoring energy, healing illness, and helping your body (and, of course, baby's body) to grow. In the beginning of your pregnancy, sleep is not likely to be a problem—unless getting too much of it gets in the way of your daily life or work activities. Those first few months in particular can be quite draining physically, as your baby requires lots of energy to grow.

But as your pregnancy progresses, and the baby begins to grow larger, your sleep cycle may be negatively impacted by the many twists and turns the baby takes—compounded by kicking at the least opportune moments! Maybe this is the baby's way of preparing you for the sleepless nights ahead, but it's just as likely that baby is simply trying to get comfortable himself. Most babies in utero sleep less than two hours at a time, and they do tend to stretch a bit in-between naps. If you are having a hard time sleeping through the night (at least eight to ten hours), you might consider taking smaller naps with baby throughout the day. This may help to coordinate your sleep schedules—a bonus after baby's born!

Change Positions

If it's difficult for you to sleep on your side, try using a full-body pillow and wrap one leg over it to help balance your spine. Or purchase a soft memory-foam mattress that better adjusts to your body's ever-changing shape. Be willing to keep trying different options until you find the one that works for you and helps you get the rest you need for the big job ahead.

Get Some Massages

Massage is known to help with sleep difficulties, since reducing the amount of stress on tired muscles can be key to achieving total relaxation. If you can't afford to visit a massage therapist on a regular basis, consider purchasing some massage oil and a few tension reducers (such as a ball or a wooden or plastic massage tool) and asking your partner to help you to relax better at bedtime.

E-SSENTIAL

Talk to your doctor or pregnancy support group if you're still having a difficult time getting comfortable when it's time for a rest. You will likely get lots of great suggestions to get the rest you need, and many you would never have thought of on your own.

Building a Support Network

It's true that you will need a support group in place to help you through this important transition in your life. Going through the birth experience alone can be a very difficult experience, both emotionally and physically. Of course, you'll have your partner and other family members or friends in your extensive support network, but who else might you include?

For starters, you should look for a good prenatal or birthing class. Ask family or friends for referrals; your doctor, midwife or doula may also know of some good classes you both might want to attend. Women's centers at your local hospital are another good resource, as many have excellent health libraries with a number of helpful books, DVDs, videos, or presentations to help you prepare for the big day.

Joining an "Expecting Group"

In addition to all of the great online parenting groups and resources out there, you may find it particularly helpful to join an online "expecting group." These support groups are typically comprised of other expectant parents either in your geographic area or with the same general due date as you. One of the benefits is that you can go through the entire pregnancy together—sharing tips, problems, solutions, and even emotional issues with one another in a private online forum. Just be sure that you don't divulge anything too personal, and take medically oriented advice back to your doctor before you consider trying it.

To join an expecting group, go to Google or Yahoo and use the "Groups" search feature with "expecting group" and your city or due date as keywords.

Making a Birth Plan

Working together on a written birth plan is a not only a good way to communicate with your doctor about how you would like your birthing experience to be, it can also be a great way for you and your partner to bond over the impending birth itself.

A birth plan lets your family, friends, and medical team know what you would most prefer in the birthing experience. Just remember, it may need to change. Your parents may have simply relied on doctors to tell them what to expect, but recent generations are generally more actively involved.

Of course, once you've finished writing the final version of your plan, don't forget to give it to your practitioner so that it can be included in your file. You might also pack an extra printout to pack in your suitcase for the trip to the hospital, since your doctor may not remember to bring it. If your practitioner isn't available on the day you go into labor, having that extra printout will be a godsend to the delivery expert on call, whom you may not have ever met before the blessed moment arrives.

What to Include in Your Birth Plan

You'll want to be as specific as possible when writing your birth plan. Here are some things you need to include:

- ✓ The method you've chosen for delivery (Lamaze, Bradley, Hypno-birthing, Grantly Dick-Read, or the LeBoyer Method)
- ✓ A section about where you intend to give birth (at home, in the hospital, or at a birthing center)
- ✓ Your plan for how you'd like to manage pain and monitoring of you and your baby
- ✓ Thoughts about the atmosphere you'd most appreciate (i.e., warm lights, soft music, or even a water birth)
- ✓ Who should be in attendance, and why you want them there (include a call list and try to limit the number of participants); note that insurance regulations or hospital rules may limit participants to your partner and possibly one other person
- ✓ Whether you'll allow any relatives to videotape or photograph the experience
- ✓ How soon you'd like to hold the baby after giving birth
- ✓ How you'd prefer to have emergency information presented to you

It May Change over Time

While it's great to have a written birth plan early on in your pregnancy, keep in mind that a lot may change over the next several months before baby's arrival. For one thing, you may well decide to change several elements in the plan based on what you've learned from your doctor, a close friend, or at a birthing class. Like any good plan, you'll need to build in some flexibility so that you can easily modify the plan later on without getting yourselves too far off track.

Screening and Diagnostic Tests

Each time you visit your obstetrician or practitioner, you'll be the gleeful recipient of a battery of tests and procedures—many of which involve some poking, prodding, and even a little pressure. None of these is cause for concern; it's all for the good of your baby's (and your own) health and well-being. There are several types of tests, and each will be given at the appropriate time during your pregnancy. Ideally, of course, you've had some testing (like Pap smears, tests for sexually transmitted diseases, and a complete blood profile) done before you got pregnant. That's the best way to ensure a healthy pregnancy—from the start!

Standard Tests

At the beginning and toward the end of your pregnancy, you may have some pelvic or internal exams. You'll have to produce urine specimens at each visit, and these will be tested for ketones (which may indicate that your body isn't processing food into energy like it should), protein levels (excessive amounts can mean you have toxemia), and glucose (high levels can mean gestational diabetes). In addition, a urine culture may be done the first month to be sure you're free of bacteria—or at anytime during the pregnancy when the doctor suspects a urinary tract infection.

E-ALERT!

If you have more serious problems in your family medical history, your doctor will likely recommend you see a genetic counselor to calculate baby's risk of developing a specific illness or condition. Some specialists also conduct tests on the fetus to inform parents of any potential problems. It's important to remember that all decisions are still your own to make.

Glucose Testing

If your urine tests show an elevation in glucose or sugar levels, you may have gestational diabetes. If that's what your doctor suspects, a GCT or glucose challenge test will be ordered, and an oral glucose tolerance test (GTT) will follow if the GCT results still show abnormalities. For the glucose challenge, you'll be told to load up on carbohydrates, then report to the doctor's office to drink a glucose solution. An hour later, you'll have some blood drawn and blood serum glucose levels will be checked. The GTT is a more extensive, three-hour fasting test and glucose challenge. If two or more glucose levels are elevated for the three-hour period, you may be diagnosed with gestational diabetes, and your pregnancy will be watched more closely.

Ultrasounds

Not only can an ultrasound give you a first glimpse of your baby, it also shows your doctor where the baby is located (ruling out ectopic or tubal pregnancy) and whether there's enough placenta to sustain the baby comfortably throughout the pregnancy. Your third-trimester ultrasounds will give the doctor a good idea of how large the baby is and whether you'll be able to deliver naturally. If the doctor wants more detail, she may order a level-two ultrasound that provides a more detailed analysis, or you may be sent to a specialist who will perform the test and report the results back to your obstetrician. It's important to remember that you have the right to ask as many questions about the procedure—and why it's being done—as you want. Sometimes just knowing why can be enough to help you relax.

E-FACT

There are two types of ultrasounds: Transabdominal, which scans over your abdomen, and transvaginal, in which the transducer is inserted into your vagina to produce ultrasonic images of your baby. Transabdominal scans are typically the norm for ultrasounds occurring after the first trimester.

Amniocentesis

Face it, the idea of having a needle inserted into your abdomen to extract some of the amniotic fluid that sustains your baby can do a number on your nerves. Still, having an amniocentesis in the second trimester can be one of the best ways to diagnose abnormalities in baby's chromosomes, and it's generally a quick outpatient procedure. Your doctor may order this test if you're older than thirty-five, have a family history of hereditary conditions, are Rh negative, or if there are other medical indications. But as an added bonus, you'll also be able to know whether your baby is a girl or a boy—so be sure to tell your doctor not to divulge if you want to be surprised!

Chorionic Villus Sampling (CVS)

If chromosomal abnormalities or genetic defects are suspected, or if there are specific genetic conditions your doctor is concerned about being passed on to baby, you may be scheduled for a chorionic villus sampling, or CVS. This test is typically performed in the first trimester (between weeks ten and twelve). Using the ultrasound machine, the doctor will insert a catheter into your placenta, either transcervically (via your cervix) or transabdominally (a needle injected into your abdomen). A small sample of tissue is then taken from placental tissue surrounding the baby. Material from this tissue is genetically identical to baby's, and can give the doctor a clearer picture of baby's general state of health.

Getting Ready

Now that you know what you need to do physically and emotionally to get ready for your baby's arrival, you should be finding more energy soon to start working on all of the other preparations. Now is the best time, for instance, to start giving some thought to potential baby names and making your house safe for your new little person.

Once more energy begins to kick in from those fantastic prenatal vitamins, you'll probably even feel motivated to tackle the more physically demanding projects, such as decorating baby's room and filling it with some furniture. Yes, if done properly, shopping and moving things around in baby's room *can* count as exercise!

Chapter 4

Preparing the Nest

In the animal world, the female prepares a special place for her young shortly before birth. In this "nest," she both gives birth and provides a safe haven for her young to rest and grow in. When it comes to your own baby's "nest," you and your partner now have the unique opportunity to create baby's first place in the world outside of the womb—a place to dream, to experience, and to grow.

Location

Since calm surroundings are so critical to a newborn's development, you should first give some serious thought to the location of the baby's room: Will it be on the same floor as your bedroom? If not, how will you monitor the room—with an audio or video monitor? Will the baby's room be near a busy, noisy street, or will it be facing a backyard where there is nothing but the sound of crickets?

Planning the best location for your baby's room is the starting point in designing the nursery. Once you have decided on the space, then you can begin filling the room with plush toys and cool designs. But there's one thing to remember: Baby may not actually sleep in his or her nursery for a few months. The American Academy of Pediatrics highly recommends that newborns and young infants sleep in their parents' room, at least until baby is older or can sleep through the night.

Decorating the Nursery

Creating just the right aura or atmosphere for your baby's room can be one of the most exhilarating things for you to do in preparation for the big event. It is, after all, one of the few things you actually have control over in this birthing odyssey.

E-ALERT!

Before you rush out to choose the décor, write down the room's dimensions; then, when you're at the baby furniture showroom, you'll have a clear idea of what pieces will fit. Such planning will save you infinite amounts of time—and heartache, if the motif you like doesn't fit well within the parameters of the room.

Choosing a particular décor depends on a few variables, such as how much you want to spend, how much space you have for the baby's room, and whether you know for certain if it's a boy or a girl. The best option is to go with something that's generic enough for both sexes; you can always add more gender-specific items after the birth, in addition to personalized items with baby's name printed on them. Good gender-neutral colors are greens, purples, yellows, and reds.

Traditional Themes

As far as motifs go, it may be wise to visit a few baby stores to see how all of the components look together for each particular style. This will also give you hands-on experience with the equipment; if you don't feel comfortable with a particular crib style, for example, you can look around to see if there is another style that coordinates well with your selected motif.

Here are a few of the more traditional themes:

- ✓ **Animals.** Kittens, puppies, teddy bears, and farm scenes are typical within this motif, as is a Noah's Ark theme. The only thing as sweet as your own baby is a baby animal, right? You could purchase everything from the sheet and comforter set to coordinating wall hangings and wallpaper—nearly every baby store out there has at least one baby animal set in stock.
- ✓ **Three-ring circus.** Clowns, lions, and tigers can fill baby's room with an exciting array of scenes; and you can create some of your own coordinating pieces—for example, fabric balloon wall hangings, crepe paper decorations for the window frame, and multicolor paint on pillars and trim.
- ✓ **Cartoon/TV characters.** Licensed characters such as Winnie the Pooh, Mickey Mouse, and Elmo from *Sesame Street* are just a few samples of what's already out there in the baby department. You can choose a character you feel sentimental about yourself or simply one that's appealing to you and your partner. The big advantage to choosing this type of theme is that there are literally hundreds of licensed products that you can purchase from a wide variety of sources—and you're not limited to the baby shops for this one.
- ✓ **Sports teams.** If you're a sports-driven family, you can decorate a room in the motif of your favorite team. You might have to order through a catalog to get some of the larger baby products (such as comforters and lamps) with the team logo on it. Smaller items

can usually be purchased in the team's gift shop or at department stores.

✓ **Pastels.** If you want to have a smooth, coordinated look that's a little on the conservative side, solid pastels in trendy shades such as sage, squash, salmon, and lavender might work best for you. This allows you tremendous flexibility in terms of coordinating items; you can mix and match pictures, lamps, wall hangings, and wallpaper borders in many different shades.

Nontraditional Themes

Okay, so maybe you don't want the off-the-shelf look of the tried-and-true traditional themes. Perhaps you are just an out-of-the-box thinker, or a cultural creative who is inspired by every home décor program. If you are a progressive thinker and want to approach the nursery from a more artistic perspective, here are a few ideas for you:

✓ **Suns, moons, and stars.** Although popular among adults for decorating, the solar or planetary motif is still fairly new for baby's room. Set your baby's room apart from the rest by painting clouds on the ceiling and hanging fabric moons and stars from it as well. Just be sure to hang them in such a way that they don't interfere with baby's immediate area; hanging them too close to the crib would be dangerous, since they could fall or be pulled by baby into the crib. Keep it safe, yet interesting.

✓ **Geometric shapes.** Geometric shapes work particularly well in black, red, and white, since many child-development specialists have recommended these contrasting colors for baby's early stimulation and brain development. Many mobiles are already sporting these colors, and there are plenty of baby toys in these shapes and colors, too. Paint the walls white, and then accentuate the windows and trim in black-and-white stripes with red highlights.

✓ **Blast from the past.** Decorate the room in rich, upbeat colors, then mix in antique furniture, family photos, and some heirloom pieces to create an atmosphere where the present meets the past.

✓ **Fairy tale/storybook.** Choose your favorite storybook or fairy tale, and decorate the room with elements that bring the story to life. For example, paint the room green and include the items detailed in the classic picture book, *Goodnight Moon*.

✓ **African safari.** Cultural themes are growing increasingly popular in the new global village. You don't have to be African American to appreciate African patterns or décor, such as a safari scene; likewise, you don't have to be British to enjoy a Victorian baby motif. Be creative—for instance, try using pastel shades to paint your "jungle."

✓ **Aquatic scene.** These gentle mammals, usually in sea-blue coordinating materials, offer such a cool, refreshing feeling to a baby's room. You'll feel like diving right in—and baby will find the cool colors comforting, too. Use sea-related wall hangings, such as seahorses, seashells, and waves, as a way of adding even more interest to the room.

✓ **Plain, bold colors.** Don't fill the entire room with bright color; instead, play colorful accessories against off-white or lightly colored walls. Mix and match accessory items such as large, flower-shaped floor lamps, pillows, and area rugs.

✓ **Denim.** Not usually associated with babies, denim can give you an interesting dimension from a design standpoint. For instance, think of mixing a denim crib sheet set with white lace trim and lace accessories. Basically anything you could match with your jeans would work in this baby's room, leaving you lots of options.

✓ **Bold fruits.** Mix strong wall colors like lime or watermelon with plaid, polka-dot or even floral fabric treatments.

✓ **Carousel.** Although the carousel is not exactly nontraditional, it can be enhanced by painting wall posts in pastel colors and by adding fabric with a spiral pattern to the wall to create a merry-go-round effect. You might even be able to find larger carousel music boxes to place around the room to create an even more realistic effect.

Whatever motif you choose, it's sure to be a special place for your baby to rest, play, and grow. If you choose a décor that's equally appropriate for babies and toddlers, you may not have to make any changes until your child enters middle school!

Baby Equipment: What You Need to Buy or Borrow

Now that you've got the baby's room decorated, you'll need to fill it with some major pieces of equipment. But with all of the equipment out there, it's hard to know what you absolutely need and what's optional. For instance, do you really need a room monitor, or is this something you can do without?

Bassinet/Cradle

Optional. Some parents feel better when the baby is sleeping closer to their bed; that's why bassinets or cradles work so well in the first few weeks after birth. On the downside, you may spend a lot of money for something the baby can stay in only a short period of time (only up until the third or fourth month). Also, the bassinet or cradle doesn't replace the crib by any means. A bassinet will also require a separate mattress, sheets, and bumper set that cannot be used in the crib.

Crib with Mattress

Required. Whatever your taste in crib furniture, try out the floor model to see how easily the side rail comes down. This is an important feature: Look for ease of use and safety for the baby. Most makes and models conform to U.S. standards and carry certification from the Juvenile Product Manufacturers Association (JPMA). In the crib itself, look for the following features: adjustable mattress heights, wheels, and the ability to convert to a toddler bed if you are not planning on having other children.

E-SSENTIAL

Mattresses for cribs come in foam or innerspring options. They need to fit the crib properly (check dimensions) and should be covered with a waterproof cover. Foam mattresses are lighter and easier to change than innerspring mattresses, and they tend to be more economical. You can also consider fitted sheets, a thin cotton or wool blanket, dust ruffle, and matching comforter.

Carriage Stroller

Required. Carriage strollers are beautiful but can be heavy. A carriage stroller is defined by the feature of allowing the baby to rest in a flat, horizontal position. Also, the seat is supported by a frame that moves on four wheels. Large, set wheels allow for a smoother ride, and are recommended for mothers planning on lots of walking activities. Carriages set on smaller, swiveling wheels are better suited for quick turns and shopping. Carriage or full-size strollers are recommended for at least the first six months, as the baby will need to fully recline. Carriage strollers also usually come with some sort of basket—either mesh or a wire rack—that is handy when hauling lots of extra items, or for shopping excursions. These strollers can weigh as much as twenty-five pounds, so consider how much you can lift in and out of your trunk before purchasing. Also consider how easily the carriage folds, some models have a one-hand fold option.

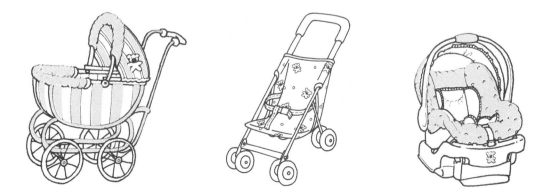

Umbrella Strollers

Optional. Umbrella strollers are designed for portability. They are completely compact, and fold into themselves for easy storage. These strollers do not typically recline to a flat position. However, they can weigh as little as seven pounds, and are great for traveling.

Car Seat

Required by law. You have the option of buying a car seat that is strictly for infants (rear-facing only, and handles an infant up to twenty pounds) or one that is for both infants and toddlers (can convert to front-facing once your child is twelve months old and weighs at least twenty pounds; most car seats hold infants or toddlers to forty-five pounds). Also, for baby, you can opt for a rear-facing infant-only seat that doubles as an infant carrier. If it's sheer economy you're going for, however, a combination infant/toddler car seat will probably do the trick.

E-ALERT!

You must have a car seat to take baby home from the hospital, and most states require that babies ride in approved car seats for travel by car or airplane. Remember, the back seat is always safest for your child, and you should never put your baby in the front seat of the car with a passenger-side air bag.

Changing Table or Changing Table/Dresser Combo

Optional—but extremely useful. Some new mothers prefer changing their babies on a table. You may, on the other hand, feel more comfortable changing baby on a floor mat. Either way, you're going to need a place to store baby's clothes and diaper paraphernalia; so decide which method will work best for you as soon as you can. In the worst-case scenario, if you choose later on not to use a changing table, you'll have a lovely piece of furniture that you can resell later.

Baby Carrier

Optional—but useful. These kangaroolike carriers strap around your waist and shoulders and hold baby close to your chest. They are very useful when baby is still too small for a stroller, and they are amazingly easy to tote baby around in. And dads can get that "bonding" feeling from carrying baby around.

Playpen or Porta-crib

Optional—but useful. Baby needs a safe place to play during the daytime, especially when you're busy. You can choose from either a stationary fold-up playpen or a porta-crib. The obvious advantage with the porta-crib is its ability to be transported to Grandma's or to any other visiting spot on baby's busy schedule—and some even function as a bassinet. Whichever style you choose, stock the playpen with soft, safe toys.

Rocker

Optional—but oh so nice. There's nothing in the world like soothing a crying baby by rocking it back to sleep. You can choose either the old-fashioned wooden high-back rocker or the more modern (and some say more comfortable) glider with ottoman variety.

Baby Monitor

Essential. For years, mothers and fathers have been able to raise children without these types of products. And let's face it; you should always be close enough to monitor the baby yourself. However, since you can't be everywhere at once, they really do come in handy. And if you have portable phones already, make sure the monitor is compatible.

Sling Carrier

Optional. Sling carriers keep baby in a good position for breastfeeding and are useful for carrying baby around the house with you as you go about your household duties. You can buy one of these used (and in good condition) at a consignment store, or you can purchase one new and resell it later. If you have a history of back trouble, skip this item.

Backpack

Optional. Some parents are more outdoorsy than others; if you like hiking in the park with baby, this is a terrific product for you. If, on the other hand, your major explorations take place in the mall, it's better to have a carrier that keeps baby in front of you. Backpacks are convenient; yet they can be a little dangerous since baby can't tell you if a branch is about to hit her face. Backpacks cannot be used with newborns.

High Chair

Required. Although you won't need it at first, since baby can't even hold his head up until about three months, you will eventually get lots of use out of your high chair. Baby does need to be confined during feeding time, and high chairs accomplish this most safely. Plus, there's a tray to protect you from wearing all of the food baby doesn't take a liking to. The tray will also serve as a "finger food" testing ground for baby.

Swing

Optional. This is a battery- or crank-powered ride that keeps baby in continuous motion. Some babies like them and some don't. You can't really know until you try; so it might be wise to take baby for a test drive. This is a great piece of equipment to borrow.

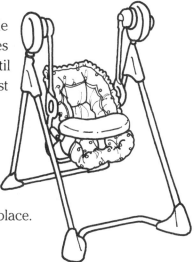

Baby Bouncer

Optional. Here, stick with the bouncer/saucer variety, which offers baby a view and mobility in all directions, yet spins and tilts in one place.

Jumper

Optional. A jumper hangs from a doorway and allows baby to swing, or push off the floor. Some children like them; others aren't the least bit interested. The safest ones are those with "bumper guards" that keep baby's body from making contact with the wall. This is another good item to borrow.

Booster Seat

Optional—but nice to have. After about six months, baby will be able to sit up. And a booster seat (with a safety belt, of course) would be especially nice for travel. They're perfect for restaurants—or when visiting relatives—that don't have their own high chairs.

Safety Gates

Required. Gates need to go at both ends of any staircase, as well as in rooms you don't want baby to have easy access to. You should equip your nest with gates, electric-socket covers, and other precautions to keep baby from doing himself harm. Safety precautions need to be taken care of as soon as baby is in any way mobile.

Diaper Pail

Required. No matter whether you use cloth or disposable diapers, you'll need something to put the dirty ones in. Deciding which to choose will depend on your choice of cloth or disposable.

Baby's Basic Layette

You've got the nursery decorated and the furniture and equipment all set up. Now, you're ready to start stocking baby's layette. Here, it's very helpful to think in terms of categories.

For Playtime

You'll need five or six undershirts (both full-snap and half-shirt varieties), nightgowns with pull strings at the bottom, and nonflammable sleepers/rompers with covered feet. You will also need at least four pair of socks or booties (depending on the climate), one sweater or light jacket, two to four waterproof diaper covers, and possibly one snowsuit (again, depending on the climate or the time of year).

For Bath Time

You'll need a plastic bathtub or tub liner, baby soap, baby shampoo, baby lotion, two to four bath towels (preferably with a hood) or receiving blankets, three to four washcloths, sterile cotton balls, and alcohol (to keep the umbilical cord area clean until it heals).

For Nap or Bedtime

You'll need a crib set (including a bumper pad, three to four fitted sheets, and two comforters), a bassinet sheet (if you're using a bassinet), waterproof crib liners, a light blanket or sheet for cover, a baby roll for propping baby to sleep on a particular side, and a music box or mobile.

E-ALERT!

Though your crib set may come with a comforter, it is best not to use it with a newborn for risk of SIDS (sudden infant death syndrome). Instead, use a thin blanket tucked in between the mattress and the crib that goes no higher than baby's chest. Then you can mount that beautiful comforter on the wall as a decorative wall hanging.

For Meal Time

You'll need four to six bottles (in both four- and eight-ounce sizes for water, breast milk, formula, or juice), a bottle brush, a bottle rack (for easy—and sterile—dishwasher cleaning), six to eight bibs and burping cloths, and, if nursing, at least two nursing bras, breast pads, and a breast pump (either manual or electric).

For Changing Time

You'll need to stock your changing table with four or five undershirts or stretchies, petroleum jelly, baby wipes (alcohol free and hypoallergenic), a thermometer, a nasal aspirator, a pair of baby nail scissors, cotton balls and swabs, washcloths, diaper rash ointment, and, of course, hundreds of diapers!

Shopping for Baby

One of the best parts of having a new baby is having a new excuse to shop. After all, there are so many things baby truly needs—and so many interesting and cute things that baby might want. The baby industry is booming, largely because manufacturers have finally figured out what motivates parents to buy for their babies: ego. They all want their babies to have the best and to look their best. But what do you really need to buy, and how much should you expect to spend at each stage of baby's development?

Buying clothes for a growing baby is a bit of a challenge at first; because none of the sizes printed on the label correspond to the baby's actual age. If the baby was large at birth (eight to nine pounds or more), you might have to skip the 0-to-3-months size right from the start in favor of the roomier size of 3-to-6-months.

What to Buy, and When to Buy It

One of the most perplexing things about buying things for baby is what to buy and when to buy it. Since you already have your layette in place by now, you should be okay for the first few weeks. What to buy after that time depends on the baby's growth spurts and your financial limitations. Not everyone can afford to buy brand-new clothes every few weeks, and not everyone can afford state-of-the-art baby toys. New or used, be sure you wash all clothing with a gentle laundry detergent before putting it on baby.

Buy It Gently Used

You would also do well to shop at consignment stores; most major cities have these, and they are well worth it, since they screen out the worn clothes in favor of the "gently used." There's also the added advantage of being able to return good-quality items for resale to get even more of your money's worth. You could spend $20 to $30 per month on clothes and slightly used toys, but you stand a chance of getting 20 percent back on a resale of the same item.

Toys for Baby's First Six Months

With so many different toys available you can't help but be confused about which toys go with which stage of your baby's development. Thankfully, most toys are clearly marked for different age groups right on their boxes. But to avoid having to read every box, here are some general guidelines about what's appropriate for each stage of baby's development.

One Month

Your newborn is still getting used to light, sound, voices, and general comfort. The best thing you can do at this stage is to provide all the comfort you can and don't expect much in the way of fun and excitement. Remember, the first month is about getting to know each other. This doesn't mean, however, that you shouldn't sing to baby; it simply means that you shouldn't expect much interaction from baby at this point. The crib mobile, some music, and perhaps a rattle or two will be all you'll need.

E-SSENTIAL

Buy toys or mobiles in sharply contrasting colors that are easier on a newborn baby's eyes—black, white, and red work best. The multicolored toys work best when babies are at least three months old and their eyes have had a chance to adjust to the world around them.

Two Months

Baby begins to wake up to the colors and sights around her—much to your delight! At this stage, you might still be using rattles, music, and maybe a stuffed animal in bright or contrasting colors. Babies at this stage become more responsive to sounds, too. So you could try toys that make simple noises—remember that babies might be frightened by loud noises.

Three Months

This is a fun stage because it's the time when your baby begins to notice more of the world around her. Babies start to notice other babies at three months and most can hold their heads up by now. Bouncing chairs, crib gyms, baby swings, and teething rattles can provide hours of fun, but so can a mirror strategically placed by the crib. Faces are most interesting to baby now—his own and, in particular, yours. Try some toys with faces, too.

Four Months

As soon as babies unclench their fists, they are ready for touching and feeling; they want to reach out and experience what things feel like. You could, at this stage, invest in some rattles and teething toys.

Five Months

Baby is better able to grasp with his or her hands this month and will appreciate toys like cups, balls, blocks, and spheres that spin on the end of a stroller or swing. There will be a lot of pounding going on, as baby's hands are truly his new favorite toy.

Six Months

The baby is now getting more and more mobile; this would be a good time to put baby in a saucer-bottom exerciser or a doorway jumper to see whether she likes such activities. Continue with cups, balls, stuffed animals, rattles, and nursery rhymes as well. Babies respond well to sounds that are alike, and for that reason, rhyming stories tend to be most popular with the younger set.

E-SSENTIAL

Don't forget to begin reading to your baby from conception on. Invest in a small library of books; often you can find great books at bargain prices at your local library book sales. At first, choose books with simple pictures and few words. Gradually work up to books with simple story lines—especially with rhymes or poetic language.

A Beautiful Reward

Getting the "nest" ready for your little one can be one of the most time-consuming, expensive, and exhausting times during your pregnancy. But it can also be the most rewarding for your family once the new baby comes home. Even though it may be weeks or months until baby actually moves into this special new room (complete with your loving touches), it should be very satisfying to know that you created a special place for your special new someone.

There's one more added benefit: Decorating and preparing your baby's room exactly as you have always dreamed it can go a long way toward bringing baby home to a stress-free environment. The more you can do to ease the stress of transition, the happier you—and baby—will be in those critical first months together. With a tall order like that, thank goodness you have a whole nine months to accomplish the nest of your dreams!

Chapter 5

Naming Your Baby

You're flipping through the pages of baby-name books, and visiting every baby-naming Web site on the Internet, but you still haven't a clue what to name baby. For some parents, all it takes is one glance at a name to know it's the perfect one. For others, it's a no-brainer; the first child simply *must* be named after a special person in the parents' lives. But if you're like most parents-to-be, you'll be so inundated with input from everyone else around you that it'll be hard to decide.

Where Do You Start?

You're about to welcome a new baby into your life, and this bundle of joy needs a name. Seems easy to figure out, right? Think back to your teens when you scribbled down dozens of great names and kept them on file for when you had a baby. If you've found your old list and still love those names, you've got a head start. If not, the search is on.

To get started, create a list of all the important factors you want to consider in choosing a name for your baby. Ask yourself the following questions:

- ✓ Is there someone you care about or admire—living or deceased—whom you want your baby to be named after?
- ✓ Are you only considering using names that begin with a particular letter of the alphabet?
- ✓ Is there a special place that you might consider using as a name?
- ✓ Is there something you're passionate about that would make a great name?
- ✓ If you're spiritual, would your prefer a name that reflects your religious heritage?
- ✓ Do you feel a strong enough affinity to your (or your partner's) family heritage to consider a more ethnic or culturally influenced name?
- ✓ How crucial is the meaning of a name in making your selection?

Thinking about your priorities and making note of these criteria will help you narrow your focus considerably.

Choices, Choices

What are expectant parents to do? From the hundreds of names available, how do you choose the one that's right for a little person you have yet to meet? One way to narrow down your choices is for each of you to keep a running list of name possibilities, and then compare your lists to see which ones are the same. Hopefully, there'll be at least one or two!

After you've created a list of your top ten favorites, practice saying each one out loud to hear how they sound. After all, your child will hear this name directed at him (or her) a thousand times over the next several years; it would be nice if the first, middle, and last names all seem to go together—and don't create open opportunities for teasing by other kids on the playground later on.

E-ALERT!

Don't make baby naming a free-for-all! To further narrow down your choices, you may want to ask key friends or relatives what they think. But do keep in mind that the more people you involve in the very personal business of naming your child, the more you open yourself up to hurt feelings later on.

Getting Dad Involved

Many times, amid the monthly obstetrician visits, the baby showers, and all the attention that's paid to the mother-to-be, the prospective father feels a little left out. But there are a few ways Dad can be even more involved in naming the new baby—of course, he'll want to have some choice in the matter!

If you're more concerned about equality, why not let Dad choose baby's first name while you choose the middle name, or vice versa? You can always switch this naming order with your next child! Using this method, you might wind up with some interesting name combinations—but you're sure to have less argument about your final decisions.

Make a Naming Date

To make name-choosing a fun opportunity for togetherness, consider going away together for a "baby naming" vacation. This way, you'll be away from all other outside influences—and you, Daddy, and baby can weigh some options without any pressure. Talk about why you like or dislike certain names, and then make a list of the possibilities that you can rank according to preference.

Family Ties: Junior, Senior, III, Etc.

Some folks believe that the highest honor you can bestow on another person is to name a newborn baby after him or her. Juniors, IIIs and IVs are done much more often with male babies, though many female children have either a first or middle name that comes with family history attached.

E-FACT

If you are absolutely set on successive naming, note that it is customary to use Jr. when the son is second in line, and Roman numerals for each successive child in the lineage. If baby is the fourth James Smith, his name would read James Smith IV.

Although this naming convention can create a great sense of pride for a family, it can also be a problem when Junior grows up. For one thing, it can create more red tape for government and credit-reporting agencies, as they often confuse one family member's name for another, sometimes with disastrous results. It can also result in mixed-up mail once Junior is out on his own. But more than that, you need to realize that you could be inadvertently forcing baby to live up to his father's accomplishments instead of allowing him an opportunity to develop his own identity in the world. So, choose carefully!

Names and Stereotypes

One thing that you have absolutely no control over when choosing a name for your baby is the associations that other people will have with it. Think about that bratty kid in your third-grade class named Henry who teased you relentlessly. Be honest: today, whenever you meet someone with the same name as a former tormentor, isn't there even the tiniest assumption that this new person has the same characteristics of the boy or girl who bugged you back then?

Similarly, some of the associations that people have with celebrity names can be just as damning—or complimentary, depending upon the name. In the late 1970s, many parents rushed to name their daughters Farrah. When you meet one of these young women today named Farrah, what's the first thing you think of?

And the nature-oriented names that hippie parents christened their kids with back in the 1960s through the mid-1970s today stand out. You may meet thirty-somethings named Cinnamon and Charity. Of course, you won't want to make a big deal out of their names, since they probably got this treatment all the time, but it will be the name itself that will initially corner your thoughts, and not the person behind the name. Of course, after you get to know the person a bit, the initial surprise about the person's name tends to fade into the background. But keep in mind that some people are never able to get past that name, and therefore make instant assumptions about a person.

But then again, a name doesn't have to belong to a celebrity or serve as a barometer of the social times to provide people with an image of the person behind the name. Some names just have a certain sound to them that helps paint a picture in our minds. Just try to imagine the different physical characteristics you would expect the following names to embody: Bertha, Wilbur, or Gladys.

Americans frequently say they shun stereotypes, but in the end, slapping a label—or in this case, a name—on images and characteristics before you get a chance to become familiar with the person is the brain's natural way to make sense of something new. Unfairly, certain names also help you to decide whether to spend the time to get to know more about that person.

Today, those big blue "hi-my-name-is" tags tell a whole lot more about you to the world than you really want. So take some time to think about what you'd like your child's name tag to convey to the world.

Exploring the Possibilities

When it comes to baby names, there are as many possibilities as there are people. One way to wade through the myriad choices is to break them into types or categories of names. For instance, you might create a list of all the old-fashioned names you can think of for both boys and girls, and then create another list that's just ethnic-sounding names you like. Breaking potential baby names into categories like this will help you narrow your choices down even further; if you can hone in on the type of names you like best, your list will instantly become much more manageable—and it'll be easier than ever to zero in on a final selection!

Use the Web as an idea-generator for baby names. Copy and paste the best options onto a list, and e-mail the list to your family and friends. Or, if you really want to have fun, conduct a name poll on your blog or Web site. Allow a space for visitors to post and vote on their own name choices.

Popular Names

Every year, it's a big news story: Which baby names are the most popular in America? If trends and popularity matter to you, or if you simply happen to like some of the names on the "Most Popular" list, go ahead and name your baby from this list. On the plus side, baby won't feel unusual or out-of-place with other children at school a few years down the road. But on the downside, nearly everyone else on the playground with the same name will turn their heads whenever a mom or dad calls out. According to 2006 Social Security Administration records, here are the ten most popular girls' names, in order of popularity:

- ✓ Emily
- ✓ Emma
- ✓ Madison
- ✓ Abigail
- ✓ Olivia
- ✓ Isabella
- ✓ Hannah
- ✓ Samantha
- ✓ Ava
- ✓ Ashley

The ten most popular boys' names, also in order of popularity, are:

- ✓ Jacob
- ✓ Michael
- ✓ Joshua
- ✓ Matthew
- ✓ Ethan
- ✓ Andrew
- ✓ Daniel
- ✓ Anthony
- ✓ Christopher
- ✓ Joseph

Old-Fashioned Names

If you're a bit nostalgic and you want a less-common name for your baby, you can always choose an old-fashioned name. Old-fashioned names are names that were in vogue 100 or so years ago, but are no longer in the top 100 popular names for babies. Not all of these names are stodgy; in fact, several may even be making a comeback. For girls, some lovely old-fashioned names include Lydia, Clara, Grace, Flora, Lilly, Harriet, Ella, Margaret, Nellie, and Martha. Boys' names that were popular more than a century ago include William, Thomas, Frank, Samuel, David, Herbert, Harold, Edward, Charles, and Henry—and, interestingly, many of these names are still classic choices for baby names.

Names off the Family Tree

If you don't have access to a good list of old-fashioned names, you may want to dust off your genealogy charts and choose a name from your own list of ancestors. Ask older relatives for stories about your ancestors, and then choose the name of one with whom you resonate. This is a very good way to preserve family legacies—and a great way to hear the amazing stories of your predecessors.

E-FACT

Generations of parents in every country and of every faith have their own superstitions about what they should or should not name a baby. For instance, a traditional Ashkenazi superstition dictates that if you name a baby after a living person, that person will instantly fall ill and die, since the baby literally took the name's energy; however, Sephardic Jews believe the opposite and honor living relatives by naming a child after them.

Celebrity Names

Celebrity names offer the most interesting, and often unique, name choices on the planet. If you choose a name that came from one of the "beautiful people," expect that your child will also garner lots of attention—though it may not always be the kind either of you would prefer. On the upside, any high-profile celebrity baby name will be instantly recognizable to anyone with a TV, an Internet connection, or a subscription to *People* magazine—so your child's name will be quite memorable. On the other hand, if the name is really unusual, like late musician Frank Zappa's children, Dweezil and Moon Unit, or actress Gwyneth Paltrow's daughter, Apple, you might be setting your child up for a life of endless teasing and intrusive questions from strangers. If you want to use a celebrity name, try to choose one that's a bit more appropriate, such as Britney, Carly, Dakota, or Dylan. If you have a favorite performer and would like to name your child after that celebrity, you might consider designating the middle name as your homage. For instance, singer Billy Joel and model Christie Brinkley named their daughter Alexa Ray Joel; her middle name was in honor of musician Ray Charles. Now as a young musician herself, she's living up to that legacy.

E-ALERT!

Don't choose names that are difficult to pronounce or spell—and don't get too hung up on a specific unusual name, since your child will likely prefer a more traditional variant later on. For a reality check, imagine your child using your name choice as a teenager or on a driver's license. Keep it real—and manageable!

Ethnic Names

Foreign or ethnic-sounding names are also becoming more recogniz-able than ever. If you want a name with the air of the exotic, or simply want to honor your ethnic heritage, an ethnic name might be just the right choice for you and baby. Here are just a few ethnic-sounding name options for girls:

- ✓ Sophia (Italy)
- ✓ Eleni (Greece)
- ✓ Matilda (Finland)
- ✓ Breana (Scotland)
- ✓ Annaliese (Germany)

Ethnic names for boys:

- ✓ Moses (Israel)
- ✓ Johann (Sweden)
- ✓ Anders (Denmark)
- ✓ Rashid (Turkey)
- ✓ Nicholas (Greece)

E-QUESTION

How can I find the name spellings of some of my ethnic relatives?
Check your family history records first. If you don't find what you're looking for there, visit *www.ellisisland.org* and look up your immigrant relatives. You might be very surprised by what you find on this site.

African American Names

If you're African American, you may want to choose a baby name that honors your heritage. For instance, naming your daughter Tanisha might indicate that she was born on a Monday, since the name is a derivative of an

African word meaning the first day of the week. For girls, names like Latoya, Latrice, Danelle, Lakeisha, and Moesha are popular. For boys, it's names like DeJohn, LeBron, Jamal, Antoine, and Isaiah that appear in the top 100 African American names list. Of course, if you are a follower of Islam, you might choose to name your male child Mohammed, Al-Jamal, or Abdul-Rahman. Muslim names for a female child include Khadeejah, Bashira, Mayesa, and Jasmin.

The use of apostrophes is also a growing African American trend in baby naming. Some popular African American names using apostrophes include Aa'Niyah, A'Lelia, Ce'Qwoia, D'Sean, D'Vonte, A'Driannah, Cha'Nice, Ka'Ren, Ky'Lee, Ma'Kayla, and Ty'Reese. Here, you can be as creative as you like— but take care not to come up with tease-inducing name combinations.

Choosing a Middle Name

Often unfairly relegated to last-minute thought, middle names offer a golden opportunity for "make-goods" with demanding family members who insist that you bestow upon your baby a name you simply don't like. But you can also use a middle name as a good differentiator between your "Joe Smith" and the thousands of others in the world. Choosing a unique middle name can really help set your child apart in a hurry!

A middle name also offers your child an opportunity to use a first initial and go by a middle name if the original first name is one that he particularly dislikes. Finally, a middle name can be a tiebreaker if you and your mate are deadlocked on two different first-name possibilities. Maybe the middle name should be called The Great Compromise!

E-FACT

In some cultures, middle names are not commonly used outside of royalty. However, in Mexico, the baby can have up to five middle names, and even takes the mother's surname! That's because Mexico is a matriarchal society, meaning lineage is recorded through the mother's ancestry versus the father's.

Putting Names Together

The true litmus test of whether you've chosen the right name for your child is to listen to how it all sounds together. For instance, do the first and last names sound melodious, or harsh? How do they sound when you add in the middle name? Listen for cadence and names that seem to roll off the tongue.

Also, while it might be tempting and even humorous to name your child "Dow Jones," "Holly Wood," or (gulp) "Frank N. Stein," consider how it will make your child feel later in life when people ask "Is that your real name?" or say, "You're making that up, right?" When it comes to names, you need to think as far down the road as possible in order to head off a lifetime of embarrassment for your child.

To Tell . . . or Not to Tell

Whether it's popular or old-fashioned, trendy or ethnic, when the two of you finally do choose a great-sounding name for your baby, the immediate temptation will be to share the news with everyone you know. But many couples are opting to keep their babies' names a secret until the child is actually born. The obvious downside to that is you will have people asking you the same question for months: "So, what's the baby's name going to be?" If you decide to keep the name a surprise, then you might do well to send out a preemptive e-mail that tells everyone in your close (and maybe even not-so-close) circle that you prefer not to be asked that particular question. Or, you might simply reply, "We haven't decided yet." That usually ends the conversation—and you should be able to keep your "secret name" under wraps until the baby's ready to be born.

E-SSENTIAL

Make guessing games about baby's name part of the whole "baby pool" that your coworkers are likely to start close to your due date. Offer a special prize to the person who correctly chooses baby's name, birth date, time, and weight! Your colleagues will enjoy the challenge!

Announcing . . . Baby!

Finally, now that you've chosen a name you both like, it's not too early to start planning for the baby announcements you'll be sending out in a few months. Of course, you can always call everyone immediately after baby's birth, or mail out more traditional-looking printed announcements. The choice is entirely up to you.

Even if you choose to work through your call list on the big day, you'll still want to jot down a little "script" to follow in order to maximize your time. In it, you'll include many of the same details you would on a printed birth announcement: name, birth date, and family members who welcome the child.

If you want to print up personalized birth announcements using your home computer and some preprinted paper, you can set up your template well ahead of baby's birth and fill in the details you already know: Baby's name, birth month and/or year, birthplace, and (of course) parents' and other family members such as grandparents or siblings. That way, when you're ready to head to the hospital for D-day, you'll have one more thing just about done in preparation for baby's world premiere.

Consider the Feelings of Family Members

When, how, and where to tell the world the name you choose for baby is a personal choice that's ultimately between the two of you. Your family has likely been supporting you emotionally throughout your life, as well as throughout your pregnancy, so show them lots of consideration when it

comes to announcing your baby's birth and name! Your parents and siblings should be the first to hear the good news, followed by extended family and friends. Don't let folks in your immediate circle be the last to know; you may regret it later—or worse yet, you may never be able to live it down.

Chapter 6

Baby Safety

Face it, when you're busy thinking about all of the wonderful days ahead in your new life as a parent, the idea that something terrible could happen is the farthest thought from your mind. And while it isn't necessarily healthy for you to go to the opposite extreme—to become consumed with horrible thoughts about your baby's welfare—it is definitely wise to prepare your house and everything in it for the inquisitive young mind about to enter. As far ahead as possible, you'll want to be sure your home is a safe, clean, and happy one for baby—and you!

From Baby's Perspective

Long before baby's arrival, you should start baby-proofing your house in order to make it the safest possible place for your child to live and grow. But how can you anticipate all of the potentially dangerous situations your little one can face in the obstacle course that is currently your home?

The best way to approach it, besides reading up on baby safety, is to bring it all down to your baby's perspective. That's right—lie down on your floor, and take a good look around as though you are your baby. Keep a notebook with you, and make note of anything that's hanging, broken, sharp, heavy, or made of glass. Review the list with your partner, and make sure you deal with each item on your list before the baby comes.

Five Common Injuries

For babies, the big, wide world can be an exciting place to explore. Unfortunately, it's also a daily opportunity for injury. According to Safe Kids Worldwide, an international information network focused on preventing accidental injury in children, most of the nearly 2 million pediatric emergency room visits are due to accidents that occurred at the child's home.

What are the five most common injuries? Falls (including things falling onto baby), accidental ingestion/poisoning, drowning (in tubs, swimming pools, or pails of water), burns, and suffocation (mostly in cribs or due to obstruction, i.e., small objects including pieces of food that choked baby).

Your Shopping List

Whether or not you need these items depends on the layout of your home and your childproofing decisions. For example, do you want to latch your kitchen cabinets, or rearrange the contents so that all hazardous and breakable items are stowed high out of reach, and store only child-safe items (pots and pans, Tupperware) in the lower cabinets? A basic baby-proofing shopping list should include:

- ✓ Outlet covers or caps
- ✓ Gates
- ✓ Drawer and cabinet latches
- ✓ Toilet lock
- ✓ Foam strips or corners for table edges
- ✓ Window guards
- ✓ Window latches
- ✓ Oven lock
- ✓ Doorknob covers
- ✓ Stove knob covers

So, You Think It's Safe . . .

When you think you've thought of everything, watch your child to see what hazards she discovers. Is she fascinated by the oven door? You may have to strap it closed. Does she like to throw toys in the toilet? You may want a toilet lock, but since these are difficult for older siblings or uninitiated guests to operate, you may prefer just to keep the bathroom door shut. Is she climbing the bookshelves? Make sure they are bolted to the wall. Some babies simply require more childproofing than others. You'll soon discover what kind of adventurer lives at your house. Here is a list of the top ten household dangers:

10. Poisonous plants

9. Venetian blind cords

8. Electrical cords

7. Electrical outlets

6. Stoves, heaters, and other hot appliances

5. Poisonous household products

4. Medicine

3. Water (even water in a bucket used to mop the floor is a hazard)

2. Coins or other small objects (choking hazard)

1. Stairs

Poisonous Plants

The following plants can cause **SEVERE POISONING** (this is not a complete listing):

Avocado leaves	Larkspur
Azalea	Mistletoe
English ivy	Nightshade
Foxglove	Oleander
Hemlock	Rhododendron
Hydrangea	Sweet pea

The following plants cause uncomfortable, though usually **NOT LIFE-THREATENING**, reactions (this is not a complete listing):

Calla lily	Philodendron
Daffodil bulb	Poinsettia
Dieffenbachia	Tomato leaves
Holly	Wisteria
Hyacinth	Yellow jasmine
Iris	Yew
Laurel	

First Aid

As the parent of a small child, you'll be administering a lot of first aid—particularly once your child is getting around on her own. You can minimize hazards by childproofing, but your baby will still get her fair share of "owies" in her first year.

Once your baby becomes mobile, you'll be patching up scrapes and bumps, pulling out splinters, and administering other forms of first aid. You'll need:

- ✔ First aid manual
- ✔ Telephone number for Poison Control
- ✔ Sterile gauze
- ✔ Steri-Strips or butterfly bandages
- ✔ Soap
- ✔ Ipecac syrup
- ✔ Activated charcoal
- ✔ Adhesive strip bandages (Band-Aids)
- ✔ Adhesive tape
- ✔ Antiseptic wipes
- ✔ Elastic bandage
- ✔ Papain (this natural meat tenderizer soothes bee stings)
- ✔ Antibiotic ointment such as Bacitracin
- ✔ Hydrocortisone cream
- ✔ Tweezers
- ✔ Old credit card (to scrape bee stings)
- ✔ Calamine lotion
- ✔ Cold packs (instant, or keep one in the freezer; use a bag of frozen vegetables in a pinch)
- ✔ Cotton balls
- ✔ Scissors

Common Injuries

Following are some common childhood injuries and ways to treat them.

Burns

Soak the burned area in cool water for at least twenty minutes or until the pain fades. You can hold the burn under cold running water or put ice and cold water in a bowl. Don't use ice alone; it can increase the damage to the skin. Do not put butter or other greases on a burn—they'll trap the heat and make it worse. And don't pop any blisters that develop; just cover them with a bandage. Redness and a slight swelling are signs of a first-degree burn (the least serious); blistering and significant swelling indicate a second-degree burn; areas that seem white or charred indicate a third-degree burn. If you suspect a second or third degree burn, see a doctor immediately.

Poison Ingestion

Take away the poisonous substance, if your child is still holding any, and remove any left in his mouth with your fingers. Keep anything that you remove for later analysis. Check for severe throat irritation, drooling, breathing problems, sleepiness, or convulsions. If you see any of these symptoms, call an ambulance. If not, call your local poison control center. They may tell you to induce vomiting by administering ipecac. Do not give your baby ipecac without checking with poison control; some poisons can do more damage when vomiting is induced. Or you may be told to neutralize the poison with a glass of milk or activated charcoal. (This processed charcoal is available in natural food stores and some pharmacies. It binds to most poisons and allows them to be excreted harmlessly. A standard dosage is eight to ten times the amount of poison ingested, mixed with water to administer. There are no known risks to taking it, but check with poison control in case it does not bind with the type of poison you're dealing with.)

Tick Bite

The faster you get the tick off, the less likely your baby is to get a tick-borne disease. Clean the area with alcohol if it's available, water if it's not. If you have nothing to clean with, skip this step. Pull the tick straight up from the skin using your fingers (tweezers are more likely to break the tick, leaving part embedded). Save the tick in case you need to bring it to a doctor. Mark the bite with a pen, and watch the area for a few days for a bull's-eye-shaped rash. This rash indicates Lyme disease, for which your baby will be treated with antibiotics. You should also watch for signs of Rocky Mountain Spotted Fever (rash on hands and soles of feet, fever).

Sand in the Eye

Try to keep your baby from rubbing his eye, but otherwise do nothing; tears will usually wash out the sand. If not, you can help them by washing the eye with a saline solution. If nothing you do seems to work, call your doctor.

Bee Sting

If the stinger is visible, try to remove it by scraping across the skin with a credit card. Do not squeeze it. Wash the area with soap and water and apply an ice pack to reduce swelling. You can also counteract some of the effects of the venom by dabbing the area with diluted ammonia (the kind you use for cleaning), sprinkling it with meat tenderizer, or spreading it with a paste of baking soda and water. If your baby has a severe reaction—swelling that extends far beyond the site of the sting, a rapid heartbeat, clammy skin, hives, or trouble breathing, call 911.

Sunburn

If you're like most people, your first reaction to your baby's sunburn will be guilt. "Oh, how can I have forgotten to put lotion on? Why did we stay at the park all afternoon? Why didn't I go home when I realized I forgot his hat?" After you're done beating yourself up about this, give your baby a bath in cool water or soak some washcloths in water and lay them over the burned area. After he's dry, spread aloe (100 percent) on the burned area.

Or soak your baby in a lukewarm bath with either a quarter cup of baking soda or a cup of comfrey tea (comfrey reduces swelling). Give him some ibuprofen or aspirin (if there are no fever or cold symptoms).
If the sunburn blisters, if your baby gets a fever or chills,
or if he seems very sick, call the doctor.

Cuts

Stop the bleeding by applying pressure directly to the cut. If the cut "smiles" (the edges gap apart farther in the middle than on the ends), is deep, or may have dirt or glass stuck inside, see a doctor. Wash it thoroughly with soap and water, apply an antibiotic ointment, and put on a Band-Aid. If the cut isn't particularly deep or long, it will probably stay closed on its own. Or you can bring the edges together and fasten with a butterfly bandage or Steri-Strip before covering it with a regular Band-Aid.

Splinters

Wash the area with soap and water. If the splinter protrudes, stick a piece of tape over it and pull the tape off—the splinter may come off with the tape. Still stuck? Move on to the tweezers. If the splinter is embedded, soak the area for ten minutes, wipe with an antiseptic, then numb the skin with ice or a local anesthetic intended for teething—like baby Orajel or Anbesol. Sterilize a sewing needle by holding it in a flame for a few seconds (make sure to wipe off any carbon on the needle) or dipping it in alcohol. Then gently, using the tip of the needle, try to tease the splinter out. If it's still stuck, try again after your baby's bath. Don't poke around for more than five minutes; it's unlikely you'll remove the splinter and you may damage your baby's skin. You can also try gently rubbing the skin over the splinter with a pumice stone—if you take away a thin layer of skin, the splinter may be easier to grab. Call your doctor if it is deeply embedded, is glass or metal and you can't get it all out, or the area becomes infected.

Bug Bites

These are not a major deal for most babies, and usually look worse than they feel. If your baby seems itchy, put ice, cortisone cream, or a paste of baking soda and water on the bite. If the itching doesn't seem to stop, or the area keeps swelling, call your doctor, who may prescribe an antihistamine.

Scrapes

Run cold water over the scrape and wash it with soap. Pat it dry with a clean cloth, dab with antiseptic cream, and bandage. Go to the doctor if the scrape is deep, bleeding heavily, embedded with gravel or dirt, or if later you see increasing redness or pus.

Choking

First give your baby a chance to cough and clear his throat himself. If he can't breathe, dial 911 then place him face down on your arm or lap so that his head is lower than his torso. Support his head and neck. Using the heel of your hand, give five quick thrusts between the shoulder blades. If he's still not breathing, lay him on the floor on his back and, using two fingers, press quickly along the breastbone five times. Keep repeating these two moves. *Do not* use the Heimlich maneuver; a baby's bones and organs are too fragile.

The ER

Sometimes, a kiss, a Band-Aid, and an ice pack aren't enough. The following injuries may require immediate medical attention:

✓ Head injuries, which may include some of the following:
  - Bleeding that won't stop after ten minutes of direct pressure
  - Crying for more than ten minutes
  - A severe fall (down a stairway, for example)
  - Seizures
  - Unconsciousness, no matter how briefly
  - Vomiting more than twice
  - Pupils unequal in size
  - Crossed eyes
✓ Cuts that are very deep or present a "smile" (the skin edges gap apart farther in the middle than on the ends)
✓ Burns that have blistering, significant swelling, white patches, or charring

Home, Sweet—and Safe

A good starting point for most parents-to-be is the electrical system in your home. Your first mission is to cover all outlets with safety covers or plugs, and fasten latches to cabinets with dangerous items inside. While you're at it, put a new battery inside your smoke and carbon monoxide detectors. Oh, and you might want to consider securing toilet lids, too, as many young children are fascinated with putting objects inside it just to see what will happen!

Don't leave window-blind cords hanging for baby's hands to grab onto; instead, wind them up or buy a product that does it for you. Also, be sure to install window guards, especially if you live in a two-story or high-rise building.

Safer Mobility

Once baby starts becoming mobile, you'll be surprised how quickly grabbing will begin. You might also use door stops to protect your baby from slamming doors, wall anchors to secure TVs and heavy pieces of furniture, padding for sharp edges on furniture, and stair rails with securely positioned foam pieces.

Pool and Water Safety

If you live near a pond or a swimming pool, make sure you keep baby as far away from the water as possible—except if you are swimming together in a shallow pool. If that's the case, then you should definitely use inflatable wings or a life jacket for baby. And never leave a baby unattended in the bathtub—not even for a second!

Keep Poison Away

Lock all harmful chemicals (cleaning solutions, medicines and even some pet supplies) in a baby-proof cabinet—preferably one that's up high and out of baby's immediate reach. If baby should get into something potentially dangerous, contact your local poison control center immediately, even if you aren't sure baby actually consumed anything. Better to be safe than sorry—and better yet to avoid potential dangers altogether by keeping as much as you can out of baby's reach.

Lead and Asbestos Dangers

If your home was built before 1978, you should have it checked for lead and asbestos. If you detect either substance, contact a professional to help you deal with the problem safely and effectively—and legally. Avoid sanding old paint altogether from the moment you decide to get pregnant, and don't let anyone else do it either, even when you're not in the house.

A Costly Proposition

Although a lead-free house is optimal, it can cost as much as $30,000 to de-lead an old house—and the home's architectural detail could be destroyed in the process. If you can't afford to do it and don't want to move, a compromise solution is checking frequently to make sure that paint is not peeling (especially on windowsills and ceilings) and remind your pediatrician to have your child's lead level checked routinely.

Asbestos removal can be pricey, but is far less so than lead removal. Asbestos can also be encapsulated for a fraction of the cost of removing it, and that's why many people feel that this alternate option is safe enough for unused, unfinished basements. The choice ultimately depends more on your budget.

Equipment Safety

Products such as cribs and high chairs should most definitely be selected with safety in mind. Parents and caretakers of babies and young children need to be aware of the many potential hazards in their environment—hazards that can occur through the misuse of products or through the use of products that have not been well designed.

Ask yourself these questions: Does your equipment have basic safety features? If not, can missing or unsafe parts be easily replaced with the proper parts? Can breaks or cracks be repaired to give more protection? Can you fix the older equipment without creating a "new" hazard? If you answer no to any of these questions, the item is beyond help and should be discarded. If the item can be repaired, repair it before even thinking of using it.

Car Seat

For birth to at least one year and twenty pounds, baby should only ride in a properly installed rear-facing seat that will better protect his or her head, neck, and body from potential impact. The seat should be secured to the vehicle by the safety belts or by the LATCH system (which stands for Lower Anchors and Tethers for Children). If you're not sure whether your car seat is the right one, consult the owner's manual of your car for recommendations and maximum seat dimensions. Also, be sure to thoroughly read the owner's manual that came with the car seat, as it should explain in precise detail how to use the seat properly. For instance, your child's car seat should recline at approximately a forty-five-degree angle. Harness straps/slots should be harnessed at or below shoulder level (lower set of slots for most convertible child safety seats), and should be snug on baby. Harness the clip at armpit level. Never use the baby's car seat in a front seat where an air bag is present.

E-SSENTIAL

You should keep your eyes and ears open for product recall information on car seats, as they tend to happen somewhat frequently. Also, it's a good idea to have your local auto service shop inspect your car seat from time to time, just to make sure it's installed and working properly.

Back Carrier

The carrier should have a restraining strap to secure the child, with leg openings small enough to prevent the child from slipping out, but large enough to prevent chafing. Check for pinch points in the folding mechanism or frame. The carrier should have a padded covering over the metal frame near baby's face. Of course, you shouldn't use a back carrier until baby is four or five months old. By then, baby's neck is able to withstand jolts and not sustain any injuries.

Bassinet/Cradle

For the first week at home, you might want to use a bassinet or cradle; just make sure it has a sturdy bottom and a wide base for stability. The bassinet/cradle should have a smooth surface (no protruding staples or other hardware that can injure baby). The legs should have strong, effective locks to prevent folding while in use. The mattress should be firm and fit snugly. Follow the manufacturer's guidelines on the weight and size of a baby who can safely use these products.

Baby Bath Ring or Seat

Bath time should always be a time for caution since, in the water, disaster can strike in a matter of seconds. For any baby bath product, make sure suction cups are securely fastened and that they securely attach to the smooth surface of the tub. Fill the tub only with enough water to cover baby's legs, and never leave baby alone or with a sibling while in the bath ring—even for a second!

E-ALERT!

Never make baby's bath water too hot! Warm water is the safest temperature for baby's bath, just be sure your hot water heater is set to 120 degrees to avoid accidental scalding. If you don't want to second-guess, purchase a baby bath thermometer and use it until you feel you can safely gauge on your own.

Changing Table

Changing tables make changing time convenient for you—not to mention easier on your tired back! But be sure your changing table has safety straps to prevent falls, as well as drawers or shelves that are easily accessible so you aren't tempted to leave the baby unattended.

Used Crib Safety Tips

An unsafe used crib can be very dangerous for your baby. Each year, about fifty babies suffocate or strangle when they become trapped between broken crib parts or in cribs with older, unsafe designs. A safe crib is always the best place to put your baby to sleep, so look for a certification seal showing that your crib meets national safety standards. If your crib doesn't meet these guidelines, you should seriously consider replacing it with a safer one. Here's what to look for in terms of crib safety:

- ✓ No missing, loose, broken, or improperly installed screws, brackets, or other hardware on the crib or the mattress support
- ✓ No more than 2⅜ inches between crib slats, so a baby's body can't fit through the slats
- ✓ A firm, snug-fitting mattress so a baby can't get trapped between the mattress and the side of the crib
- ✓ No corner posts over ¹⁄₁₆ inch above the end panels (unless they are over 16 inches high for a canopy) so a baby can't catch clothing and strangle
- ✓ No cutout areas on the headboard or footboard so a baby's head can't get trapped
- ✓ A mattress support that does not easily pull apart from the corner posts so a baby can't get trapped between mattress and crib
- ✓ No cracked or peeling paint
- ✓ No splinters or rough edges

E-QUESTION

How should I tell my in-laws that their "heirloom" crib is unsafe?
Go to the U.S. government's consumer safety Web site and download the crib safety checklist. Share it with your in-laws and then brainstorm other creative ideas for the antique piece; perhaps you can use it as a toy display on the other side of baby's room.

Check the Slats and Sides

On a crib, slats should be spaced no more than 2⅜ inches apart, without any missing or cracked slats. The mattress should fit snugly—less than two fingers' width between the edge of the mattress and the side of the crib and the mattress support securely attached to the headboard and footboard. The corner posts should be no higher than ¹⁄₁₆ inch (1 mm) to prevent entanglement of clothing or other objects worn by baby. Since they can allow head entrapment, there shouldn't be any cutouts in the headboard or footboard. Drop-side latches should securely hold sides in a raised position, not be moveable by an active or adventuresome baby. All screws or bolts that secure the components of the crib are present and tight. When baby reaches 35 inches in height or can climb and/or fall over the sides, it's time for a toddler bed.

Crib Toys

Parents always want their kids to be occupied—even when they're tucked away in their cribs. But crib toys need to be limited to just a few that are chosen with care, if they have to have any at all. Toys with strings with loops or openings should never be dangling near the crib. If you use a crib gym, remove it when the child is able to pull or push up on her hands and knees or reaches five months of age, whichever comes first. Toys with small components are a choking hazard and should never be left in a crib. Never leave large stuffed animals or pillow-like stuffed toys and other soft products in a crib with a sleeping baby.

Other Equipment Concerns

In addition to cribs some other pieces of baby equipment have safety concerns you should look out for. Remember to periodically check all your baby gear for wear and tear, loose pieces, and chipped paint.

Gates and Enclosures

Until babies are old enough to do more exploring on their own, gates are a good way to keep little ones out of areas that aren't childproofed. Openings in gates should be small enough to avoid entrapping baby's head, with a pressure bar or other fastener that can resist forces exerted by a determined "explorer." To avoid splinters, use plastic-molded gates or expandable enclosures with large v-shaped openings along the top edge or with diamond-shaped openings within.

Your baby might enjoy playing in an exercise "saucer" that includes a seat that spins and a rubber disc under baby's feet. These are generally very safe, and lots of fun for active babies. Thankfully, the unsafe, wheel-driven baby walkers of the past are not as readily available, and most experts strongly discourage their use—so politely decline one, even as a hand-me-down.

High Chairs

Baby's high chair should have waist and crotch restraining straps that are independent of the tray, which should lock securely. The clasp on the waist strap should also be easy to use. A good high chair has a wide stable base, with caps or plugs on the tubing firmly attached. If you have a folding high chair, it should have an effective locking device to keep it from collapsing. Always use restraining straps; otherwise the child can slide under the tray and strangle or fall onto the floor below.

Hook-On Chairs

Hook-on chairs are great for visits to grandma's or a dinner out with family and friends. Just make sure yours has a restraining strap to secure baby, along with a clamp that locks properly onto the table for added security. The caps or plugs on the tubing should be firmly attached and unable to be pulled off by curious little hands, since they may be a choking hazard. Don't position the chair anywhere the child can push off with his feet—and, of course, never leave your baby unattended in a hook-on chair.

Pacifiers

Pacifiers are great for babies who love to suck on things. But they can also present opportunities for danger. To prevent accidental strangulation, leave off any attachable ribbons until baby is at least six months old. The shield of the pacifier should be large and firm enough to not fit completely into the child's mouth, with ventilation holes so the baby can still breathe freely when it's in her mouth. Throw away any pacifiers whose nipples have holes or tears that might break off into baby's mouth.

Playpens

Most playpens today are the pop-up variety and don't allow one side to be open. But if you're using a hand-me-down, be sure the mesh has no tears, holes, or loose threads. It should be securely attached to the top rail and the floor plate, and the top rail cover shouldn't have any tears or holes. If there's a thin mattress, be sure it's secure; even a very young infant can roll under the mattress and suffocate.

Rattles, Squeeze Toys, Teethers

Rattles, squeeze toys, and teethers should be large enough so that they can't lodge in a baby's throat. Rattles need to be sturdy enough to prevent breakage during use. Squeeze toys shouldn't contain a detachable squeaker, since these can sometimes be squeezed out of the toy and lead to choking. To prevent suffocation, always remove rattles, squeeze toys, teethers, and other toys from cribs or playpens—especially when baby is sleeping or unattended.

Strollers and Carriages

A stroller can be a fantastic way to get baby out and about in the world—just be sure yours secures correctly so that it doesn't collapse on baby when you least expect it. The seat belt and crotch strap should attach securely to the frame, with an easy-to-use seat belt buckle. Be sure the brakes securely lock the wheels. Always secure the seat belts, and never take a baby in a stroller on an escalator. Keep baby's hands away from pinching areas when the stroller is being folded or unfolded or the seat back is being lowered. If you're using an heirloom baby carriage, be sure the brakes work and that the mattress can't be pulled over baby's head.

Toy Chests

Toy chests offer the best opportunity to keep the floor clean in baby's play room—and eliminating opportunities for falls is a good safety precaution. But make sure the lid can't trap your baby, and that any hinged lids can't pinch baby's tiny fingers. The best toy chests for a baby's room are the plastic-molded ones.

Toy boxes should be checked for safety. Use a toy chest with a lid that will stay open in any position when raised, and that won't fall unexpectedly on a child. For extra safety, be sure there are ventilation holes for fresh air. Watch for sharp edges that could cut, and hinges that could pinch or squeeze.

Think Toy Safety

When buying toys, choose them with care. Keep in mind the child's age, interests, and skill level. Look for quality design and construction in all toys for all ages. Make sure that all directions or instructions are clear to you, and when appropriate, to the child.

Do Your Own Safety Checks

Toys can be lots of fun for both baby and you, but the responsibility for keeping them safe and clean is entirely yours. To properly maintain toys, check them periodically for breakage and potential hazards. Don't be a packrat—throw away any broken toys!

It is best not to use wooden toys with baby unless they are smoothly sanded and painted with a nontoxic, protective coating. Just make sure there aren't any splinters. Also, check all outdoor toys or play areas regularly for rust or weak parts that could become hazardous.

To store toys properly, teach older children to put them safely away on shelves or in a toy chest after playing so that trips and falls can be prevented.

Old—and Dangerous

Older toys can break to reveal parts small enough to be swallowed or to become lodged in a child's windpipe, ears, or nose. The law bans small parts in new toys intended for children under three. This includes removable small eyes and noses on stuffed toys and dolls and small, removable squeakers on squeeze toys.

Cords Can Be Deadly

Toys with long strings or cords are dangerous for infants and very young children. The cords may become wrapped around an infant's neck, causing strangulation. Never hang toys with long strings, cords, loops, or ribbons in cribs or playpens where children can become entangled. Remove crib gyms from the crib when the child can pull up on hands and knees; some children have strangled when they fell across crib gyms stretched across the crib.

E-SSENTIAL

Look for and heed age recommendations, such as not recommended for children under three. Look for other safety labels, including "Flame retardant/Flame resistant" on fabric products and "Washable/hygienic materials" on stuffed toys and dolls.

Age-Appropriateness Is Key

All toys are not for all children. Keep toys designed for older children out of the hands of little ones. Follow labels that give age recommendations; some toys are recommended for older children because they may be hazardous in the hands of a younger child. Teach older children to help keep their toys away from younger brothers and sisters.

E-FACT

Protecting children from unsafe toys is the responsibility of everyone. Careful toy selection and proper supervision of children at play is still—and always will be—the best way to protect children from toy-related injuries.

Once Baby's More Active . . .

Right now, it's hard to imagine that within the next few months, baby will become more and more mobile in your home. After all, baby isn't even full-term yet! But from the moment baby starts crawling, you'll need to start moving room to room with a fresh set of eyes. The most treacherous places in your home for baby are the kitchen, the family room, and your home office—so do your best to minimize risk in each of these rooms.

Kitchen and Home Office Safety

In the kitchen, move all appliance power cords out of baby's reach, and never cook with baby in your arms (or within arm's reach of a hot stove). In the family room, keep all smaller objects and electronic devices out of baby's reach as well; items like your sewing kit or an older child's toys with small components should never be left out within baby's grasp. Finally, keep your home office off-limits to baby, except for portable cribs or an exercise saucer. There are just too many power cords—not to mention your client files or important papers!

E-SSENTIAL

Do a "feng shui" space clearing in your home before baby arrives. Get rid of all potentially harmful objects, but also things that you just don't need anymore. Once baby comes, you'll be surprised at how quickly your home fills up with stuff again!

Keep It Clean

Finally, keep your home as clean as possible at all times. Dirt and debris can become hiding places for all kinds of vermin—both seen and unseen. Mice, rats, and ants love leftover and improperly stored food items, as well as boxes to hide in or near. Dust mites from infrequent sweeping can fill your home with nastiness that can create allergies in small children and affect your own well-being. If you've never been very tidy before, there'll never be a better time to start than before baby arrives!

Chapter 7

Your Baby's Pediatrician and Other Medical Concerns

Before you became pregnant, you probably only saw a doctor once a year for your annual checkup. But now that you're expecting a baby, it's time to get used to the idea of seeing many more medical professionals on a regular basis, since there will most likely be monthly visits to monitor growth and assess needs. That's why it's very important to choose a medical team with which you feel comfortable. At your childbirth class, you'll learn how to make the best choice for you and your baby.

...g a Good Childbirth Class

...your obstetrician or call your local hospital to find out where and when ...birth classes are held. Some places charge a nominal fee for these ...es; others offer them free of charge. Either way, you need to have some education before embarking on a birthing journey for the first time; it may be called "natural" childbirth, but for first-timers there is often the feeling that nothing is going to happen naturally.

E-ALERT!

If you have already planned on a completely natural, unmedicated birth (and your physician has given the okay), you still need to learn about Cesarean births, because there is no guarantee that you won't have one should an emergency arise.

Choosing a class that suits your needs may seem like a daunting task at first; recognize that what's most important is that ultimately you feel comfortable with the teacher and the methods being presented.

Different Approaches to Childbirth

Most good childbirth instructors teach a little bit of all of the childbirth methods, to give first-time parents a good base from which to choose. These methods include:

✓ **Lamaze.** This method stresses relaxation techniques and conditioning to combat labor pain.

✓ **Grantly Dick-Read.** The originator of the idea of including fathers, this method relies on a combination of relaxation technique and mental preparation to get through labor.

✓ **The Bradley Method.** This childbirth method employs diet and exercise as a sensible way to work through the pain in a medication-free manner.

Some classes take bits and pieces of each method to combine the best advice available; you can decide what will work best for you. Whatever you choose, you should sign up early in order to begin the class no later than your seventh month. You want to make sure you'll finish the course before the baby arrives.

E-SSENTIAL

Though you may feel silly panting and blowing with a pillow up your shirt and a roomful of other couples doing the same, these types of exercises can actually help alleviate your delivery-room fears well in advance—not to mention give you and your partner something to joke about on the way to the hospital.

Finding and Choosing a Pediatrician

From birth to around age eighteen or even twenty-one, your child will be seeing a doctor on a regular basis, and preferably someone you've spent a lot of time in choosing. A professional you feel comfortable discussing your developing child with is tantamount to a having a healthy child.

The first step in finding a good pediatrician is to talk with other parents, your obstetrician, or your regular family doctor. You should then look in your insurance directory to make sure that the recommended physician is covered by your plan.

Next, you should call the pediatrician's office to listen for a friendly voice. If his or her staff seems rushed, or impatient, or just plain rude, hang up and call the next one on your list. Medical professionals should realize that they are representatives of the physician and practice; therefore, they should always be kind and patient with anyone on the other end of the phone—no matter who or when.

Set an Appointment

When you get a positive feeling from a receptionist or nurse's aide, you should set up an appointment to interview the pediatrician. Most will not charge you for this time with them; it should be considered a sales call, since you are in effect interviewing them for the job of caring for your little one; it is not a job you would entrust to just any name on the list.

Ask Questions

Once you have an appointment scheduled, jot down some questions you might like answered by the pediatrician. Always take your notes with you into the meeting; you'd be surprised how much you can forget when you're busy taking it all in.

Here are some questions that you should ask:

✓ Ask the doctor about his or her general approach to working with children. Questions such as, "What do you find most fulfilling about working with youngsters?" will net you some telling answers. If the doctor says, "I most enjoy helping kids to grow, learn, and adjust to their world," you've got a good one. If, on the other hand, the response is that it was either this or become a veterinarian, continue on your search.

✓ Find out what the doctor's policies are, especially about whether your child will have to sit in a waiting room filled with sick kids. Ideally, there should only be a few children in the waiting area at a time—and the really sick kids (those with contagious illnesses) should be sequestered in an examining room, away from other children. If such separation is really important to you, look for an office with separate sick and well waiting rooms.

✓ Does your insurance cover everything the doctor orders? Finding out early in the process will help you avoid troublesome decisions later. Call your insurance company; doctors simply can't know every detail about all policies.

✓ What rules and regulations does the pediatrician have (if any)? A doctor once gave out a handout three pages long—topped with the words: "I will decide what an emergency is and will call you back accordingly." This same doctor said she would not tolerate a patient being five minutes late for an appointment; yet she evidently felt it was okay to leave new patients in a waiting room full of sick children for forty-five minutes. Needless to say, she didn't get many new patients.

✓ What are the doctor's parental philosophies? Is the doctor a parent, too? If so, what is her approach to parenting? You may feel more assured calling a pediatrician who has also experienced a frantic night with a baby's temperature soaring.

E-SSENTIAL

Once you've chosen your pediatrician, it might be a nice gesture for you to let the doctor know why he was chosen. If it's the doctor's responsiveness that impresses you, say so. If it's the calm, quiet atmosphere you like, mention that, too. Being as specific as possible will help the doctor keep up the good work.

What Happens at the Early Checkups?

The first visit with the pediatrician usually occurs at the hospital within hours of birth. During this visit, the doctor will examine the baby from head to toe, making sure that all of the baby's vital signs are stable and consistent with those of other newborns. The doctor will then report all of her findings to you in your hospital room; you will begin hearing about "percentiles" (benchmarks against other typical newborns) and how your baby measures up against others his age. (Be forewarned: Some parents share their baby's "percentiles" in a highly competitive manner, even though these are statistics that you cannot change. Just smile politely!)

Within three to five days after delivery, you will return to the pediatrician's office for another checkup. All of the vitals will be checked again, including your baby's weight and an exam for jaundice, and you will also have the chance to discuss any feeding, sleeping, or related problems with your pediatrician.

Record Your Concerns—or the Doctor's

Always take your notebook with you for these visits, as you will be able to look back for reference after you leave the doctor's office. Of primary concern at this time is baby's weight; if he has dropped a pound or more since leaving the hospital (and most babies do) but has not gained any of it back yet, the doctor may make recommendations and may ask you to return a few more times in the next two weeks for a weight check.

Well-Baby Checkups and Immunizations

"Well-baby" visits need to be scheduled at one, two, four, six, nine, twelve, fifteen, eighteen, and twenty-four months, and here the doctor will cover everything from a brief physical to a discussion of baby's particular growth stage to track his physical, emotional, and motor development. You will constantly be talking about baby's eating habits. After two years of age, your child will need only an annual checkup.

Immunizations should occur at two, four, six, twelve, fifteen, eighteen, and twenty-four months. These immunizations protect against the following diseases: diphtheria, pertussis (whooping cough), mumps, measles, tetanus, rubella, hepatitis A and B, prevnar, chicken pox, rotavirus, and haemophilus influenzae type B.

Hepatitis B Vaccine

This vaccine, which helps protect infants at risk of developing the disease from infection passed by the mother, is often given to babies first at birth and then at two and six months. Some babies, albeit a small percentage, develop minor, temporary side effects such as a rash. This is nothing to worry about and will go away on its own within a few days.

Polio Vaccine

Your baby will need to have the inactive polio virus immunization, and this vaccine is given at two, four, and eighteen months. Babies used to get the active virus version, but since there was a 1 in 750,000 chance of contracting the disease with the first dose, many physicians felt that was too risky. In concordance with these fears, the Centers for Disease Control and Prevention (CDC) made a new recommendation for U.S. polio immunization, so the enhanced inactivated polio vaccine (eIPV) is now the only option.

E-FACT

Perhaps the best news of all is that there are now combination shots for some immunizations. These shots eliminate the need for three injections at one time—something that all babies (and some weak-stomached parents) will definitely appreciate.

DTP Vaccine

This is the combination diphtheria-tetanus-pertussis vaccine, given at two, four, six, and eighteen months. The good news is that there is a newer-class version of this vaccine (acellular DTP, or DtaP) with fewer side effects than the old one. However, there is still a chance baby will have a minor adverse reaction within hours of the shot. Watch baby carefully for signs of discomfort.

Hib Vaccine

Given at two, four, six, and fifteen months, this shot protects baby from haemophilus influenzae type B. Some babies show signs of discomfort afterward; report any unusually high-pitched crying or redness and swelling to the pediatrician.

MMR Vaccine

This is the measles, mumps, and rubella vaccine, which baby doesn't get until he is fifteen months old, when the immune system is even stronger.

Up to 15 percent of babies show adverse reactions, not immediately after the shot but within two weeks of immunization. Symptoms such as rash, fever, or swollen lymph glands could indicate a reaction; and it is best to notify your pediatrician immediately if you notice such reactions.

Building a Good Working Relationship with Your Pediatrician

Once you've established a partnership with your pediatrician, how can you keep the relationship a positive and productive one? First, you should follow the rules and policies of your pediatrician. Keep the doctor's information sheet handy, and refer to it often. Parents who expect special treatment or who think they are somehow above the rules, will ultimately turn off a pediatrician and damage their working relationship. Also, to save the doctor time, come in with as much information as you can muster. Things like temperature, symptoms, and general behavior of the baby will provide some clues to baby's illness.

Listen and Wait (If You Can)

Be willing to try what the doctor says. If she doesn't feel that a medication will nip the problem or that the illness must simply run its course, don't argue, but do ask questions if you are not convinced. If, on the other hand, you try leaving baby to fight off the problem and the symptoms get worse, do call the doctor back to try another approach.

E-ALERT!

Don't use your baby's appointment as an opportunity for all of your other children to be seen by the doctor. Pediatricians agree that this one-stop-shopping approach not only takes too much of their time (affecting other scheduled appointments) but also is unfair to them. If others in your family need to be seen by the doctor, schedule a separate appointment for each.

If you can wait until morning, do so before calling the doctor. Leave the nighttime and weekend calls for emergencies only. This is a hard concept for first-time parents, to whom anything unusual may seem like an emergency.

Take Care of Yourself, Too!

Finally, realize that part of having a healthy baby is for the baby to have a healthy you. Take care of yourself, and alert your pediatrician to any problems you might be having (such as postpartum depression, breastfeeding concerns, or even general worries about parenting). Your pediatrician can be a valuable resource to help you learn more about your role as a parent.

When to Call the Nurse

First-time parents tend to worry about their baby more than veteran parents do, mainly because every new noise or cry makes them worry about illness. But it's important to remember that baby operates much like you do. There can be occasional bouts of diarrhea, some gas or tooth pain, and even crying for no real reason. Your baby might even have a constipated moment or two. None of these problems is necessarily an indication of serious illness, so you need not worry if they happen occasionally or seem short lived.

Fortunately, most pediatricians' offices have nurses on staff to field calls from worried parents. A pediatric nurse can quickly discern between acute and serious conditions, and will immediately refer the more serious cases to the pediatrician. Here are some times when a call to the nurse at your pediatrician's office is absolutely necessary:

- ✓ When baby's temperature is higher than 101 degrees (rectally), or above 100.4 degrees if the infant is less than three months old.
- ✓ When baby sleeps long or doesn't wake easily.
- ✓ When baby is unusually fussy or irritable.
- ✓ When baby refuses to feed well or eats only a small amount before crying in a high-pitched manner.
- ✓ When baby isn't wetting at least one diaper every four hours or so (for a grand total of six to eight per day).

✓ When baby vomits excessively at more than two consecutive feedings, or vomits green bile (if this occurs, call doctor immediately).

✓ When baby has labored, distressed, or rapid breathing.

✓ If baby's color tone changes (look for blueness in the lips or fingernails or yellowish skin or eyes).

If the baby exhibits any of these symptoms and is under two months of age, you should treat it as an emergency situation and call the nurse at your doctor's office for proper guidance. A pediatric nurse call may also be warranted (during regular office hours) for minor irritations, such as a rash that doesn't ease with cream or air-drying; constipation, diarrhea, or a cold; or a minor injury.

Common Ailments

There are several common ailments that can affect your baby. While many of them can be scary for the parents they are often not too serious for the baby. Some of the most common health concerns and their symptoms follow.

Rashes and Skin Irritations

These are common problems among very young babies; everything from laundry detergent to your perfume can cause red, flaky, and itchy skin for baby. The most common culprit, however, is spillage of milk into the folds of the neck. Be sure to keep a bib on baby, and wipe the area after feeding time. Also, use a good baby cream in the affected areas two or three times per day. Eczema, or atopic dermatitis, can occur when infants have rough, red, itchy skin and often improves with moisturizers and a topical steroid cream. Call the doctor if you suspect your baby has eczema.

Keep Skin—and Air—Moisturized

When baby has eczema or other skin conditions, you should use lots of baby cream and keep baby's nails trimmed to avoid excessive scratching. A daily bath can be okay for a baby with eczema, as long as you use a mild soap and apply a moisturizer within a few minutes of getting out of the bath. Use a cool-mist humidifier to keep baby's environment moist. Avoid overdressing baby, and stay away from scratchy materials. Soft cotton outfits that leave baby's neck open to the air are preferable. Be sure to lay a cotton receiving blanket on play areas. Take note of any foods that seem to trigger a rash, and eliminate them from baby's diet. Call the doctor if the rash seems to be getting worse or if it doesn't seem to go away even after your home treatment.

Fever

The scariest thing a new parent will face is baby's first real fever. (Note: For infants under three months old, a fever is anything above 100.4 degrees.) If baby has a slight temperature, you may be able to bring it down with over-the-counter baby pain reliever. Some fevers are caused by teething pain or perhaps are a reaction to an immunization; these can usually be treated with infant pain reliever as well. However, if the fever is 100.4 degrees or more, you will need to call your doctor immediately. If the fever is accompanied by a rash or if it seems to be hanging on for longer than a few days, call the doctor.

E-FACT

For newborns and younger infants, always use a rectal thermometer to get the most accurate temperature. You can still use the digital type for back up. Also, do not use products containing aspirin. They have been associated with Reye's syndrome, a brain disorder.

The Common Cold

Particularly if you live in a changeable climate, your baby could be susceptible to colds throughout the fall and winter. Colds are usually passed through airborne particles or through hand-to-hand or hand-to-mouth contact with an infected person. If someone in your family has a cold, ask that person to please keep a distance from baby—and to not kiss or hold the baby until the cold has completely passed. You should also frequently wash their hands and cover their coughs and sneezes. Babies can develop a fever prior to showing full-fledged cold symptoms, such as a runny or stuffed-up nose, a cough, red, watery eyes, and lack of appetite.

Keep Passages Clear and Open

If you think baby has a cold, you should use a bulb syringe and infant nasal drops to keep nasal passages clear and open. Put a pillow under the baby's mattress to keep his or her head elevated (or use a product called crib shoes to elevate the head of the crib); never place baby's head directly on a pillow, because baby can pull it over and suffocate. If baby becomes fussy, has trouble breathing, is not eating well, or seems otherwise unhealthy, call your doctor for advice.

Ear Infections

Middle-ear infections occur in nearly all children before they reach their second year and are more common in children who are around other kids on a regular basis (such as at a daycare). You should treat an ear infection as soon as you can, since they can be quite uncomfortable for baby and can cause delays in language development (because of hearing difficulties). Ear infections are more frequent in babies than in adults because a baby's Eustachian tube is smaller than an adult's, allowing bacteria a quicker route to the middle ear.

Common Symptoms

How do you know when baby has an ear infection? Usually a high-pitched cry and tugging of the ear will tell you. The more you try to lay the baby down to rest, the worse the crying becomes. Fever is also common. Finally, baby may eat less because it hurts to swallow. Call your doctor for her advice.

E-SSENTIAL

If your pediatrician has recommended a prescription medication, use it exactly as indicated. Most antibiotics (amoxicillin is the most pre-scribed) need to be taken until completely gone. Also, be sure to take baby back to the doctor for a follow-up exam.

More Common Problems—and What to Do

Sometimes, baby's health problems are very common—though that may not bring you immediate comfort when your precious little one is suffering. Still, knowing how to deal with the more routine problems will go a long way toward calming your nerves so that you can help ease baby's discomfort. The key to successfully treating most of these health challenges is quick recognition by you.

Diarrhea

The primary causes of diarrhea are a viral or bacterial infection, or intolerance to a new food. If baby has one or two loose stools in a day or so, there is no real cause for alarm; however, you should call the doctor if the diarrhea contains blood or if baby is dehydrated.

Signs of dehydration include a significant decrease in wet diapers (low urine output—less than five wet diapers per day); dry mouth; and sometimes weight loss.

Constipation

If baby is straining or having difficulty in producing stools, the best thing you can do is try curling the baby's knees up as he is straining; this can help baby use gravity to push the stool out. If there is still a problem, you could try an increase in water or diluted juice. Note that it's common for breastfed babies to only have bowel movements once a week or so, so it's likely not constipation if the baby is feeding well and the bowel movements are soft.

Vomiting

As with diarrhea, your primary concern should be to keep your baby hydrated. Feed baby formula, breast milk, or an electrolyte solution to replenish fluids more rapidly. Vomiting typically is more short lived than diarrhea but can be indicative of a more serious problem. Try to give baby about a teaspoon of fluid every five to ten minutes, and then call your doctor. (Note: Spitting up after feeding is not considered vomiting.)

Gas Pain

Your baby is crying incessantly, and nothing seems to be wrong—until you notice that baby has passed a tiny bit of gas. Where there is a little, there is usually more; so try some gas-relief drops to help baby get rid of the tummy pain. In and of itself, gas poses no real threat to baby's health; in fact, it is healthy for baby to pass as much gas as necessary. By the way, most babies have gas and most babies cry—so these two "signs" are not always indicative of a problem.

Teething Pain

It can take up to two (long) weeks for baby to cut a tooth; imagine how long baby will fuss and cry if left to fend for herself! Gums will be sore, and baby will drool buckets. These are your major symptoms; now that you know what they are, how can you best help baby? Give her some pain reliever (either acetaminophen or ibuprofen if the baby is more than six months old; or you can try some topical pain reliever such as Anbesol). Provide lots of cool teething toys for baby to gnaw on; always keep at least one in the refrigerator. Keep a bib on baby as often as possible, and change it as frequently as it becomes wet.

Only the Best for Baby

As a new parent, you'll certainly want only the best possible care for your baby. One of the best ways to ensure that you've got the best medical care available in your area is to chat with other parents to find out as much as you can about the pediatricians and children's hospital nearest you. Let these more experienced parents tell you everything they know—good, bad and ugly—about all of the pediatricians that may be on your list.

In some cases, you may find that the best doctors are located a little bit farther away than some others, but in the end, what matters most is not how close they are to your home, but how accessible they are to you when you need them.

It might also be a good idea to do a little bit of research on the Internet. By conducting your own "background check" on specific pediatricians, you may well ensure that you and your baby will get the best pediatrician in town.

Chapter 8

The Blessed Event

By now, you're no doubt tired of hearing all of the unsolicited comments from well-meaning friends and relatives: "Haven't you had the baby yet?" "Are you still here?" Certainly you're getting tired of carrying around your full-term baby—even if you were really excited about having it in the first place. You really can't help but sit in the nursery for hours on end, staring with anticipation at the empty crib. When will you finally hold your baby in your arms?

the last month of pregnancy, as you await your sweet arrival, it's hard to stay positive about the whole experience. On the one hand, you have those well-meaning people constantly commenting on how "ready" you look (even weeks before you actually are—further prolonging your agony). On the other hand, you have your own feelings of anxiety and concern over everything from whether the baby's room is really ready to trying to imagine a pain you've never felt before (but, no doubt, have been frightened by—thanks to the stories of every other mother you know).

What to Pack for Yourself

One of the best ways to get ready for the big "D" (for delivery) day is to start packing your bags. Take advantage of this quiet time to pack for both you and your baby—as sensibly as possible. Planning ahead will ensure you have easy access to all of the practical and comfort items you'll want to have on hand at the hospital, including a list of everyone you want to call to announce the wonderful news!

Practical Items

You'll need a robe and a nightgown, unless you like wearing the standard hospital issue. If you're going to breastfeed, choose a gown that opens easily in the front. Next, some warm, nonskid slippers would be nice, though the hospital typically has nonskid socks. Hospital floors can be slippery, and you'll be walking to the nursery at least once during your stay. You'll also want to pack a good nursing bra, as well as some nursing pads, in case your milk comes in sooner than you expect. If you're not going to breastfeed, bring a bra that's slightly smaller than you would normally wear to help your breasts return to their prepregnant state.

Comfort Items

Nonperishable snacks for your birthing coach are always a great thing to pack. Your baby's father is bound to get hungry, especially during a long labor, and you don't want him having to spend time waiting in line at the hospital cafeteria when he could be rubbing your back instead! For easy backrubs, pack a tennis ball or back massager. These items will help him provide extra pressure—a godsend if you have back pain. Finally, pack some toiletries, including your toothbrush, toothpaste, hair brush, makeup, deodorant, and a box of large maxi pads with wings, as you'll need them after the birth.

E-SSENTIAL

To make your birthing experience a little bit more comfortable, bring some soft music on a portable CD player (or several CDs that you like, since it might take a while), a picture of a pleasant scene to focus on during labor and a special toy or meaningful item from one of your other children.

Comfortable Clothing

You'll need one outfit to come home in after the delivery; make sure it's loose enough to accommodate your body comfortably, as you will not lose incredible amounts of weight immediately upon delivery. Include a few pairs of maternity panties and several pairs of socks—you'll need them for the delivery and afterward.

Packing for Baby

If you thought packing for yourself was a challenge, try packing for someone you haven't even met yet—your baby! Since the normal tendency is to overpack, you'll want to prepare baby's travel bag a few weeks before your due date. The easiest way to pack mindfully is to lay out all of the items you think baby will need on your bed, and take a good, hard look at how much you're packing. Are there items that seem extra or unnecessary? If you really want to be sure, invite a friend over to take a look, then toss aside any items beyond the bare minimum: clothes, diapers, and nail scissors.

Clothes

Pack at least two gowns that are open at the bottom or that have a pull string, as well as one going-home outfit. By now, you should have lots to choose from. Decide what you want to dress the baby in for its first pictures, since Dad will probably take several shots of you leaving the hospital. Bring a light or heavy blanket, depending on the climate or the time of year. Finally, if it's winter and you live in a cold climate, pack a snowsuit. The hospital may give you a cap for baby, but pack one anyway because your newborn's head needs to be covered when you walk out the door, no matter what season it is.

Diapers

If you are planning to shy away from disposables, bring four or five cloth diapers, and be sure to include a waterproof diaper cover to catch any diaper leakage. The hospital will provide all the disposable diapers you will need.

Nail Scissors

Most hospitals won't cut baby's nails, which can grow quite long in utero. Special baby scissors with clean, sharp edges are the best buy.

The Breech Baby

A breech baby is simply a baby who is presenting its feet first—instead of its head—toward the birth canal. Today, almost all breech babies are delivered via C-section. What if your baby is in a breech position prior to birth? Is there anything you can do to help the baby to turn?

E-FACT

Some experts suggest that you try getting on your hands and knees, rocking your pelvis while arching your back, to get the baby to move naturally. This does not always work, but it can sure help ease any back pain you might be experiencing.

See a Specialist

Another option is to go to a specialist who can turn the baby through external manipulation and use of ultrasound to check baby's position. However, some doctors insist that a breech baby is in that position because it is most comfortable—that the baby, in fact, knows that it has a cord around its neck and that moving makes it tighter. They are growing increasingly skeptical about this procedure, since a few infants have been lost because the umbilical cord was wrapped around the neck at the time of inversion—with the specialist completely unaware.

Try an Alternative Method

Some women have used acupressure or other nontraditional methods to encourage their babies to move into birthing position. Some women have even tried putting a radio between their knees while lying on their backs, hoping the baby might turn its head in the direction of the music! Whichever method you decide to try, do consult your doctor first. Remember, the baby can still turn at the last minute—even during labor!

Birth—and How You Get Through It

You have made it this far; so take some comfort first of all in knowing that labor and delivery comprise only a small portion of the total birth experience. Do you feel better now? Okay, with this new perspective in mind, you can move on to the three stages of birth and what you can anticipate.

Stage One: Labor

Labor itself takes three stages to accomplish its mission: early labor (about five to eight hours, but possibly longer if this is your first baby), which brings with it irregular contractions that open your cervix to about four centimeters; active labor (about two or three hours), which brings intensifying contractions that are closer together and open your cervix to about eight centimeters; and transition (thirty minutes to two hours), which is hard labor and opens your cervix to the ten centimeters needed for pushing.

False Versus Real Labor

Many women dash off to the hospital at the first sign of contractions, but just because there are a few labor pains happening doesn't necessarily mean you're in active labor. False labor is sporadic and unpredictable, and it may disappear altogether if you change position or get up and move around a bit. Real (or active) labor is marked by pain occurring in regular intervals, increasing in intensity until it becomes difficult to breathe or talk through each contraction. In active labor, the breaking of the bag of waters can also be a telltale sign that labor is real. Often, a small amount of blood-tinged mucous may pass from the vagina prior to your water breaking—and sometimes, your water won't break until the doctor or midwife makes it happen in the delivery room! That's why you need to rely on timing and intensity of contractions as an indicator of labor.

E-SSENTIAL

If you're feeling a little anxious about the details of the birth, it might help you to learn as much as you can about the stages of labor. If you're like most women, you've already flipped to this section before reading any of the early pregnancy information—to mentally prepare yourself for the moment you've likely dreamed about for quite some time.

Stage Two: Birth of the Baby

This is that glorious stage where you get to push the baby out of your body and into the world. You will be totally focused on getting the baby out, and your partner may need to stay close to your head to help you stay focused. At this point, if you feel like it, you can try whatever position makes you feel most comfortable (sitting up, lying down, squatting, or a side position). As the baby moves further down in the birth canal, you will feel more and more like pushing. If your doctor says it's okay, do so. If he asks you to pant or blow instead, do as you are instructed, since you might have to have an episiotomy if the doctor thinks you might tear your vaginal opening. This will only take a minute to do and most doctors will perform it only if it is necessary (though you should discuss this ahead of time). Stitching you back together after episiotomy generally takes another thirty to forty-five minutes.

Water Birthing

According to the National Women's Health Information Center, more and more women in the United States are using water to find comfort during labor and delivery. In water birthing, laboring women get into a tub of water that is between 90 and 100 degrees. Some women get out of the tub to give birth. Others remain in the water for delivery.

The water helps women feel physically supported. It also keeps them warm and relaxed. This eases the pain of labor and delivery for many women. Plus, it's easier for laboring women to move and find comfortable positions in the water.

E-SSENTIAL

Water birthing is relatively new in this country, so there's very little research on its benefits. Even so, some women say giving birth in the water is faster and easier. Plus, women may tear less severely and need fewer episiotomies in the water.

Water birthing may be gentler for your baby too. It may ease the baby's transition from the womb to the new world. The baby is born into an environment that is similar to the womb. Plus, the water dulls the lights, sound and feel of the new world. Once the baby is born, it's brought to the surface of the water and wrapped in blankets.

Ask your doctor or midwife if you are a good candidate for water birthing. Water birth is not safe for women or babies who have health issues.

Stage Three: After Birth

This is the stage where your hormones trigger delivery of the placenta, and it is either pushed out by you or removed by your doctor. The doctor will then check it over for signs of any problems and assist you in the beginning of your recovery by suturing any tears or incisions from an episiotomy.

He will likely give you some bonding time with baby and then visit you later with aftercare instructions and tips.

Where Are They Taking My Baby?

It's the moment you've anticipated—you've finally given birth. And immediately after doing so, you expect to hold your newborn infant, just like in the movies. Suddenly, a nurse rushes to the doctor's side, and your baby gets whisked off to an incubator—where a series of tests are completed. What is the baby's coloring like? Does it have all of its fingers and toes? Can it grasp and use its reflexes?

The Apgar Scale

Using a rating scale called the Apgar (after Dr. Virginia Apgar, who devised the method of testing newborns back in the 1950s), a neonatal nurse evaluates the baby to determine its health immediately after birth; she then repeats the test one or two more times in the five to ten minutes following birth. This is standard procedure and nothing to be alarmed about; you should ask your doctor in advance of the birth how soon you'll be able to hold the baby; that way it won't be a disappointment to you if this is a moment you've envisioned for some time. Realize that waiting a few minutes to make sure baby is healthy is worth it for the peace of mind it will bring about baby's general health in the days to come.

Aftercare Precautions

Immediately after the baby is born, you will need to watch for the following signs of trouble and call your doctor immediately if you experience any:

- ✓ Discharge from your vagina that is heavier than normal, is bright red, or is foul-smelling.
- ✓ Fever or sudden rise in temperature.
- ✓ Burning on urination or difficulty in doing so.
- ✓ Soreness or irritation in your legs or in your breasts.
- ✓ Any adjustment problems that interfere with care of the baby.

Working with a Doula or Midwife

If you live far away from relatives and want to have the kind of nurturing care that your own mother might provide, working with a doula can be a wonderful reassuring experience. A doula will stay with you from the moment you go into labor through the birth, and will sometimes even serve as a lactation consultant. If it's a long labor, a doula might give your baby's father a rest and hold your hand through some contractions.

E-QUESTION

What's the difference between a doula and a midwife?
A doula is more like a coach, someone who provides emotional and physical assistance to a couple during the birthing process. A midwife has actual hands-on medical responsibility for everything from prenatal exams to delivery.

If you prefer a nonsurgical, homelike atmosphere, you can always opt for a midwife-assisted birth plan. This often, but not always, means giving birth at home.

The At-Home Birth

In spite of the fact that births predominantly occur in hospitals, there are still a high number of at-home births (usually performed by midwives). These births are permitted if there are no signs of imminent danger to the mother and the baby seems to be progressing normally.

At-home births differ from hospital births in that you are free to include whomever you'd like in the process. If you'd like your whole family over to have a "welcoming" party for the baby, this option is more available to you than it would be in a hospital birth. Families who already have other children often like to include all of the children in the birth of their new sibling, and this is more easily and comfortably accomplished at an at-home birth. Of course, as with any birth, you should prepare for the possibility of an emergency. Should any complications arise, your midwife will call 911.

When Baby's Late

Some babies are just plain reluctant to be born. When a baby is more than a week beyond its due date, a physician may make the suggestion to you that the baby be induced.

When a baby is induced, the first step is often placing a prostaglandin gel on the mother's cervix to encourage dilatation. Some women spontaneously go into labor with the gel alone, while others require further medication in order to get things rolling.

Inducing Labor

If you should need more medication, Pitocin is usually the drug of choice. It is given through an IV, and it usually spurs labor on within a few hours. On the downside, many women say that Pitocin causes fast and furious labor pains. The pains are generally more intense and closer together than in a natural labor, but the benefit is that the labor is also generally shorter with induction. Most Pitocin-induced labors are over within a few hours.

Forceps Delivery

When labor seems difficult or extremely prolonged, and the natural force of your body doesn't seem to be enough to nudge baby out of the birth canal, some doctors will use forceps to deliver your baby. Forceps are two metal blades built to fit gently onto baby's head; the doctor applies some pressure to draw the baby out. Forceps deliveries are not as common as they were in the last few decades, primarily because some babies have been hurt in the process.

What If You Need a C-Section?

If baby is really late, too large or not well positioned—or when the lives of either the baby or the mother are in jeopardy—a Cesarean section may be performed. If your doctor chooses to perform a C-section (as it's more commonly called), you'll be given a spinal, or epidural, an anesthetic that numbs you and allows you to be awake for the surgery. A tent is placed over your abdominal area, and your husband or partner is usually near your head. Delivery of the baby is usually within minutes, and in most cases, you can see the baby immediately after it's removed through incisions in the abdomen and uterus. Afterward, the placenta is removed and examined, and the doctor will usually perform a check of your abdominal cavity. Once that's accomplished, you'll be stitched up and taken into the recovery room.

E-SSENTIAL

Take the time to discuss your feelings and fears with your doctor well in advance of the possible surgery. It might be a good idea to ask the doctor exactly how the determination for a C-section is made so that you are prepared for that option and not surprised when surgery is mandated.

Ask Questions about C-Sections

If your doctor should decide to perform a C-section, ask as many questions about it as you feel a need to; then try to put it all in perspective. If you had your heart set on a vaginal delivery, don't let the prospect of a C-section ruin your birthing experience. You are still a mother giving birth to her child, regardless of the way it actually happens. And the best thing you can do is put the needs of your child first, which is exactly what a C-section is about, since it is performed as a safety measure for the baby.

Recovery after a C-Section

When recovering from a C-section, you will be encouraged to turn and move around while still in the recovery room so that your muscles don't get cramped. You should make sure that you raise the head of your hospital bed before attempting to turn your body; then place a pillow over your abdomen to keep from popping stitches when attempting to sit up. Try to move into a sitting position carefully, stretching your legs to the floor as far as you comfortably can. Then, with some help from your partner, try to stand for a few minutes. Alert your doctor to any discomfort beyond that which is expected after a C-section.

Postpartum Issues

After the blessed event has passed and all of the guests have departed from the ceremonial "viewing of the baby," you will be left to adjust to your new life as a parent. You will suddenly be faced with a lot of situations you never had to deal with before baby came along.

First is the adjustment to being totally responsible for this new and completely dependent little life. This feeling can be overwhelming, particularly to those who were entrenched in their careers immediately prior to giving birth. Instead of daily status meetings and power lunches, you find yourself changing diapers, feeding like a milk truck, and monitoring baby's every move to make sure she is still okay.

E-SSENTIAL

It might also take awhile for you and baby to get used to each other's cues. For instance, baby may cry incessantly for an hour or so before you can figure out exactly what's wrong; expect that this might happen, try not to get frustrated, and allow yourself a little time to learn baby's way of communicating.

Don't Rush Recovery

Physically, you may be feeling extremely tired from the birth experience itself, and your body will need at least four to six weeks to recuperate. Giving birth is something akin to the decathlon. Your body uses muscles you didn't even know you had to accomplish a monumental feat: bringing a new life into the world. Don't underestimate the fact that your body will take its own time to get back to normal after the birth. If you try to rush your recovery, your body could respond with negative side effects and complications, thus extending the recovery period.

Give Yourself Emotional Leeway

Expect your emotions to run the gamut from euphoria to depression. There are plenty of ways you can deal with any stress you might be feeling.

First, write down your concerns or worries and share them with someone close. Try a change of pace; vary your daily routine.

If that doesn't seem to work, get a babysitter for a few hours and just do something for you: a massage, a facial, shopping, or even lunch alone at your favorite restaurant. Or take a warm bath and cuddle up in bed with a good book. In those first few weeks home, go easy on yourself—and always make time for you.

When to Call for Help

If the stress is too much or becomes more severe (leading to depression), seek professional assistance. You should call your doctor if you experience any of the following:

- ✓ Lethargy or the inability to motivate yourself to do much except meet the baby's primary needs
- ✓ Periods of moodiness or irritability that lead to further depression
- ✓ Anxiety
- ✓ Insomnia
- ✓ Difficulty concentrating or making decisions
- ✓ Crying jags or periods of sadness that do not go away easily

All of these symptoms are signs of postpartum depression (PPD), a condition that affects about 10 to 15 percent of new moms (although that number could be considerably higher, since many are afraid to tell anyone what they're experiencing).

Is It PPD . . . or "Baby Blues"?

Postpartum depression is different from the more common (and shorter-lasting) "baby blues," which typically occur within days of the birth and last a maximum of two weeks. With PPD, a new mother experiences depression that cannot be alleviated without the use of antidepressants, or therapy, or, in some cases, both. Risk factors for PPD include problems with your marriage, depression or anxiety during the pregnancy (or a stressful event), lack of support from your partner or significant others, a history of premenstrual syndrome, or a previous case of PPD.

E-ALERT!

Another form of this disorder is postpartum psychosis, which affects a very small percentage of the population but has symptoms of wishing to harm yourself or the baby. These thoughts are serious enough to warrant immediate attention (and intervention). Call for help if you experience such thoughts; with professional help, it is absolutely possible to overcome this disorder!

Beginning a New (and Separate) Life

After nine months together, you and your baby are now embarking on separate, unique lives. And even though you had a life before baby's conception, the one you have now entered into is entirely different.

Before baby's birth, you were your own person. During your pregnancy, you were the mother-to-be. Now, you are baby's mommy. If you want to have a separate identity outside of your child, you'll need to decide how and where it will be. Perhaps it will mean returning to work (see Chapter 16 for options) or simply joining a group such as a book club or parent's group.

Whatever you decide, know that your life will never be the same. Rather, it will be much richer and much fuller than you ever dreamed possible—full of more possibilities than ever before, especially now that you and baby are finally two separate entities!

Chapter 9

Sharing Baby

Little did you know in those first moments after birth that you would be bringing baby not only into your and your partner's life but also into a whole new world. You probably gave little thought to expanding your own small world to include relatives, friends, and daycare providers. But before you can consider the assortment of folks who will play a role in baby's life, you might need to take a look inward to make sure you're okay with some of the changes you're experiencing.

Adjustment Issues for New Moms

For women who have been used to running a business or working in the outside world, the prospect of spending an entire day changing diapers and breastfeeding is not exactly an easy one to adjust to. The pace is much slower, and everything takes longer than it used to. Even getting in and out of the car is more cumbersome than before, with the added diaper bag, stroller, and car seat. If you're not prepared for these kinds of changes, they can be quite a jolt.

The First Six Weeks

The first six weeks after your baby's birth are consumed with new detail; every day you learn something that you didn't know before and that you were unprepared for. It's a time of trial and error—a time for you to get used to having a baby to care for and for the baby to get used to being cared for by you.

E-ALERT!

Be prepared to be tired a lot and more than a little overwhelmed. The incredible sense of responsibility for this tiny little life can be scary to many new mothers. Friends who have recently given birth will tell you that this sense of responsibility was something they could never have imagined or prepared themselves for properly.

You're Not the Only One Who's Overwhelmed!

Your partner may be feeling some of this new responsibility, too, and may be as overwhelmed as you are. Don't be afraid to share your feelings openly with each other; you will both need each other's support during this time in your lives.

Above all else, don't be too hard on yourself, particularly if this is your first time being a mother. If you have a hard time dealing with parenting issues, seek the help of a support group for new parents or check out an online support group (see Appendix A for Web sites). There is help out there; you're not alone in feeling overwhelmed.

Separation Anxiety—How to Get Through It

New parents need time for themselves. Many new parents simply wish for an evening out among other adults; some prefer a quiet dinner alone. But how can you ease the inevitable separation anxiety you or your baby will experience?

First, involve those who will care for the baby "in small doses" before leaving for a longer period of time. Have Grandma come to the house and spend time holding the baby long before you decide to leave; this way, baby and Grandma will be more comfortable with your absence.

If you sing to the baby before naptime or bedtime, consider leaving a tape recording of your voice for the caregiver to play while you're gone. Or, have your babysitters or caregivers come to the baby's most familiar surrounding (your home) rather than taking baby to their home. The more familiar everything is to baby, the less stress he will feel. Although you may think they are unaware, babies spend their entire first few months painstakingly taking note of everything in their new world.

If you want, check in with your caregiver frequently—but not too frequently. One or two calls per outing is acceptable, but not a call every hour.

E-SSENTIAL

Time away from baby should not be a guilt-inducing experience but a pleasurable way of re-energizing and maybe even gaining new perspective. Don't feel as if you're a bad parent just because you need a break; in fact, the best parents know when to take time for themselves.

Information Sheet for Babysitters

When you start making time for yourselves again, you'll need to leave some pertinent information at home for anyone who is babysitting your little one. Here's a list of information you might want to keep on the refrigerator door or near the phone.

- ✓ We are out at:
- ✓ We will return at:
- ✓ A number you can call to reach us is:
- ✓ If you can't reach us, call:
- ✓ Baby's mealtime is:
- ✓ Baby's naptime is:
- ✓ For a snack, baby can have:
- ✓ Baby is allergic to:
- ✓ Baby's bedtime is:
- ✓ In case of emergency, call the pediatrician at:
- ✓ Police number:
- ✓ Fire Department number:
- ✓ Special instructions:

Build Your "Village" and Keep It Thriving

Senator Hillary Rodham Clinton was right on target when she wrote that it takes a village to raise a child. Even though you are the center of your baby's universe, there are others who will influence and guide your child through life: grandparents, aunts, uncles, cousins, friends, and even celebrities.

That's why you need to be as careful as possible in selecting those who will be part of your child's "inner circle." Choosing those whom you'd like to include in baby's "village" is a critical first step in baby's development, since you cannot be there every moment of every single day. This is one reason many cultures and religions encourage parents to select godparents for new babies; they are the charter members of baby's village.

Set Healthy Family Boundaries

In terms of family members, you really don't have much choice—family is family, after all. Still, you can choose more interaction with the family members you're close to and limit involvement with the ones you're not. This may be the first time in your life that you've set such healthy boundaries—and that couldn't happen at a better time!

Other Options

But what about those people you will rely on to help care for the baby, particularly if you are dependent on two incomes? What are your options for excellent care of your baby if you return to work? There are two primary ways to get quality home care for your baby. First, you could leave baby with a relative. Grandparents are a great choice (if they are capable and willing), but sisters, aunts, or even older siblings could work just as well. Your situation may dictate that you have more than one person on call to watch the baby.

E-ALERT!

Should you decide to rely on family and friends, create a contingency plan in case something unexpectedly comes up. Also, be sure to show your relatives your appreciation on a regular basis—with money, a gift, or simply a card with heartfelt thanks. A little appreciation goes a long way toward keeping everyone happy; and it can lessen any feelings of being taken for granted.

Second, you could form a babysitting "pool" with friends and neighbors. Particularly if you work part-time hours, you might be able to form a group in your neighborhood or with friends in similar circumstances. Each of you then takes a turn with the babies while the others go to work.

How to Interview a Baby Sitter

Particularly in light of television-show investigations of nannies, au pairs, and babysitters, many parents are leery of letting anyone outside of the family watch or take care of their children for fear of their babies being mistreated by someone they didn't know enough about.

You'll need to interview each candidate, ask for references, and make sure you feel 100 percent comfortable. Start the process as early as your fifth month of pregnancy to give yourself plenty of time to hire the right people.

E-SSENTIAL

Ask potential babysitter questions such as: How long have you been babysitting? Do you have references? What do you enjoy most about working with children? What do you enjoy least? Why do you think you would be a good sitter for my child? What would you do in an emergency situation? Is your schedule flexible?

Be as Careful as Possible

Remember that this is one of the most important jobs you will ever hire anyone to do. It's not out of bounds to consider running a background or police check on someone you'd like to hire. If you're looking for more than occasional babysitting, you'll need to be even more cautious, and ask more questions. (See Chapter 10 for advice on how to find a daycare situation that meets your needs.)

Tips for Sibling Adjustment

The arrival of a new sibling can be a joyous occasion for a young child. But it is not without its challenges, since some children would prefer that they be the apple of Mom's (or Dad's) eye.

The hardest part for children to understand is not necessarily *that* there's a new baby coming but rather *why*: "Why do you need to have another baby, Mommy? Aren't I good enough for you?" "Why do I have to share my room with the baby?" "Why do I have to give the baby my old clothes and toys?"

The pregnancy itself may frighten the child, especially if you're experiencing morning sickness or other less-than-desirable side effects. But for most children, the waiting is the hardest part. Even the most excited siblings-to-be will find the nine-month wait to be painfully slow.

Ways to Get Siblings Involved

There are several ways you can get your child or children more involved in the birthing process. One way is to make the pregnancy seem real from the start. Buy or borrow books on the development of a new baby; some are geared for children under the age of ten; others can be of interest to the whole family. Use these books at story time to explain to your child the intricate process of growing a baby. Be sure to relate the pictures the child is seeing in the books to his or her own development; nothing helps a sibling-to-be understand the process more than the story of his or her own birth.

E-SSENTIAL

Allow your child some hands-on experience feeling the baby move. Also, if you can, take your child with you to the doctor's office. Hearing the baby's heartbeat and seeing an ultrasound are good ways to make the experience more real to your child. If your child can't attend an ultrasound for some reason, ask the doctor for a good picture to take home with you.

You should end each conversation about the baby with, "Do you have any questions or anything more you'd like to know about the baby?" This gives your child the opportunity to air any fears or concerns in a quiet, giving atmosphere.

Involve Your Child in Preparing the Nest

Take your child with you to buy baby clothes, diaper bags, strollers, and crib sheets. Ask whether he likes a particular décor for the baby's room and if there's anything he would like to donate to the baby. It's better to have the child feel involved in the process and to feel as though he has a choice in what to give baby (as opposed to your taking toys away or announcing that the siblings will have to share something). If your child does need to give up a crib or a room, make these arrangements as early as you can so that the sibling can adjust to the change. You might give an older child the bedroom furniture that had been your own as a child; he may be very touched by the special nature of having something that was once Mommy's, as well as by the idea of getting "big-girl" or "big-boy" furniture.

Bring Out Your Child's Baby Scrapbook

Your child may wish to relive babyhood for a little while; don't be worried about this or show disapproval, since it is likely to be a quick phase your child is passing through. If your child wants to play with baby toys, it's okay. Maybe you could encourage him to think of ways to play with or teach the baby with these toys.

Explain What Will Happen at the Hospital

Many hospitals have classes for siblings; see if you can get into one anytime from mid-pregnancy on. Go over the "action plan" with your child; explain where he or she will be taken while you are giving birth. Let your child know when he or she can come to the hospital to see the baby, and be honest about what will happen when you bring the baby home from the hospital. Explain that you will be tired and that at first the baby will mostly sleep, eat, and cry. The child needs to know that the new baby will require lots of care and attention and that he will be a helper more than a playmate in the beginning.

Pack a Special Present in Your Hospital Bag

Give your child a special gift when presenting the new baby. Also, when guests come for the ceremonial "viewing of the baby," you might ask them to pay special attention to the new big brother or sister. Kids feel very left out when the baby is getting all of the attention—and the presents. Even a small token can go a long way in making the sibling feel more comfortable.

Honor Your Child's Feelings, Even If They're Negative

If a sibling is feeling negative about the baby, listen to his feelings in a nonjudgmental way. Try to work through these feelings by addressing the child's fears; most often, the child is afraid you won't love him as much as you used to. If the child begins acting out the negative feelings (by hitting or abusing the baby), seek professional help and limit contact between the two until a resolution becomes clear.

Set and Keep a "Special" Time Together

Create activities that you can do together while baby is napping or otherwise occupied. If there were special things that the two of you used to do, try and preserve as many as you can to help the child feel a sense of security and continuity.

E-ALERT!

Keep in mind that your child has a lot for his young mind to deal with; this thought will help you keep a good perspective through your family transition. Offer your child as much individual attention as possible, and remember that you can never say, "I love you" often enough.

Helping Pets Adjust to Baby

Is your pet treated like a member of the family? Do you shower your dog or cat with affection the minute you return home from work? If so, the baby's arrival will signal a definite change in the dynamics of your relationship. If Fido is used to greeting you and having a little game of Frisbee, imagine how he might feel when you start heading for baby's room first and merely pat him on the head.

The next thing you know, you have a contented baby but a pet who has begun exhibiting some annoying new habits: Suddenly your cat starts urinating on the carpet or your well-behaved dog starts chewing up your shoes. What does this bad behavior mean? In a nutshell, it means your pet is jealous.

A Smooth Transition

Believe it or not, there are plenty of ways to get you (and your pet) through this new transition smoothly. For starters, you must watch any interaction between pet and your infant carefully, especially if this is the first interaction of its type for both. Check for signs of aggressiveness, and if you see any, keep the interaction limited until more time has passed and the two seem better acquainted with one another.

Help your pet get used to the idea of a new baby in the house by letting the animal get used to the baby's scent. If he seems interested in doing so, let him sniff everything from baby's nightshirt to the rocking chair.

Create "Special Time"

Create a new "special time" with the animal, just as you might with a sibling. Your pet needs to know that she is still special to you, even though you have new responsibilities.

As a good precaution, never let your pet and the baby be alone together, for any period of time. Close the baby's door during naptime or crate the animal. Some parents use baby's naptime as their "quality time" with their pet, and a pet would hardly complain about that.

Keep Up with the Basics

Practice regular grooming and cleanliness measures with your pet. Don't let litter boxes fill up, and check regularly for fleas. Take your animals to the groomer if you don't have time to maintain their cleanliness yourself. For hygienic purposes, anyone playing with the pet should make sure to wash his or her hands before handling the baby.

E-SSENTIAL

Getting into a new routine is half the battle. You can circumvent some problems by working with your pet before the baby is born. You could, for instance, involve the pet in the decorating of the baby's room, particularly by letting the pet smell every piece of furniture and perhaps by letting it sit on the baby's rocking chair. Also, before baby is born, it would be a good idea for you to take your pet to the vet for a routine checkup—just to make sure the animal is healthy.

Respect Your Pet's Feelings

The most important thing to keep in mind is that although there are plenty of folks who don't think that animals have feelings, they truly do. They know from the time you announce your pregnancy that change is in the air, because your attentiveness to them is affected from that moment on. As you become consumed with thoughts about the new baby, your pet may be pondering his position in the roost. Being aware of your pet's needs and tending to them in a caring, sensitive manner may be all you need to do to preserve the peace.

Adjustments to Your Relationship

Before the baby came, you were like any other pair of young lovers, basking in the glow of your love. You went out to fancy restaurants, went sailing at the drop of a hat, and made love whenever you wanted to. What's going to happen to that wonderfully independent lifestyle now that baby's here?

The complete turnabout that your love life may take can be very unsettling, especially for the couple used to being on the go. Now there are bottles, diapers, strollers, and naptimes to consider. There is the question of who actually has the car seat this time, where baby's pacifier is, and just why that kid is still crying after all the calming methods you've tried. It seems as though everything revolves around baby—and it does!

Preserve Your Own Time

Once the baby is here, you might feel like you're moving in slow motion. Everything takes at least an hour longer than it used to. Your patience is tested at every turn, and it's getting harder just to talk to each other, let alone spend any meaningful moments together. What can you do to bring the intimacy back to your relationship? The answer is simple: Always make time to talk to each other. It's easy to get bogged down in the daily details of new family management; thus, the two of you as a couple need to reserve time on a daily basis just for "catching up" with each other. It needn't be an hour; it could be accomplished in twenty minutes per day. All you need to do is be open to talking and listening to each other.

Some Words of Advice . . . for Dads

When listening to any problems your partner is experiencing, be sure to repeat back what you've heard to let her know you've understood her correctly. Many men leave this critical stage out of their communication process, only to wind up with the "you-just-don't-understand" argument. If you want to avoid a fight, it's best to respond with empathic statements such as "This must be a tough situation for you" or "I'm hearing that you aren't comfortable with the way I'm doing things." Then ask what she wants from you next. Don't be accusatory or show anger; instead, be gentle, loving, and intent on solving the problem.

Even though the new mother's responsibilities now include someone who demands a lot of attention, you are still the man she fell in love with and the one with whom she is building this new family. Together, you are both an important part of this family's life!

Leaving the Cocoon

There are lots of people (and pets) with whom you will want or need to share baby. But only you can know when you're truly ready to do so. If you feel a need to fiercely protect your time with baby, especially in the first few weeks home, you shouldn't be made to feel like you're being selfish. In fact, it might not be a bad idea to create a cocoonlike home atmosphere for the first few weeks home. Not only will you have some fantastic bonding time with your new baby, but you'll also limit any opportunity for the spread of germs that could make your baby sick.

Waiting until the baby's immune system kicks in can be essential to helping protect your baby from illness—and in those first weeks, that's one less thing to have to worry about.

If you work outside the home and have the luxury of being able to take an extended maternity leave, plan to do so. Since your baby's first days, weeks, and months can represent a time of enormous growth, you won't regret the extra time you get to share with this incredible new little life.

Later, when you decide you're finally ready to share your baby with others in your circle of family and friends, you'll find that your baby is even more adaptable due to the warm moments of building love and trust with you.

Chapter 10

Daycare

Although you may not prefer daycare for your baby, the reality is that many families need to rely on the incomes of both parents. Inevitably, this means you will probably need a caregiver for baby while you're both at work. This could be a friend or relative, or it could be someone you haven't even met yet. Even though you're still pregnant, you want to find a daycare that meets all of your expectations—with room on their roster for one more little one.

Start Planning Now

Quality daycare is in high demand—and some daycare centers even have waiting lists months long. If you wait until after the baby is born, you may have trouble finding a daycare situation you feel totally comfortable with—and waiting too long could mean you'll have to settle for less than your ideal.

Planning is really the key to finding a good daycare; taking the time to develop your plan well in advance of your baby's birth will eliminate additional stress later on. Start checking out daycare options as soon as possible—as early as your third month of pregnancy.

Daycare Centers

Daycare centers are one of the most popular options for working parents. In a center, your child will be cared for in a group setting by adults who are trained in child-rearing and child-development issues. To begin checking into daycare centers, ask your state child-care or child-welfare agency for a list of licensed centers; most states now require commercial child-care providers to be licensed.

Check Out the Basics

Next, call each center for basic info such as fees and availability of space. Ask about the ratio of children to child-care providers. A quality daycare center should care for infants in a separate room, away from toddlers and older children (who can present safety hazards to infants). Infant child-care providers at daycare centers should care for no more than three infants apiece, and two is an even better number.

E-SSENTIAL

It's essential to check out each daycare center on your list. Many unscrupulous daycare operators will say they are licensed when they are in fact not. If you still have doubts or questions, you can contact the National Association for the Education of Young Children (*www.naeyc.org*) for more information.

You should also ask about how many babies are kept in each room. More than six infants in a room, whatever its size, can make for a chaotic, institutionalized setting (and you don't want your baby kept awake constantly from other babies' crying).

Pay a Visit

If the center checks out so far, you may want to schedule a visit. Ask the center director when the older children generally nap, and avoid visiting at that time, since you'll want to see how well the child-care providers manage when most of the children are awake. Here are some things to look for during a visit to a daycare center:

✓ Do the children at the center seem happy? Do they look reasonably clean?

✓ Are the rooms bright and airy? Do they have natural light?

✓ Is there a good selection of toys? Centers should have plenty of age-appropriate, safe toys that encourage creativity and motor development.

✓ Is the center clean? In particular, check the bathrooms and food preparation areas. Do you detect a strong odor of urine anywhere?

✓ Is there a safe outdoor play area?

✓ Is the center thoroughly childproofed? Ask to see fire exits and first aid supplies.

✓ Do the child-care providers seem attentive to the children's needs?

✓ How noisy is the center? Happy kids do make noise—but total chaos is a problem.

✓ How capable do the child-care providers seem at setting limits for the children? At resolving conflicts between the children?

✓ Does the staff seem willing and eager to talk with you? Do they appear interested in getting to know your baby?

✓ Are you meeting everyone who works at the facility, from the operator to instructors to clean-up help? You should be able to meet anyone who might possibly come into contact with your baby. It's also a good idea to ask about the turnover ratio, since a lot of new kids coming in can mean exposure to a lot of new germs.

Once you have narrowed your choices down to one or two centers, ask for at least three references. Call them all and ask for feedback. If they do not give you glowing reports, look elsewhere.

E-FACT

In a good situation, your child will have other children of a similar age to play with, facilities that are expressly designed for her needs, child-care providers who are knowledgeable and experienced, and a wide variety of age-appropriate activities. Daycare centers can also be moderate in price, especially when compared to the cost of hiring a trained nanny.

Weigh the Negatives

When you are choosing child care for a young infant, you may find daycare centers a bit institutional and potentially overwhelming for your baby. Another negative consideration is the issue of staff turnover. Even good centers can experience a lot of staff turnover, and too many child-care providers in too short a time can interfere with a baby's long-term ability to form lasting attachments to other people. Finally, any time you take your child outside of your home for care, you are in for a certain amount of inconvenience.

Family Daycare

This childcare option is growing in popularity. Unlike a daycare center, a family daycare provider cares for children in her own home. Often, one or more of the children in the group are her own.

Most states have licensing requirements for family daycare, but some providers operate illegally, either because they cannot meet the health, safety, or educational requirements of their state licensing agency, or because they do not want to declare their daycare income to the IRS (these will insist that you pay them in cash). If you live in a state that licenses family daycare operations, resist the urge to check out that nice, but unlicensed, child-care provider down the street, and only consider licensed child-care providers.

E-ALERT!

Since some state requirements are fairly minimal, it is important to check out even licensed family daycare situations carefully.

Make a List of Providers in Your Area

Start your search by obtaining a list of licensed child-care providers in your area from your state child-care or child-welfare agency. Ask friends and neighbors if they know of any good family daycare providers and check to see if those people are on your list. Call those names first and ask if they have room for your child. It can be harder to find family daycare for an infant than for a toddler, since child-care providers typically can accept only one or two infants into their group. If a provider is recommended but doesn't have room for your child in the near future, ask her to recommend someone who might.

Make an Appointment

If a provider meets your requirements, make an appointment to visit her during the day. She may ask you to come during naptime, but make sure you see her in action while all the children are awake too. Spend some time there and check the place out as best you can. Ask other parents for their feedback as well.

E-SSENTIAL

Depending on the age of your child and the provider's requirements, you'll need to have a diaper bag packed each day with diapers, wipes, bottles, bibs, a few changes of clothes, and so on. Coupled with having to get your child fed, dressed, and ready (and getting yourself ready, too), all this can make early mornings at your home a bit hectic.

Clean, Safe, and Happy

The house where your baby will spend lots of time in the near future should be clean. The kitchen and the bathroom should be sanitary. Also, unless you are standing right next to the diaper pail, you should not detect a strong odor of urine anywhere.

Look carefully at the area in which the children spend most of their time (most likely the living or family room). Is it light and airy? Is the furniture comfortable for small children? Since babies and young children play a lot on the floor, carpeting should be vacuumed frequently, especially if there are pets. The house should also be childproofed, with clearly visible gates on the staircases, latches on kitchen cabinets, and covers on visible electrical outlets.

E-FACT

Don't expect as many toys as you might find at a daycare center, but the provider should have at least a few age-appropriate, safe toys that encourage creativity and motor development, for both the infants and the older children. The provider may also allow you to bring over some of your child's own favorite toys and leave them there.

Is there an outdoor play space? Is it safe and fenced off? If the provider does not have an outdoor play space, ask her where she takes the children for outdoor play.

Finally, the children should look happy and the atmosphere should be calm. The daycare provider should seem relaxed, not tense, when she is dealing with the children.

Check References

Finally, check at least three references—ideally, parents of children she cares for or has cared for in the past. If they don't seem enthusiastic about her, keep looking.

In a good family daycare situation, your child will spend her day in a homey atmosphere and will benefit socially by having other children to play with. If you stay with the daycare provider over the long term, your child may come to regard her as a second mom and be treated as part of the family. In many areas of the country, family daycare is also relatively inexpensive and a more economical option than are daycare centers. As with a daycare center, though, you sacrifice a certain amount of convenience when you take your children outside your home for child care.

Child Care in Your Home

If you want your child to have one-on-one attention, child care in your home can be a good choice. There are two basic types of home child-care providers: nannies and au pairs. Many people think the two are basically the same thing, but there are many important differences.

Nannies and Nanny Placement Agencies

A nanny takes care of your child in your home. She may live in your home or live out of it. Many nannies have formal training in child care and child development. Others have no formal training but rely on life experience.

There are many agencies that will, for a fee, help you find a nanny. While agencies vary in their screening and training processes, they should, at minimum, do a complete background check of potential candidates (including a police check), provide you with references, and find you at least a couple of candidates to choose from. Fees vary, but in larger cities nanny agencies may charge you fees of $1,000 or more (although if your first choice doesn't work out, the next search may be on the house).

E-QUESTION

What if you don't want to pay a nanny agency?
Ask your relatives, friends, or neighbors if they can recommend someone. Or, place an ad in your local newspaper. Specify the number of children, their ages, whether you want live-in or live-out care, whether the nanny will need a car, the town you live in, and the minimum amount of child-care experience you would prefer.

Be Prepared to Pay

Nannies are in high demand in most areas and you will need to offer a competitive salary. Live-out nannies working in major metropolitan areas typically earn $14–$20 an hour, depending on their level of experience. For full-time nannies, this can mean a monthly salary of $2,600–$4,000, in addition to medical benefits, paid sick leave, and vacation time, and a variety of other benefits such as health-club membership or travel discounts. If you're working through a nanny placement service, it's usually the agency that takes care of the nanny's benefits out of the fees you pay them for the nanny's services. You'll pay less if you can find a live-in nanny (you'll need an extra bedroom for this option) who will take part of her compensation as room and board.

Be Realistic in Your Expectations

Keep your expectations realistic. Outside of hands-on child care, a nanny should be able to prepare your children's meals and perhaps do a little light housework that pertains to their care (like picking up toys or doing your children's laundry). She is not going to clean your house from top to bottom and cook gourmet meals for you while your baby naps.

Au Pairs

Despite popular misconceptions, an au pair is not a nanny. She is typically a college-age, eighteen- to twenty-six-year-old foreign student who comes to this country for a year to experience American culture. Au pairs agree to commit to living with a family for a year's time and provide child care and light housework in exchange for room, board, a stipend, and sometimes tuition expenses. Since they are also students, their workload cannot be more than forty-five hours per week.

If you are considering hiring an au pair, keep in mind that the program was not created to provide child care for Americans. Instead, it was designed to provide a foreign living experience for young people. You should also keep in mind that in other countries, au pairs generally have fewer responsibilities than they are often expected to assume in this country, and they rarely serve as the sole care providers for children while their parents are out of the house.

E-ALERT!

You will need to hire an au pair through an agency. The agency is supposed to do a thorough background check and provide you with references. It is also supposed to provide the au pair with a certain amount of child-care training, as well as CPR training. Make sure you know in advance exactly what experience and training you can expect an au pair to have.

While you will probably not have the opportunity to interview a potential au pair in person, you can ask some of the same questions you would ask when interviewing a nanny over the telephone. Try to get a sense of the person's experience and interests, and whether the person is interested in and likes children.

A More Affordable Option

A main attraction of au pairs is cost. If you have an extra bedroom, this is almost always the least expensive child-care option short of your relatives. Even when agency fees and an au pair's transportation and tuition are factored in, costs rarely exceed $300 a week, plus room and board, for a maximum of forty-five hours of child care and some light housework. You should be aware that while you may end up with a wonderful, nurturing, experienced live-in child-care provider, you may also spend a year trying to train a homesick teenager in the rudiments of baby care. You can always ask for a more experienced au pair prior to making a commitment to the au pair agency.

Do Your Own Background Check

If you are not working with a child-care provider network or agency and want to do a background check of local candidates, you can easily use online services to do so. Start with a strong search engine such as Google, or visit your local sheriff's Web site to see their sexual offender listing, which (in most cases) can be searched by zip code.

You may also try using some commercial software or Web services such as Net Detective, Web Detective, KnowX.com, or LocatePeople.org. To respect privacy laws, it's generally a good idea to get permission in writing from the person you are investigating. Most standard job application forms (available at your local office supply store) now include a check box for the applicant to grant permission for a criminal background check only.

The Final Choice Is Yours

With so many child-care choices ahead of you, it's easy to feel overwhelmed. The bottom line is, if you don't feel comfortable—if something about the daycare center or individual child-care provider bothers you, no matter how small or seemingly unimportant, you owe it to yourself to either address the issue or to move on to the next center or person on the list. If you start with a list of most desirable qualities in a childcare provider and rate each one accordingly, a final decision will be much easier to make. The basic things to look for are communication, access and honesty.

Communication, Access, and Honesty

Child-care providers shouldn't make commitments they can't or don't intend to keep. They shouldn't cover up problems or accidents that occur. Providers should give you frequent and complete updates about your child's progress and problems. If they keep you informed, you can develop ways to deal with problems and build on the activities and accomplishments of the day.

E-ALERT!

If providers feel that they can't abide by certain wishes, they should be candid about their inability to do so. Providers should also abide by parents' wishes on matters such as discipline, TV viewing, food, adult smoking, and toilet training.

There should always be open access to a home-based or commercial daycare. Parents must be welcome to visit at any time, even without calling first. Providers should also allow parents to make a reasonable number of phone calls to check on their child's well-being, especially in the case of minor illness or separation anxiety. You and the provider should work out the best times for these calls and determine in advance how many are reasonable.

E-QUESTION

Should providers criticize or advise parents on child rearing?
Not unless parents ask for their advice. If asked, they should always offer advice in a noncritical way. Of course, if providers see something that is seriously wrong (i.e., signs of abuse, neglect, or malnutrition), they should discuss the problem with the parents and, if necessary, contact the proper authorities.

Advance Notice of Changes

Since it is often very difficult to find adequate alternate care, providers should tell parents well in advance if they are going to change their hours or prices—or if they plan to close down or limit the number of children in their care. Parents need at least a month's (or, better yet, six weeks') notice if they need to find a new care provider for their child. A center or family daycare provider should also clarify holiday schedules, so parents know which days are covered and which are not. Not every calendar holiday is a paid holiday for working parents. And except in the case of emergency, parents should be given at least two weeks' notice even if the provider won't be available on a nonholiday day.

Stay Connected

Once your baby arrives and you're ready to go back to work, you'll feel a mix of emotions at the prospect of being separated from your child for several hours a day. However, if you've done all of your homework beforehand, you can also feel a strong sense of relief that you've made the best possible choice. Now all you need to do is follow your child-care plan—and find ways to stay connected despite the fact that you are at work.

The best way to remain involved in your child's daycare experience is to stay connected. Set weekly or monthly "in-touch" meetings with your child-care provider to ask questions and discuss your child's progress. Drop in when you can for parties or special events. If getting time away from work is an issue, offer to set up a blog, chat room, or online group where you and your child-care provider can stay in contact throughout the day. Or simply offer to donate snacks, hand sanitizer, or disinfectant for toy clean-up days. With a little effort on your part, you can stay connected to your baby in the most important way of all—ensuring a safe, healthy, and loving "village" of care.

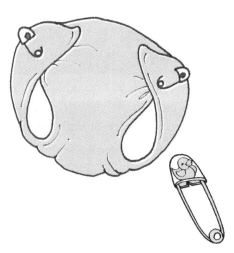

Chapter 11

Bonding with Your Baby

Your baby is just waking up from a nap, and you tiptoe carefully into the room. You walk up to the crib, look over the rail, and you see a glimmer of a smile from your baby—a gift from baby to you. Is baby as attached to you as you are to him? Yes, but you are each attached for different reasons. Unlike adults, babies do not make attachments based solely on love; they also feel a biological imperative to bond.

Will You Bond?

If you're concerned about your ability to bond with your new baby, you should be relieved to know that you are not alone in your fears. Most new parents feel some uneasiness over whether they will be able to form a close family. After all, you've never had to do the work of building a family before; up until this point, you've only had to be a member of one. However, if some time has passed and you still don't feel a real bond with baby, call your obstetrician, since it could be a sign of postpartum depression. Not to worry—help will be on the way if you simply reach out!

What Baby Really Needs from You

At every stage of their tiny lives, babies will depend on you for different things. For the first two months, your baby will simply need to have basic needs met; you will bond with baby while feeding, changing, or rocking baby. Until the first spontaneous smile is given to you, you won't have tangible evidence of bonding.

After two months, baby begins to develop a personality, building on patterns established during those first few months. Baby is becoming your little buddy. At this stage, you begin to notice patterns. When baby is wet, the cry is even pitched; but when the baby is hungry, the cry may become quite high pitched. Baby is dependent on you at this point to learn his or her signals.

Baby S.O.S.

Baby's distress signals are relatively easy to deal with. All you have to do is go down the list of baby's basic needs: Does the diaper need to be changed? Is baby hungry again? Does baby need a nap?

A contented baby is a happy, quiet little one who seems perfectly at ease in whatever she is doing at the moment. For instance, a contented baby will swing for a half hour and not cry frantically when she is picked up to go to bed.

Mystery Emotions

Other emotions are a little more perplexing. A baby's smile, for instance, gives rise to arguments over whether the baby is truly happy or has just passed gas.

What is baby really smiling about when he or she flashes that toothless grin? Babies begin life with little if any muscle control in their faces; thus, the first smiles are actually reflex smiles. After the baby is a few weeks old, the smile becomes more controlled but is still quite random. Baby will smile at happy voices or at tummy gas, but the smile is not directed to anything specific. The best smiles, of course, come between four and six months, when baby begins to smile at the puppy, or the toy, or directly at you (returning your smile).

E-QUESTION

Do babies get angry?
Yes—but not usually until they are at least six months old. That's because anger is primarily about something that has changed or been taken away, and baby doesn't usually notice such disturbances until he or she is at the six month mark. The emotions of an infant are, at best, crude attempts to get needs met.

How Babies Learn

Since you don't always see outward evidence to the contrary, you might think baby has a one-track mind based on whatever need is most immediate. To some extent, that's true, but rest assured, there's more going on in that growing brain than a self-assessment of hunger, wetness, or need for sleep! Your baby is actually quite flexible in how she grows and learns. Baby's brain is growing and changing, also. The things your baby sees, hears, and does help her to learn about the world, and also generate an interest in the people and things in the immediate environment.

Your baby's growing little mind has come into the world like a super-absorbent sponge, ready to absorb all kinds of interesting things. But most important, your baby is learning from you how to be a person. At the same time, you are learning to be a parent, watching your baby for cues that will help you communicate more effectively. Learning to pay attention and respond positively to each other will help you both to bond.

Making Sense of It All

Since before birth, your baby has been taking in lots of information—starting with the sound and rhythm of your heartbeat, and remembering the sound of your voice. Baby learns from what she sees, hears, smells and touches; after seeing or hearing something several times, she can remember whether she has seen or heard it before. Early on, repetition is precisely how she learns.

Your baby's brain grows and changes in important ways every day. The experiences your baby has are important for these changes. Some parts of the brain are most important for learning, while other parts are critical for remembering new things. These parts will continue to grow and change as your baby learns new things every day!

E-SSENTIAL

Experts say that responding to your baby in a loving and attentive way helps him to learn—so talk to your baby often! Provide your baby with a variety of experiences (talking, singing, playing games) to help baby explore his world safely, positively, and imaginatively.

Baby Quality Time

Creating special moments that will last a lifetime isn't a difficult thing; all you need to do is be sure to catch baby at the right time. The best time during the first few months for bonding with your baby is right after feeding and changing. At that time, most of baby's needs have been met, and baby will generally be in a happier mood.

If you work outside the home, concentrate on spending quality time with your baby when you return home from work. Quality time is time you set aside for baby—and baby alone. Focus entirely on the baby, and have a great time doing so. If the phone rings while you're playing with baby, you can let the answering machine or voice mail answer it.

What can you do during quality time with baby? It needn't be anything elaborate. Many first-time parents, guilt stricken over their time away from the baby, try to fit every single activity into a half hour with baby in the early evening. This practice not only is unnecessary (since baby doesn't have a concept of time) but also can lead to overstimulation for the baby; and the parents could misread the baby's irritability as an expression of dissatisfaction with their being away all day.

E-SSENTIAL

It's hard not to take baby's tears personally when you feel uneasy about your situation, but realize that the baby isn't keeping track of your hours together. All babies know (and need to know) is that there are people in the world who love them, care for them, and spend time with them.

Give yourself credit for all that you do accomplish with baby, and give baby a break whenever she needs one. Babyhood is not about how many toys one has or how much time Mommy and Daddy have to spare. It's about the quality of the time spent and the depth of the bonds of love that are expressed between parents and their babies. Creating a lasting bond depends more on sincerity than on longevity.

What to Say When You Talk to Your Baby

How many people do you know that talk baby talk to babies? More than you'd probably care to think about. Is baby talk bad for babies? Well, it doesn't really hurt, but it doesn't necessarily help baby's language development, either.

It's best to talk to a baby just as you would talk to any other person. Just work at keeping it simple. (Reading *War and Peace* to your baby isn't going to help him or her learn the language any faster.) Start with simple sounds and then build to short, concise words.

E-ALERT!

Don't expect too much in the beginning! Make sounds slowly, mouthing and saying "o-o-o" and giving baby ample time to hear (and eventually repeat) it. After about a month of this, baby should finally repeat the sound, and baby's language development skills will be off to a great start.

Other tips for talking to your baby include:

✓ Keep it short and sweet. Use short, simple words like happy, ball, puppy, and kitty when you talk to your baby. Babies can only process a few syllables at a time; so go slow and keep it simple.

✓ Use toys as visual cues. Find a toy that is a favorite of baby's to play with; tell baby the name of the toy (bear, rattle, etc.), and use its name frequently. Give the toy to baby right after saying what it is.

✓ Involve baby's body. Clap baby's hands along when you play word games. Physical activity can help baby associate learning new words with something that feels good to do.

✓ Narrate everyday activities. Narrate the things you do during the day, for baby's sake. When baby is on the changing table, for instance, you could say, "Now, I'm going to change your diaper. See, di-a-per. All clean!" When you show baby a diaper and then say the word, baby starts to associate pictures with words.

✓ Use baby's name often. Dale Carnegie was right when he said that there is no sweeter sound to a human than the sound of his own name. This is how baby's sense of personal identity develops.

✓ Read to baby. Short, simple books that have a touchy-feely approach (such as mirrors for baby to look into or fake fur to pet) are a good starting point, since much of a baby's early processing occurs through sensual, hands-on experiences. Books of rhymes are good, too, since there is repetition of sounds.

Using Baby Sign Language

Baby sign language is a relatively new concept for parents who want their babies to express their needs in a special, and often more direct, way. Despite its initial challenges, it can be a great way to bond with your child until more language skill is acquired.

If you choose to sign with your baby, start slowly when the baby is at least six months old. Begin with just a few simple concepts like "milk," "sleep" and "eat" before moving on to more descriptive words. Always use the sign with the activity so that baby can connect visual cues to the hand signal for each specific concept. Most of all, relax and enjoy the experience of communicating in an entirely new way with your baby. It can truly be an amazing experience!

There are a variety of detailed instructions, flash cards, books, Web sites and DVDs to help you learn how to teach your baby sign language. See Appendix A for more information.

E-FACT

Proponents of baby sign language say that babies who sign can communicate their wants or needs earlier, more frequently, and with less frustration than other babies. Some experts say that signing babies may even be able to learn foreign languages more easily later in life!

How to Have a Well-Adjusted Baby

Your baby begins life with the most important ingredient to development: love. Loving your baby is the first step in building a secure environment, one in which baby can grow and learn and feel your support every step of the way. Take your time with day-to-day activities, such as feeding, rocking, and singing to baby. If baby feels rushed (because you're on a cellular phone and have the baby propped up with a bottle for your own convenience), there could be emotional or eating disturbances later. Set the tone for good habits early.

E-ALERT!

Remember that babies can do no wrong. They aren't capable of distinguishing behaviors, so you cannot punish a baby. Never shake or hit a baby. Be caring and supportive. You will get your chance to teach baby when he or she becomes a toddler and is more capable of processing right and wrong.

Be Positive

Encourage baby with your vocal intonation. When baby achieves something, enthusiastically say lots of, "Good girl!" The first time baby tries to talk, encourage her with your voice, even though baby's sounds don't make sense yet. Have you ever known a puppy (or a person) who didn't keep trying after being positively encouraged?

Use your baby's name often, and associate it with different things. Say, for example, "Kelsey is a good girl" or "Andrew can talk!" Build language skills early in your child by planting positive pictures in her mind.

Let your baby experience other gentle, loving people (and even pets). A well-balanced child can spend time with anyone and doesn't cry for Mom or Dad every time someone new comes into the room.

Baby's Personality

From that very first smile, you were probably convinced that your baby was the best baby ever. But while your baby may indeed be expressing some joy, the truth is, it may not necessarily be directed at you. Still, every baby has a unique personality—traits that you will discover through lots of great daily interaction. Just remember that, at least in the beginning, many of baby's actions are simply mirroring your own antics; that's why it's really important to set a positive tone with baby through fun, yet calm, interaction, Keep stimulating baby's mind, and nourishing baby's psyche with warm, loving thoughts. Do those two things on a daily basis, and you'll find that you do indeed have the best (and most emotionally secure) baby ever!

Is Baby Adaptable?

Some babies readily accept new situations, people, toys, or surroundings without so much as batting a tiny eyelash, while others can't seem to move from one room to another without a crying jag. For those slow-to-transition types, it's best to move slowly from one activity or place to another, giving baby time to accept that something has changed in his or her environment. For some babies, changes create insecurity. If that seems to be the case with your baby, it's a good idea to do anything you can to help baby learn that he or she is always safe with you. Hold baby close, swaddle baby, or sing softly as you slowly (and gently) move from one situation to another. Over time, baby will build confidence and learn to be more secure, making him a much better playmate for other babies in social settings.

How to Start (or Be in) a Playgroup

Picture several parents sitting around in a circle, babies on their laps. As they sing, "The Wheels on the Bus," they clap baby's hands together or bounce their knees in time to the music. After the song is over, the babies play "So Big," with parents stretching their arms and legs to show how big they are (and, of course, to exercise them). Someone brings out a xylophone, and babies then get to try their tiny hands at making music.

This is not a scene from a TV show, and these babies are not necessarily "gifted" children. They come from all social, economic, and ethnic groups, and from different backgrounds. The only thing they have in common is their love of play.

Join Up!

If you aren't a member of a playgroup, you might do well to consider joining one. Such groups can be a fun way to explore new activities with your baby and with other parents who may offer you interesting (and fun) suggestions. Such groups often use music, art, and educational (yet fun) toys to create new experiences—and as a bonding aid between parent and child.

Playgroups are especially good for new families living in a place that is far away from family and friends; you can connect with others who experience the same tribulations and joys that you do. It can also be a positive experience for your baby, since babies love to look at and play with other babies.

Finding a Playgroup

Word-of-mouth is the best way to find a local playgroup. Ask other parents you see at the park or grocery store. Find out if your church sponsors one. Often, your community newspaper is a good source for such groups. If you don't see an ad in the paper, call an editor to ask whether she knows of a good playgroup.

Or Starting Your Own

If all else fails, why not start a playgroup yourself? Place a classified ad in your local paper or post flyers at the grocery store or at your church. There are plenty of good resources to guide you in what games to play and what kinds of toys to have on hand. If you can get enough parents interested, you can ask for a small membership fee to cover expenses such as toys, extra diapers and wipes, snacks, and so forth.

Babies need socialization in the same way that puppies do. Finding a group you and baby feel comfortable with can be a great bonding experience for both of you.

The Upset Baby

The doorbell rings and the dog barks like crazy. Or you accidentally set off your car alarm. Whatever the cause, there are several things that may move baby out of her comfort zone during the first year—setting off a panic that results in seemingly uncontrollable tears. There are often three major causes of distress in babies: loud noises, separation anxiety, and improper handling.

Loud Noises

Approaching baby quickly and loudly can cause her to cry. Some people, especially those who have never had children before (but adore them nonetheless), just don't realize that excessive gushing can scare the you-know-what out of a baby. Loud music can also startle or upset baby, so tell the teenagers (or neighbors) to tone it down.

Separation Anxiety

Being away from Mom or Dad can also cause baby to let out a wail or two. Even if the baby knows that Grandma is nice or that the babysitter is sweet, he or she also knows that you are leaving—and that is a scary thought for a baby. In truth, however, separation anxiety can be harder on parents than on babies.

Improper Handling

Limit contact with small children and pets, at least until you're sure how they will do with your new baby. Small children can accidentally hurt baby. They just don't understand that baby is too small yet to be a playmate. Pets can also frighten or even harm baby. Slowly integrate them, and always maintain your supervision. It is absolutely unsafe to leave pets alone with baby, even for a minute. Even the sweetest little pet can cause the baby injury if jealous or accidentally provoked.

Is Baby Overstimulated?

Many first-time parents aren't sure when to stop playing with their babies; they think baby's crankiness is a signal for them to switch to yet another toy or an expression of dissatisfaction with their parenting ability. But how can you tell when enough is enough? Baby's sounds and body language will tell you all you need to know.

When a baby is overstimulated (either by too much noise or overzealous playing), you will know it by baby's crying. There may even be some rubbing of the eyes, strong kicking, and stiffness when you attempt to comfort baby through rocking or holding.

The best thing you can do is put the baby in bed, dim the lights, and put on soft, gentle music. Any other noise or fussing on the part of parents will only serve to annoy baby further. All babies need some quiet time alone (just as adults do); so respect that need in your baby. Sometimes, fussiness is the only way baby can tell you that he wants to be alone for a while.

Regular Communication Is Key

Whether you choose to sign with your baby or communicate with words, the best way to stay on top of baby's needs is to listen and observe as much as possible. Often, the needs are quite simple and the recommended course of action fast and direct. You won't have too many unusual demands from your baby—at least in the first year of life!

Anticipate your baby's most basic needs by keeping food, fresh diapers and clothing close at hand, and always be ready to share giggles and smiles, since those are a natural part of bonding. Radiate warmth, love, and encouragement, and you will find that you have a baby whose entire world happily revolves around you.

Chapter 12

Caring for Baby— and Staying Fit

Once you've had your baby, the thing you'll be most concerned with is how to properly care for her. Remember that the overall health and well being—including nutrition and exercise—of both you and your baby are your top priorities. It doesn't matter which methods you choose, as long as you choose what's right for both of you. But remember, your postpregnancy routine should be focused on gradual change and development rather than on immediate results.

Breast or Bottle?

Baby's first-ever need from you is food. Many babies, in fact, feed in those first few moments after birth. But whether you choose to breastfeed or bottle-feed, there are plenty of important considerations to mull over prior to making a decision. You'll need as much information as possible to ensure that the final decision is one that you feel good about and that baby draws the most benefit from in the long run.

E-ALERT!

If you don't feel comfortable with the way you are feeding your baby, your discomfort level will become evident to the baby, and you could wind up with some feeding problems.

You've probably heard from both sides on the issue of breastfeeding. Some mothers (and some doctors) will tell you that breastfeeding is the only way to make sure that baby is getting proper nutrition. Others will say that formula feedings now have better nutrients than they used to contain. Both of these arguments are actually correct. Formula is better than it has ever been, and breast milk provides excellent protection against illnesses. So, what's a new parent to do? All things being equal, it really boils down to your own personal comfort level and core belief system.

Breastfeeding: What You Should Know

Breastfeeding is the most highly recommended form of providing proper nutrition for your baby. Your own milk not only has the right amount of fat and nutrients to help baby grow but also contains compounds that help build baby's immune system. In fact, researchers at the University of Texas Medical Branch in Galveston say that breastfeeding helps protect the roughly 19 percent of babies who would otherwise have been highly susceptible to chronic ear infections due to genetic abnormalities. These protective benefits lasted long past infancy.

Nursing your baby should begin immediately upon birth, to give you and baby a chance to get used to this new method of meeting baby's nutritional needs. Remember that up until this point, baby has only fed on your food and prenatal vitamins—and had room service deliver it via the umbilical cord!

Now, baby has to work a little bit harder for her food. So, when you first begin to breastfeed, expect that it may take a few tries before the two of you get the hang of it. Invest in the services of a lactation consultant who can ease your mind by showing you the proper positions for breastfeeding and how to tell if baby has a good latch.

E-FACT

Contrary to popular belief, breastfeeding is not as easy as it looks—at first. What mothers are made to believe comes naturally may often be trial and error until they get used to it; so don't lose your cool until you're absolutely sure there's a problem that will permanently impede your breastfeeding efforts.

Mastitis (a painful infection of the milk ducts) is one reason mothers stop nursing their babies; the other common reason for discontinuing nursing (besides needing to return to work) is the mother's belief that she'll never get it right. In the latter case, try not to give up until you've discussed the problem with your doctor or a lactation consultant, since it may be an easy problem to fix.

Nurse as Often as Possible

Of course, you'll want to nurse every time the baby seems hungry. At the hospital, if you are sure you want to nurse exclusively, be sure to point this out clearly to the neonatal nurses. So often, well-meaning nurses offer to feed the baby glucose water or formula so that you can rest. If you don't want this to happen, be clear and direct in your instructions that baby be brought to you every time he seems hungry. The more you nurse, the more milk you will produce. Experts agree that you should try to feed at least eight to twelve times per day.

Don't Worry about the First Few Days

The first few days, you will not see (or feel) a whole lot of milk. However, your pre-milk has plenty of nutrients in it for baby to consume, and baby actually doesn't need much more in the first days. It takes regular stimulation to make more milk. When your milk is delivered, you'll know it: Your breasts will swell, and they may even feel like cool water is running through them. Some women report a tingling feeling. Whatever symptom you experience, you'll know it's time for feeding your baby when your breasts are ready.

Practice Makes Perfect

Position baby's chin and nose against your breast, and then make sure baby gets the entire nipple in his mouth. If you just let baby attach to the tip of your nipple, you will not have a good latch; and while baby can still get milk, your nipples will feel like they are nearly being pulled off of your body. If you see tiny sores or blood on your nipples, you likely aren't positioning baby correctly, and your nipples are probably starting to abscess. Good positioning is everything!

E-SSENTIAL

You should try to nurse for at least ten minutes on each side to encourage milk production in both breasts. You should also drink lots of fluid before, during, and after feeding. You'll need to stay hydrated in order to produce more milk and to keep your own body in a healthy balance.

Is Baby Getting Enough Milk?

Most new mothers are concerned about their babies getting enough milk. In the first few days, when you're in the hospital your baby should stay with you in your room if there are no complications with the delivery or with your baby's health. Don't expect the baby to wake you up when she is hungry. You will have to wake the baby every one to two hours to feed her. At first you will be feeding your baby colostrum, your precious first milk that is thick and yellowish. Even though it looks like only a small amount, this is the only food your baby needs. In the beginning, you can expect your baby to lose some weight. This is very normal and is not from breastfeeding. As long as the baby doesn't lose more than 7 to 10 percent of her birth weight during the first three to five days, she is getting enough to eat.

Keep Tabs on Diapers

You can tell your baby is getting enough milk by keeping track of the number of wet and dirty diapers. In the first few days, when your milk is low in volume and high in nutrients, your baby will have only one or two wet diapers a day. After your milk supply has increased, your baby should have five to six wet diapers and three to four dirty diapers every day. Consult your pediatrician if you are concerned about your baby's weight gain. You should visit your pediatrician between three to five days after your baby's birth and then again at two weeks of age.

After you and your baby go home from the hospital, your baby still needs to eat about every one to two hours and should need several diaper changes. In the early weeks after birth, you should wake your baby to feed if four hours have passed since the beginning of the feeding. (If you are having a hard time waking your baby, you can try undressing her or wiping her face with a cool washcloth.) As your milk comes in after the baby is born, there will be more and more diaper changes. The baby's stools will become runny, yellowish, and may have little white bumpy "seeds."

Your Breasts Will Regulate Milk Amounts

You can feel confident that your baby is getting enough to eat because your breasts will regulate the amount of milk your baby needs. If your baby needs to eat more or more often, your breasts will increase the amount of milk they produce. To keep up your milk supply when you give bottles of expressed breast milk for feedings, pump your milk when your baby gets a bottle of breast milk.

Other signs that your baby is getting enough milk are:

✓ Steady weight gain after the first week of age. From birth to three months, typical weight gain is four to eight ounces per week.
✓ Pale yellow urine, not deep yellow or orange.
✓ Sleeping well, yet baby is alert and looks healthy when awake.

Remember, the more often and effectively a baby nurses, the more milk there will be. Breasts produce and supply milk directly in response to the baby's need or demand.

Make It Easier on Yourself

Hospital nurses mean well and are often quite knowledgeable about breast-feeding. Yet, there are still many who don't really know how to help you. Ask for the lactation consultant first; and if your hospital doesn't have one, ask who the best nurse is on staff to help you. Don't take the advice of just anyone passing by unless it's from someone you trust.

Also, once you're home, keep baby in a bassinet next to your bed. That way, you don't have far to go when baby gets hungry in the middle of the night. And breastfeeding babies nearly always will be hungry a few times at night.

E-QUESTION

Did you know that your baby will tell you when she is full?
Cradle your baby's head, but not so closely that baby can't turn away from you when she is finished eating. That's baby's way of telling you she is done.

Protect Your Nipples

To build up nipple durability and keep from getting too tender, try expressing a little bit of breast milk and rubbing it into your nipples. Let the milk air dry. This offers your nipples natural protection from dry or chapped skin. Another solution is to use lanolin cream on your breasts; it provides a safe, harmless barrier to skin problems. It isn't necessary to use soap on your nipples, and it may remove helpful natural oils that are secreted by the Montgomery glands, which are in the areola. Soap can cause drying and cracking and make the nipple more prone to soreness.

Follow Your Prenatal Diet

Be sure to follow your prenatal diet (and stay on the vitamins as long as you're breastfeeding). Eat a well-balanced diet, and keep the fluids coming. Don't drink too much fluid, however, since this can defeat the purpose. A dozen or more servings a day is probably too much.

Benefits for You, Too

The benefits of breastfeeding are not limited to baby. You too can reap some rewards, including weight loss (if you breastfeed for at least three months); a uterus that contracts more quickly (since feeding stimulates contraction); and a lower chance of breast cancer (for you and, believe it or not, for female babies who were breastfed). Also, breastfed babies tend to spit up less than formula-fed babies do. Best of all, it's free and always available, no matter where you are. You can also use a breast pump for times you can't be there, to ensure that baby is getting breast milk at all times.

E-FACT

At first your breasts contain a kind of milk called colostrum, which is thick and usually yellow or golden in color. Colostrum is gentle to your baby's stomach and helps protect your baby from disease. Your milk supply will increase and the color will change to a bluish-white color during the next few days after your baby's birth.

How to Make Breastfeeding Work for You

Breastfeeding can be a wonderful experience for you and your baby. It's important not to get frustrated if you are having problems. What works for one mother and baby may not work for another, so just focus on finding a comfortable routine and positions for you and your baby. Here are some tips for making it work, from the National Women's Health Information Center:

✓ Get an early start. You should start nursing as early as you can after delivery (within an hour or two if it is possible), when your baby is awake and the sucking instinct is strong.

✓ Nurse on demand. Newborns need to nurse often. Breastfeed at least every two hours and when they show signs of hunger, such as being more alert or active, mouthing (putting hands or fists to mouth and making sucking motion with mouth), or rooting (turning head in search of nipple). Crying is a late sign of hunger. Most newborn babies want to breastfeed about eight to twelve times in twenty-four hours.

✓ Feed baby only breast milk. Nursing babies don't need water, sugar water, or formula. Breastfeed exclusively for about the first six months. Giving other liquids reduces the baby's intake of vitamins from breast milk.

✓ Delay artificial nipples. A newborn needs time to learn how to breastfeed. It is best to wait until the newborn develops a good sucking pattern before giving her a pacifier. Artificial nipples require a different sucking action than real ones. Sucking at a bottle can also confuse some babies when they are first learning how to breastfeed.

✓ Breastfeed your sick baby during and after illness. Often, sick babies will refuse to eat but will continue to breastfeed. Breast milk will give your baby needed nutrients and prevent dehydration.

✓ Air dry your nipples. Right after birth, you can air-dry your nipples after each nursing to keep them from cracking. Cracking can lead to infection. If your nipples do crack, coat them with breast milk or a natural moisturizer, such as lanolin, to help them heal.

✓ Watch for infection. Signs of breast infection include fever, irritation, and painful lumps and redness in the breast. You need to see a doctor right away if you have any of these symptoms.

✓ Promptly treat engorgement. It's normal for your breasts to become larger, heavier, and a little tender when they begin making greater quantities of milk. This normal breast fullness may turn into

engorgement. When this happens, you should feed the baby often. To relieve engorgement, you can put warm, wet washcloths on your breasts and take warm baths before breastfeeding. If the engorgement is severe, placing ice packs (or frozen vegetable bags) on the breasts between nursings may help.

✓ Eat right and get enough rest. You may be thirstier and have a bigger appetite while you are breastfeeding. Drink enough noncaffeinated beverages to keep from being thirsty. Get as much rest as you can. This will help prevent breast infections, which are worsened by fatigue.

E-SSENTIAL

If you're on a strict vegetarian diet, you may need to increase your vitamin B12 intake and should talk with your health care provider. Infants breastfed by women on this type of diet can show signs of not getting enough vitamin B12.

When to Stop Breastfeeding

Although children in some countries continue breastfeeding until they're four or five years old, most American moms prefer to have their children weaned much earlier. Typically, that means weaning baby off the breast starting at six months of age—at the same time more solid foods are being introduced. To stop breastfeeding, you may alternate solid and formula feedings with breastfeeding until baby gets used to eating more of the newly introduced foods. Some women also begin wearing a bra that is one size smaller than their current size; this creates a binding effect that constricts the amount of milk produced until the milk ducts dry up.

Formula Feeding

What if you decide, for health reasons or convenience, that baby will be formula fed? Should you feel like you have to explain it to everyone who asks? The decision to feed your baby formula is a personal one; and whether or not other folks agree, formula is better than ever at mimicking breast milk in terms of nutrients.

The first discussion about formula feeding should be with your partner. If you both agree this is the way to go, then you need to talk with your pediatrician about the appropriate formula for your baby. Many pediatricians suggest using cow's milk formula with iron; however, if your baby has an intolerance to cow's milk, you will need to switch to a soy-based or elemental formula. Neither is a poor choice; it just depends on what baby's specific needs are.

Tips for Hassle-Free Formula Feeding

If you can, buy the premixed cans of formula. These are the most convenient to use, since they are already of perfect consistency. The powders take longer to prepare and are thus less convenient, especially when traveling. Premixed formula costs a bit more, but that's worth it when you have a crying baby at 2 A.M. and no bottles ready. Here are some other bottle-feeding tips:

- ✓ Alternate the positions you feed baby in, for variety and proper balance on your arm muscles.
- ✓ Sterilize all bottle pieces thoroughly, and always keep your hands and kitchen area clean. Use antibacterial soap to clean.
- ✓ Feed baby every three or four hours the first few months. Follow what your pediatrician tells you about increasing frequency.
- ✓ Don't heat the formula in the microwave, as this may cause uneven heating and hot spots in the mixture that could burn the baby. Instead, put warm water into a dish or bowl, and then place the bottle inside. This will help the formula heat up uniformly—and prevent burns for baby.
- ✓ Tip the bottle over and sprinkle some formula onto your wrist to make sure it's the right temperature. Lukewarm is a good temperature.
- ✓ Don't reuse formula if baby doesn't drink the whole bottle of milk. Using a bottle over again promotes bacterial growth, which is not desirable with a little one.

✓ From birth to about four months, feed baby five to six ounces of formula at a feeding. Many doctors are starting babies on solid foods after four to six months, with six months being the more common goal.

✓ Stop halfway throughout the feeding and burp the baby. Burp again after baby is finished. Keep the bib on for about fifteen minutes after feeding—formula-fed babies often spit up in that time frame, and you'll want to be ready.

E-SSENTIAL

Enjoy your bonding time with baby every bit as much as you would if you were breastfeeding. Cuddle, kiss, and love the baby while feeding; share the joy of bonding with baby with others in your family. Let others have a try at feeding baby (with the exception of small siblings who aren't ready to hold baby yet).

Formula feeding can be a wonderful, healthy experience for you and baby, and some breastfeeding moms use formula as a supplement when they need to.

Graduating to Solid Foods

When your baby reaches the age of four to six months, or starts showing signs of readiness, such as no longer being satisfied with straight milk at regular feedings, your pediatrician may recommend that you start him on solid foods. That doesn't mean you're suddenly going to serve steak and potatoes, but it does mean that baby is moving on to new (and more challenging) fare. You'll start with rice or oatmeal baby cereal, before moving on to jars of baby food and finger foods. Finger foods can be started as early as eight to nine months, or once baby has developed a pincer-grasp.

What Baby Can Eat—and When

One of the biggest mysteries of new parenthood is what to feed baby at each stage of his development. Here's a quick rundown of what baby may try to eat and when he will probably feel like trying it:

✓ **Four to six months:** Breast milk, formula, baby cereals; if baby is still not satisfied, you can try some fruits and vegetables.

✓ **Six to eight months:** Breast milk or formula (or both), cereals, fruits and vegetables, fruit and vegetable juices, and protein-rich foods such as yogurt, cheese, or egg yolks. This is the ideal time to try strained turkey or chicken and vegetable dinners (in jars).

✓ **Eight to ten months:** Breast milk or formula, fruits and vegetables, cereals (move on to breads and muffins), and chicken or turkey meals. You could try pureed beef or lamb at this stage, too.

✓ **Ten months to one year:** Breast milk, formula, or whole milk; oatmeal, breads, and cereals of thicker consistency; soft-cooked fruits and vegetables cut into tiny morsels for baby to feed with his own hands; and tiny portions of whatever you're having for dinner, as long as baby can chew it (baby will be more interested in "Mommy" or "Daddy" food by this time, and you can let baby experiment, within reason).

Food Allergies, Pesticides, and Organic Solutions

Some babies develop food allergies, which is why your doctor will recommend that you try a specific food for at least two to three days in a row before moving on to another new item. This way, if a rash develops, you'll be able to quickly identify the reason behind it. Babies can develop allergies to nuts, egg whites, and strawberries; that's why many pediatricians recommend avoiding foods containing these ingredients. Of course, nuts are very bad foods for babies, since they can be choking hazards; keep peanuts and cashews far from the reach of tiny (and curious) hands!

If you're worried about pesticides, buy only organic baby foods or make your own baby foods. You'll need good puree equipment and perhaps a juicer. Many parents prefer this option, since it allows them to feed their babies more whole grains and less sugar.

Some doctors recommend sticking with baby cereal for as long as baby will eat it. Their reasoning is that baby cereal is better tolerated and less likely to cause allergic reactions than other foods. Also, many doctors recommend limiting fruit juice to four to six ounces per day for a baby over the age of six months—diluting it to prevent diarrhea.

Tackling the Diaper Dilemma

After feeding the baby, the inevitable will happen. You'll have to change a dirty diaper. One of the first choices you'll make as a new parent is which type of diaper to use on your baby. Here you'll need to explore the pros and cons of all options. The "bottom" line is this: You should choose what is most comfortable for the baby and convenient for you.

Cloth Diapers

You can purchase a set of fifty or more diapers and wash them for reuse. Your baby may go through six to eight diapers per day. Pros: You can save a lot of money on diapers. Cons: It's a lot more work, and you'll go through tons of heavy-duty detergent in the process. Some reports indicate that home washing machines don't sterilize the same way commercial units do. Also, cloth diapers often leak—leading to more wet clothes.

You can hire a service that drops off clean new diapers and removes the dirty ones once per week. Pros: It's convenient and environmentally responsible. Cons: It's costly and annoying, particularly if you miss your dirty diaper pickup.

Disposable Diapers

You can buy these virtually anywhere, and their manufacturers claim that they are friendlier than ever to the environment. Pros: They are convenient and readily available; these diapers are also great for travel. Cons: They can be expensive, and are not always readily available.

If You're a Diapering Rookie . . .

Diapers can be a scary experience for first-timers, since you can never really be sure what's inside a dirty diaper until you are brave enough to open it. Once you do, you will learn something you never knew before about babies: their stool can change colors dramatically. Once you get past that initial shock, everything else becomes more practical.

E-ALERT!

When changing a diaper, you should first be sure you've put all of the changing table supplies within easy reach. Never leave the baby alone on the changing table, not even if there's a safety belt on it. Babies can roll quickly and fall off the table before you even notice a problem.

Here are some more diapering tips for newbies:

✓ Take off the dirty diaper, wiping away as much stool as you can with the front of the diaper and using a warm wash cloth or baby wipes for the rest.

✓ Be aware of the differences between boys and girls, and wipe accordingly. For girls, you should always wipe from front to back (and never in the opposite direction) to prevent any debris from getting into the vagina. Even baby girls can get urinary tract or kidney infections, and fecal matter in the vaginal area is a primary cause. For baby boys, clean a circumcised penis with warm water and apply a thin layer of petroleum jelly to the tip. For boys who have not been circumcised, wash with a warm cloth and do not retract the foreskin.

✓ Let the baby "air dry" without a diaper for a few minutes to minimize the chance of diaper rash. Then apply some petroleum jelly to the diaper area to keep baby's skin soft and protect it from irritation.

Dealing with Diaper Rash

To deal effectively with diaper rash, you'll need to keep baby's skin dry, and change wet diapers as quickly as possible. Allow the baby's skin to air dry as long as you possibly can, since that will help keep skin from getting irritated. Launder cloth diapers in mild soap and rinse well. Don't use plastic pants. Avoid irritating wipes (especially those containing alcohol) when cleaning baby's bottom. Ointments or creams may help reduce friction and protect baby's skin from irritation; however, powders such as cornstarch or talc should be used cautiously, as they can be inhaled by the infant and may cause lung injury.

Making a Splash with Baby's First Bath

Bathing a newborn can be a challenge, but it can be one of the most fun times you have with your baby. Of course, when you're reading about it, it will seem easy; but you may find it difficult at first if you're not used to a wet little one trying to squirm out of your arms. Try to keep calm, and have your partner with you (at least the first time) for backup assistance.

Feed your baby at least an hour before the bath, so that baby can relax and go to sleep after a pleasant bathing experience—and so that you can avoid any unpleasant surprises in the diaper region.

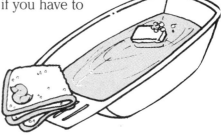

Bathe your baby in a warm bathroom. This will help drain baby's sinuses, and it will cut down on the chances of baby catching a chill. You might also want to keep all bath supplies within immediate reach, including that rubber ducky you've been saving for baby's special moment. Put baby's towel on the floor (preferably on top of the soft bathroom rug) so that you have your hands totally on baby as you take baby out of the tub.

Wet babies can slip easily, and especially so if you have to let one hand go to reach for the towel.

How to Do a Sponge Bath

To give baby a sponge bath, first fill a bowl or small bucket with lukewarm water. Put a sponge in the water, and add a little baby bath if you want. Place a large bath towel on a flat surface (such as a bed, carpeted floor, or kitchen counter). Put the baby on the towel, folding a part of the towel over the baby to keep the warmth in. Be sure to keep one hand over the baby at all times. Wash the baby's face and the rest of his body. Be gentle, talk to the baby to comfort him, and don't move too quickly. Wipe the baby gently to dry.

What about Mom?

This chapter has spent a good amount of time talking about how to care for baby, but what about how to care for yourself postpregnancy? Getting your body back to its prepregnancy shape can be a challenge; after all, when do you have the time to exercise?

Hollywood and glamour magazines don't make it any easier on new moms, showing us skinny young things who claim they've just had babies and are merely returning to the gym for some "toning." These depictions only serve to antagonize new moms more, giving you the feeling that you are a long way off from ever wearing those size 8 jeans again.

Lose Weight in a Healthy Way

Both pregnancy and labor can affect a woman's body. If you're trying to lose some additional pregnancy weight, make sure you do it in a healthy way and consult your doctor before you start any type of diet or exercise plan. If you want to diet and are breastfeeding, it's best to wait until your baby is at least two months old. During those first two months, your body needs to recover from childbirth and establish a good milk supply. Then when you start to lose weight, try not to lose too much too quickly. This can be harmful to the baby because environmental toxins that are stored in your body fat can be released into your breast milk. Losing about one pound per week (no more than four pounds per month) has been found to be a safe amount and will not affect your milk supply or the baby's growth.

Keep Calories Within Reason

You can safely lose weight by consuming at least 1,800 calories per day with a well-balanced, nutritious diet that includes foods rich in calcium, zinc, magnesium, vitamin B6, and folate. Diets in which you consume less than 1,500 calories per day are not recommended at any point during breastfeeding. This can put you at risk for a nutritional deficiency, lower your energy level, and lower your resistance to illness.

E-QUESTION

What's the best postpregnancy exercise?
For the best (and easiest) program in fitness and convenience, try a walking program. Places to walk are always available, and you can take baby along in a stroller if you need to—so there's no excuse for not doing it!

Get Movin'!

It's highly recommended that you begin every exercise session with a good warm-up. Stretch your calves, hamstrings, quadriceps, and hip flexors, holding each stretch for about five to ten seconds.

To lose serious weight, you'll need to exercise for a longer period of time (thirty minutes to an hour per day, three or four times per week). And feel free to mix and match—walking, swimming, aerobics, or fitness equipment (such as a NordicTrack). Join a health club that has a babysitting room for maximum benefit—and the option to work with a personal trainer if you decide you need one.

When you finish exercising, remember to cool down. After exercising is when your muscles most need a stretch, so don't forget this step. Do a few knee lifts or kicks (as high as you can) or march in place to bring your heart rate down after exercising. Then repeat the stretches you did in the warm-up, holding each for ten to fifteen seconds.

Belly-Tightening Exercises

To get your prepregnancy abdomen back, lie on the floor with your knees bent; slowly breathe in, expanding your chest and abdomen with each inhale. Pull in your abdomen, spreading out your ribs, then exhale slowly and repeat. On the second rotation, press your lower back against the floor, holding the position for a few seconds before releasing on a slow exhale. Repeat this exercise ten times a few times per day.

Sit-Ups

While it may not be possible to do sit-ups in those first few weeks after delivering your baby (and longer if you had a C-section), this is a very beneficial exercise to do as soon as you can manage. Lie on the floor with both of your knees bent and your feet flat on the floor. Put your arms behind your head and try to sit forward as far as you can. When you feel able, try touching opposite elbows and knees. Repeat ten times. A variation of this exercise is to lie flat on your back and raise both knees toward your chest as far as you can, with your back flat on the ground.

Rebuilding Your Back Muscles

Sitting on the floor with one knee bent and your foot flat on the floor, rest your clasped hands around your knee and use your back muscles to stretch your entire body toward the ceiling. Keep your abdomen pulled in tightly but your shoulders as loose as you can. Alternate knees and do five repetitions per leg. Both exercises will help your back regain its original prepregnancy strength.

Keep It Fun—for You and Baby

Exercise need not be a painful, miserable experience. All you need is a little encouragement, support, and direction. Of course, the motivation to return to your prepregnancy shape is what will really put you over the edge.

Make exercise time fun time for baby, too. Prop baby up in his or her car seat while you're working out. It can be a fascinating visual experience for baby, and you won't get judged on your thigh size, either! Most of all, don't be too hard on yourself. Just because you can't wear an evening gown the month after you've given birth doesn't mean your life is over. Losing weight and returning your body to its prepregnancy fitness takes perseverance and time. Go easy on yourself—and enjoy the great bonding experience of working out with baby!

Chapter 13

Getting Baby to Sleep

You've heard the horror stories. Like the one where you put the baby to bed softly and without incident. At first, all seems well. But then, out of nowhere, you hear that unmistakable cough, then a sputter, followed by a very loud, "WAAAAAA!" You wonder what could possibly have happened in those first few minutes to make your baby morph from a contented little angel into a holy terror. Now the only question is, what can you do to get this baby back to sleep?

A Major Issue

Getting your baby to sleep is the biggest (and most common) challenge a new parent can face. It is, in fact, such a big deal that many new parents greet one another with comments like, "Oh, she's so cute . . . does she sleep through the night?" Sleeping is one of the major obsessions of new parenthood—and not without cause.

The Baby Sleep Cycle

One of the first questions from just about every new parent is, "How much should my baby sleep?" At first, it may seem like baby sleeps too much, but then again, there may be times when he doesn't seem to sleep enough (especially when you're trying to get some sleep!). The real answer to this question, however, is that the number of hours your baby sleeps will change a bit over the next several months.

Since babies generally sleep about sixteen out of each twenty-four hours, that means they typically aren't able to sleep more than a few hours at a time. In terms of sleep cycles, then, babies experience about seven asleep/awake cycles, often evenly spaced every day.

E-SSENTIAL

Sleep cycles change over the first six months of baby's life. By the age of six months, your baby will most likely sleep about eleven hours each night, with a one- to two-hour late-morning and late-afternoon nap. Keeping baby on a routine will go a long way toward developing good sleep habits as baby grows.

Making Sure Baby Gets Good Sleep

Many first-time parents believe (mistakenly) that babies are supposed to sleep all day and night until they are a few months old. This is not true. Babies, especially newborns, do require lots of sleep to grow, but they should only sleep at two- to three-hour intervals during the day. The main reason for waking your baby, if she is sleeping longer than three hours at a stretch, is to make sure the baby is getting proper nourishment. If the baby is not getting enough food at regular times throughout the day, it will only serve to make your nights longer.

Teach Baby to Sleep

Some parents actually lie down near baby and pretend to sleep, just to get baby to fall asleep in a more emotionally secure way. Of course, the downside here is that you could really fall asleep, even before baby does, and if you think that might happen, be sure baby is safe in her crib before putting your head on a pillow. It's dangerous for baby to sleep in your bed!

Don't Interfere with Self-Comforting

If baby prefers thumb sucking as a calming way to drift off to sleep, resist the temptation to pop the thumb out of baby's mouth. Thumb sucking can be a healthy way for any child under the age of five years old to self-comfort—and self-comforting is something you'll learn to appreciate once you start getting a good night's sleep as a result! While some babies choose their thumbs, others comfort themselves with a pacifier (though they're not adept with it at first) or by rocking themselves to sleep. At least for a few years, whatever gets baby through the night is generally alright—so relax! Enjoy the fact that baby knows how to provide some comfort and let you get some well-deserved sleep.

Other Reasons Baby Can't Sleep

There are plenty of other reasons why some babies don't sleep through the night. The baby could have gas or have teeth coming (temporary reasons, of course!) or just want to be rocked in your arms for comfort. Some babies don't sleep well at night because they are allowed to sleep for long stretches during the day. And some babies are just colicky.

Of course, you won't figure out why your baby is sleepless until you narrow down the possible reasons. Let's take a look at all of them—and some ways you can make it all better for your newborn or young infant:

✔ Is baby hungry? Sixty percent of the time an empty tummy is what makes a baby cry. Offer a bottle or a breast.

✔ Check baby's diaper. Change the diaper as quickly and quietly as you can; making a big fuss over the diaper can actually irritate baby more.

✔ Try comforting baby. Gently rock the baby in a rocking chair. Or standing up, rock slowly back and forth, gently patting the baby's back. Maybe there's an extra burp in there that needs help getting out.

✔ Use the swaddling technique. This technique can be very helpful on a sleepless night, but it's important to note that It's only safe for younger infants and newborns. Swaddle or wrap the baby tightly in a blanket, just as the nurses did in the hospital nursery. Place the blanket sideways, with a point at the top. Next, place the baby at the top point, and then tuck one side under the baby's body. Pull up the bottom fold, and then wrap the remaining side over the baby's body. You're not cutting off circulation here, but you are providing that feeling of womblike security for your baby.

✔ Give the baby a pacifier. Like them or not, they are often temporary solutions to crying problems. Some people may say that pacifiers are more for the mother than the baby, and so what if that's true? At least you've bought yourself a few moments of quiet to collect your thoughts while trying to figure out what's wrong.

✔ Try to work out tummy gas. Put the baby on his or her stomach, and gently rub baby's back or pat baby's bottom. Or lay baby on his back while gently moving his legs back and forth. Use gas drops (available over the counter) as a last resort.

✔ Give baby a warm bath. There's nothing as soothing as a warm tub. Many babies calm down as soon as they hit warm water. Add an infant massage, and you'll have yourself one calm baby.

✔ Do a song and dance. Try singing to your baby, and move around the room as you do so. Babies have short attention spans, and can be easily redirected.

✔ Take baby out for a spin. Take baby for a walk or a ride in the car. Babies love motion, and the motion of an automobile somehow

serves as anesthesia for babies. You'd be surprised to know how many miles are put on a car just for a baby's sake.

✓ Put baby to bed. Like all people, baby can get irritable when tired. Put on the baby's lullaby tape or music box, dim the lights, and then walk out. Older babies over six months can be left to cry for at least ten minutes before you return to the room (unless, of course, you're absolutely convinced there's really something wrong). Some crying before falling asleep is normal for most babies.

E-ALERT!

Don't swaddle baby if the temperature is set high in baby's room. Swaddling babies who sleep in very warm rooms has been associated with sudden infant death syndrome, or SIDS. If you choose to swaddle baby, don't forget to turn the temperature down a few degrees.

Keys to Baby Relaxation

There are two basic words to remember when trying to calm your baby into sleeping mode: atmosphere and routine.

For atmosphere, dim the lights, put on soft lullaby-by-the-sea tapes, and rock your baby to sleep. Let your baby feel your heartbeat; it's calming and comforting to the baby, reminding him or her of that special time in the womb.

Stick to your routine with baby as much as possible. Write it down if you find it hard to remember. Figure out ways to stick with your routine even when you're on the road—stop and feed your baby at the same time you would have at home. Routine helps a baby to feel secure, and a secure baby is a well-adjusted (and relatively quiet) one.

Do Babies Dream?

Babies probably do, in fact, dream, although their dreams are not as elaborate as adults. No one is really sure what they are dreaming about, since they can't tell the details or whether or not the dream was in color. But there is brain activity and some babies even respond to dream-related stimuli by laughing or frowning in their sleep.

E-QUESTION

How can you know when your baby is dreaming?
You can watch for signals, such as a twitching leg or mouth movements. These motor movements indicate that baby's brain is sending these signals to muscles, and brain activity is a positive sign of dream activity.

Can you give your baby good dreams? Probably not, but you can influence how secure your baby feels when asleep by providing a happy, cheerful environment during waking hours. It is a known fact that happy, secure babies calm down more quickly by themselves and that they fall asleep faster than babies who live in stressful homes.

Colic and Related Sleeping Problems

We've all heard of colicky babies—the holy terrors of the baby world. What do you do when His Sweetness suddenly embarks on a reign of terror, complete with crying jags, pouty face, and flailing limbs? (Most new parents would say, "Run and hide!")

Colic is a period of crying and fussiness in a baby. Pediatricians sometimes refer to colic as a baby's "daily freak-out," particularly if it occurs around the same time every day. For many parents, this period of fussiness tends to occur in the 7–9 P.M. range.

Why do babies get fussy later in the day? Perhaps because they are at the halfway point in their eating schedule; their little bodies may have had a lot to process thus far and yet have a way to go before resting for the night. Occasionally a baby who has frequent awake times during the day will get cranky by sunset, possibly as a result of overstimulation.

An old wives' tale states that if you feed a colicky baby especially well before bedtime, you'll have a peaceful little creature who sleeps all night long. This is a fallacy. If that were true, there would be thousands of fat little babies who slept all the time.

E-ALERT!

Filling a baby chock-full of formula before going to bed, even if it is laced with infant cereal such as rice, can actually make the situation worse, since the baby's intestines get overloaded with work. Problems with tummy gas or spitting up may result from such overfeeding; so be careful how much you feed baby before bedtime.

What to Do When Nothing Seems to Work

When should you be concerned about colic or about a baby who won't calm down? When the baby cries for a prolonged period of time (half an hour) or the cries seem pierced by high-pitched tones, you might decide to take a different approach. If you are worried that something is really wrong or that such crying is totally out of character for your baby, there are still some things you can do to set your mind at ease.

First, try giving the other parent a shot at it, especially if you are tired or stressed out. You'd be surprised how much good a small break can do for you as you try to cope.

Next, take baby's temperature. If your little one has a fever, crying is definitely a way of letting you know. Call your pediatrician for advice (especially if your baby has a fever). There could be teeth coming soon.

When all else fails, call your pediatrician. If baby just doesn't seem right or isn't responding to any of the suggested methods of calming, your pediatrician may be able to help you with other suggestions.

Should You Stay or Should You Go?

There are two basic schools of thought on crying babies who won't sleep. The first is to simply let the baby cry itself to sleep, only returning to the crib if something seems seriously wrong. Some parents who have tried this method swear by it, saying that the crying time gets smaller and smaller each day until baby can finally go to sleep without crying. In the old days, this method was employed to keep parents from "spoiling" the baby with too much attention.

Other parents prefer a more hands-on approach and aren't afraid of spoiling a small baby with on-demand cuddling or comforting. Their point of view is that babies need to know they can depend on their parents when they need them and that babies are really too young to be manipulative about their parent's attention.

It's important to note, however, that most experts don't believe that you can spoil a young infant by holding them too much. Comforting your baby is one of the most loving things you can do!

The Ferber Method

The most popular proponent of the "walk-away" method of getting a baby to sleep is Dr. Richard Ferber. Widely known as the Ferber method, this approach suggests that you put the baby to sleep at night when he or she is still somewhat awake, so that baby learns to fall asleep without you. Soon after you put baby down in the crib the first night, Ferber says, you need to leave the room. You can go back into the room after five minutes have passed, but just to console baby with a tummy pat or stroke of the cheek for a short time. Ferber advises against picking the baby up or rocking the baby, as these are comfort solutions that baby could learn to use in place of good sleep habits, or as a stall tactic when he is older.

E-ALERT!

There is still controversy over which method really works best. However, most pediatricians discourage new parents from letting a colicky baby cry it out. They reason that a colicky baby is usually less than two to three months old, and that's simply too young to be left alone to cry for long periods of time.

When you leave the room a second time, you should wait ten minutes before reentering the room, and if there's a third time, wait fifteen minutes before returning to comfort baby. With the Ferber method, you increase each wait time by five minutes each night, until baby learns to fall asleep without you. Though it may be difficult to listen to baby's crying, it's important to remember that this method is safe and that your child will learn that crying to bring you back into the room isn't worth the effort.

The No-Cry Sleep Solution

For parents who don't want to let their babies cry it out, Elizabeth Pantley's book *No-Cry Sleep Solution* is a welcome approach. Pantley advises parents to set realistic expectations for baby's sleep routine; for instance, if you have a six-week-old that wakes up two or three times each night to eat, that is considered to be normal. However, for sleep issues that fall into the problematic category, Pantley recommends that you:

- ✓ Develop a bedtime routine
- ✓ Set an early bedtime
- ✓ Follow a more predictable daytime routine that's still a bit flexible
- ✓ Have baby take regular naps each day
- ✓ Help your baby learn to fall asleep without your help

Of course, your baby may still cry or fuss about your bedtime routine, but this approach stresses that you won't be leaving baby alone to cry it out; rather, you will log baby's sleep patterns, create a personal sleep plan, and change your baby's sleep "associations" so that sleep time is a more peaceful, restful transition.

Relaxation Techniques to Improve Sleep

Dim the lights, put on some soft music . . . and give your *baby* a bath? Adults like quiet, soothing baths, so why wouldn't a baby like them, too? Your baby doesn't necessarily need a tubful of squeaky toys to enjoy bath time. Many babies equally enjoy a bath in peaceful surroundings, with little extra stimuli except for warm water, a few bubbles, and the soft hum of your voice.

Speaking of music, you might sing to baby—whatever comes to mind. The song itself doesn't matter; the baby won't mind if your song isn't record quality. If you like listening to soft, classical music while bathing, perhaps baby will, too.

Give Baby a Massage

Giving your baby regular massages will not only stimulate baby's muscle development, it can also generate lots of good bonding experiences for both of you. It also has a long history as a folk remedy for colic. You can even take it a step beyond massage by giving baby her regular, soothing bath, followed by an infant massage with baby cream. Here are some tips to help you give your baby the "spa treatment."

First, start with baby lying on her back. Put some baby cream in your hands and rub your hands together to create warmth. Rub some cream on baby's face, then neck, and then stomach. Using more cream, repeat the warming process, and then start rubbing baby's shoulders, working your way down the arms. Massage each wrist and hand, working out to the tiny fingertips.

With additional cream, work on your baby's legs. Thighs are particularly good areas to massage a little bit more deeply on a baby, since they are the largest muscles the baby has at this stage.

If baby will let you, turn him over to lie on his stomach. Warm some baby cream in your hands, and then begin to massage from shoulder to buttocks. Massage the legs again, and then work on the feet, beginning with the balls of the feet and gently massaging each tiny toe.

The Latest on SIDS

Sudden infant death syndrome, also known as SIDS or crib death, is the unanticipated death of an otherwise healthy baby under a year old. For some reason, boys and children of younger moms are at higher risk than others; so are bottle-fed and lower-birth-weight babies.

The current thinking about SIDS is that it could be caused by rebreathing carbon dioxide, a birth defect or brain abnormality, or simply problems breathing when baby's on his or her stomach. Since the cause is unknown, remember that risk factors for SIDS include putting a baby to sleep on his or her stomach or side, allowing baby to get overheated, and exposure to second-hand smoke. Infants and children under the age of two should never be allowed to sleep with pillows; infants should always sleep on firm mattresses and be put to sleep on their backs. The national "Back to Sleep" campaign encourages babies to sleep in this position, as it minimizes opportunities for oxygen depletion.

E-ALERT!

Doctors do believe there's some correlation between smoking and SIDS. Babies whose mothers smoked during or after pregnancy are at elevated risk of SIDS. So, if you smoke, there's never been a more important reason to quit. Do it for the health of yourself and your baby!

When baby is old enough to roll over in the crib, he may wish to sleep on the stomach versus the back. However, by this time, the baby will be well past the age of highest risk for SIDS.

Not every case of SIDS can be traced back to smothering. Doctors believe there could be several other factors at play, such as brain stem abnormalities involving imbalances in the way the brain processes the neurotransmitter serotonin. Researchers hope to soon develop a diagnostic test for this brain stem defect.

Get on a Schedule

The most important thing of all is to get yourself and your baby on a sleeping schedule or routine as soon as possible. Humans have internal clocks that tell them when to sleep, but babies often take fuller advantage of sleep during the day; hence, the saying, "She has her days and nights mixed up."

If sleep is still a challenge, watch how your baby prefers to fall asleep; in the beginning, it was likely to be right after nursing or being bottle-fed. Keep a ten-day record of baby's rhythms, like what time he wakes in the morning, when naptimes seem to occur naturally, and what seems to work best to relax baby at night. If you follow your baby's natural rhythms, you might find that this is the best way to get baby on a sleep schedule that really works—seamlessly and painlessly!

Make Sure Everyone's in the Loop

Once you're all on the same page, as well as on a better schedule, discuss your nap routine with your daycare provider to be sure baby isn't getting too much sleep during the daylight hours. Write baby's sleep schedule on a wipe board in your kitchen, so that you don't forget. Try to schedule busy activities (such as a trip to the zoo or the library) at peak-awake times versus during restful naptimes.

Remember, try to stick to a schedule of two to three shorter naps during the day for baby, followed by a (hopefully) full night's sleep. If you can manage a daily routine like this with little fluctuation, you'll all be able to reap the benefits of a good night's sleep—every night!

Chapter 14

Traveling with Your Baby

Maybe your company gives you a use-it-or-lose-it vacation option; or maybe you just plain need a break. Maybe it's a bonding thing with your new family, and you simply can't wait to get started spending some time building memories. Whatever the reason for your vacation, you can look forward to having the time of your life traveling with your baby. That's because everything, down to a blade of grass, will be a new experience for you and your baby.

Gearing Up for Travel

If you thought it was a challenge to pack yourselves for a trip, just wait until you start packing the baby for a vacation. Not only do you need to pack several additional sets of clothes, toys, bottles, and diapers, you'll also need to be sure that you spread out all of baby's "accessories" so that you're covered should a suitcase full of key supplies get shipped to Honolulu when you're on your way to New Mexico!

With changes in airline baggage policy, chances are you'll only be able to pack a diaper bag as a carry-on. However, if you purchase a separate seat for your baby (always a good idea, since you can secure baby in a car seat), the diaper bag will count as baby's carry-on baggage, so you'll be permitted to take on one additional carry-on for yourself.

Start with a Plan

Before hitting the road (or the family-friendly skies), you would do well to investigate all of your options with a professional travel agent. That way, you can be sure that all of your destinations and accommodations fully support adults who are traveling with infants. If you want to go to a resort, you'll want to be sure it's not an adults-only paradise!

Be Flexible

Keep as much flexibility as possible in your itinerary, since baby may not be on the same schedule as you. When you make your final plans, be sure to include bits and pieces of baby's regular routine. Just because you're on the road doesn't mean that baby should throw caution to the wind and give up on naptime.

Set Some Limits

Don't try to pack too much activity into your vacation, since babies can't handle too much change at one time. Do have backup ideas in mind in case you have to make a change. For instance, you might need to switch from an outdoor flea market to an indoor museum if it starts to rain. Or maybe you'll need to schedule that zoo visit to happen before baby's afternoon nap. Stay in tune with your baby's regular rhythms and you'll avoid lots of crankiness on the road.

Pack Light—and Smart

When you travel with a baby, take the following items with you for transporting baby around: a car seat, a stroller (the umbrella type is easier for traveling), a cloth-front carrier (good for keeping baby close to you), and a backpack (if you'll be hiking or at lots of outdoor functions). You'll most likely be able to rent other equipment, such as a crib, playpen, or high chair. For every daily activity or excursion you take, be sure you've packed at least one diaper, one bottle, and one change of clothes for every hour you'll be gone. There's nothing worse than being out in the middle of a scenic tour with an empty bottle or a dirty diaper—and no more replacements!

E-FACT

New passport regulations require everyone, including infants, to have a passport when traveling outside of the United States. This includes trips to Mexico and Canada. Be sure to apply for your child's passport as soon as you know you might be leaving the country.

Practice Makes Perfect

Before embarking on a week-long trip, try doing practice runs with smaller excursions around town. Pack up the baby and visit a museum in your city—or go to a park for an afternoon stroll around the duck pond. Make note of anything you forgot to pack, or something you wish you had for the next trip. Chances are, you'll get lots of use out of anything that's portable, packable, and practical.

Places to Go, People to See

Generally speaking, the best vacations with infants are those with open schedules, decent weather (not too hot or too cold), and lots of things to see. But you (and baby) may also enjoy visiting relatives from afar. After all, what child doesn't enjoy being spoiled and cooed over incessantly?

Some of the best places to travel with a baby are those where you would go as an adult; however, these experiences may be a little more exciting for baby:

✓ A zoo or petting farm
✓ An outdoor music and arts festival
✓ A day at the beach, playing in the warm sand
✓ A park with a sandbox or swings for babies

Obviously, vacations that are primarily or specifically of interest to adults might not work as well for baby: a European tour, a romantic bed and breakfast, Las Vegas, or a Caribbean cruise.

It's All about Togetherness

Your baby will most enjoy the experience of being with you, wherever you decide to go. It takes very little to amuse and surprise a little one, because everything is new. You can have a great time traveling with a baby for that very reason; and things you took for granted will become more appreciated as you share them with baby.

Traveling can be a wonderful bonding experience with your baby. You get to explain every new site or attraction to a captive (yet appreciative) audience. Your baby's smiles will make any minor inconveniences seem worth it. Suddenly, you won't mind the wait at airports. Room service delays won't make you pace impatiently. And baby will have the best time of all, no matter what you choose to do, because she will get to see plenty of new faces.

Your Baby, the Road Warrior

So, one day you and your partner look up from your morning paper at the same moment, lock eyes, and exclaim, "Road trip!" What was once easy to do is now, with a baby in tow, more difficult. How can you drive long hours to get to your destination, without enduring long hours of a crying, fussy baby?

The good news is that you can travel on the road with a baby. In fact, road travel is sometimes easier than air or sea travel, simply because the motion of the car serves as a kind of anesthesia for babies; they almost always fall asleep in the car.

But before you hit the open road, you should plan ahead with some survival strategies, especially for those really long road trips.

E-ALERT!

Never take your baby out of the car seat—even for a few minutes— while the car is in motion. If she starts to cry hysterically while you're on the road, pull over and tend to her needs.

Use Car Seats Safely

Always use a rear-facing car seat for small infants, and position it correctly. If you're not sure of the correct position, read the manual for instructions. You'd be surprised how often well-meaning parents don't take the time to read the manual and do it right. If you think baby just needs to see a friendly face, sit in the back with him or her for a few miles. Attach baby's toys to the car seat (and stroller) so that they stay with you on most of the trip.

Make Pit Stops

Stop frequently to change baby's diaper and/ or to feed baby. Just because baby is sleeping well doesn't mean you should try to make it to your destination nonstop. Believe me, if you let baby sleep the whole way to wherever you're going, you will get no sleep once you're there. Try to adhere to baby's regular schedule as much as possible.

Even though you want to make pit stops, don't stop too much. Avoid lots of starting and stopping. Take a smooth freeway ride and avoid the traffic and noise of the city whenever possible.

Feeding Your Traveling Bundle of Joy

You've got your baby all packed and ready to go on vacation . . . but what are you going to feed him while you're out? If baby is on formula and cereal or has graduated to finger foods, you are in luck. All you have to do is pack enough bottles and snacks to feed baby during your trip. (Just be sure to keep bottles on ice until you're ready to feed; then ask an eating establishment for a cup of hot water to set the bottle in for warming.) Of course, if you're breastfeeding, packing baby's food will be a breeze!

The best news about formula is that you can now buy it ready-made, in small, use-as-you-go sizes (eight-fluid-ounce containers) or prebottled. It doesn't get any easier than that. If baby prefers nice, warm bottles, you can purchase a bottle warmer with a car adaptor.

E-QUESTION

What about breastfeeding your baby while you're on the road?
If you're breastfeeding, you need not feel like you are doing something indecent if you have to feed him in a public place. Wear a loose, comfortable shirt and a nursing bra, and bring a light blanket to cover up so you can nurse discretely.

Food Preparation

Preparing special foods for baby while you're traveling can be a bit of a challenge, but with some good planning it's still entirely possible. Plan to stay in a hotel with a kitchen in your room, and pack any small appliance you might need (since most hotels with in-room kitchens only provide the basics). Some parents recommend bringing along a food grinder to mash food into tiny, baby-size pieces at restaurants. This is rarely necessary unless baby will eat nothing else but pureed natural foods. Otherwise, a good knife can be used to cut baby's meal into bite-size pieces. If you're in a restaurant, you can also request pureed food; most chefs will be happy to accommodate your little eater.

Breastfeeding Options

Breastfeeding while traveling can also be somewhat challenging—although less of a challenge than pureed food. Look for family restrooms in large shopping areas, as most of these now include breastfeeding rooms with privacy curtains. If you feel uncomfortable feeding your baby in the middle of a busy restaurant, you can go outside or even back to your car (if you're traveling with one). Or gently place a napkin over the baby's head to shield your breast area from exposure to the general public. You don't need to go into the restroom at a restaurant or gas station (which can often be unclean or uncomfortable) to breastfeed your baby. Most important, if you are nursing baby while on vacation, stay well hydrated yourself. Travel can take a lot out of you—and, indirectly, the baby—if you don't get the proper food and rest.

Pack Things That Aren't Easy to Find

Finally, pack the things you aren't sure you can find while out on the road; however, you can leave some things to chance. For instance, if baby likes bananas for a snack, you can easily locate one at a deli or supermarket. There's no need to pack a week's worth at one time. Snack items that do pack well (and stay fresh longer) include crackers, string cheese, cereal (such as Cheerios), apples, pretzels, and rice cakes.

Flying the (Baby) Friendly Skies

It used to be that babies were allowed to sit on the laps of parents while traveling on an airplane, but the FAA has re-examined this practice and now recommends that parents purchase a seat for baby. That way, the baby can travel more safely because she will be fastened into a car seat. Use logic: If baby can only travel in a car seat on the ground (by law), shouldn't the same be true in the air—and for the same reasons?

The other benefit to purchasing a seat for baby is that it leaves your hands free to do other things—like read, knit, or get a bottle ready—when you need or want to, for at least part of your flight.

E-SSENTIAL

If you decide to take baby on an airplane, it would probably be a good idea to postpone a feeding until you are either taking off or landing. That way, if baby's ears have difficulty popping, the swallowing will help alleviate the problem. If you can't get baby to feed in the air, try using a pacifier to solve the problem.

Be Prepared

Bring the diaper bag and plenty of wet wipes with you on the airplane. Also, you might consider using an umbrella stroller, since these can fold easily and are lightweight enough to put in the overhead compartments on airplanes.

Most important, leave plenty of time for boarding and deplaning. Take advantage of the preboarding call for parents with small children by being at the departure gate at least thirty minutes early. Be prepared to fold up your stroller to put it through airport security; some airports may require you to do so. And get used to being the last one off of the plane, since most folks are in a hurry and do not have the patience to wait for you to retrieve your stroller, diaper bag, and other carry-ons. There may be the occasional kind soul who will hold back the line for you, but don't count on it.

E-ALERT!

If you are traveling to a foreign country, don't forget to bring baby's immunization records and passport or birth certificate. And always ask your travel agent for information about what inoculations your baby should have before going to a specific country.

Baby-Friendly Hotels and Motels

Many hotel and motel chains offer to let kids under the age of twelve stay free, as long as they are in their parents' room. No matter how nice the accommodations, your first step upon check-in should always be a child-proof inspection.

Get down on all fours, just as your crawling baby would, and look at the room from a baby-eye view. Are there any electrical cords, phone cords, or other items that could lead to danger for baby? If so, move them out of the way, or decide who will take turns watching the baby while in the hotel room. You'd be surprised how easy it is for a baby to pull a heavy hotel phone onto his tiny head, resulting in a serious injury.

Here's a list of family-friendly accommodations:

- ✓ Days Inn (1-800-325-2525) offers a Kids Stay and Eat Free program for children under twelve.
- ✓ Four Seasons (1-800-268-6282) offers a Kids for All Seasons program (with special activities, child-proof rooms, and milk and cookies for toddlers and up). You can also get a Single Parents Weekend package.
- ✓ Hilton (1-800-445-8667) offers a summer-long "vacation station" with welcome gifts and availability of toys and games.
- ✓ Hyatt (1-800-233-1234) offers special activities for the younger set, as well as babysitting services.
- ✓ Marriott (1-800-228-9290) offers babysitting services, cribs, and toys; call ahead for information.
- ✓ Radisson (1-800-333-3333) offers child-proof suites and other programs.
- ✓ Residence Inns (1-800-331-3131) have a homelike environment, complete with a kitchen.
- ✓ Westin (1-800-228-3000) has a "Kids Club" program with night-lights, juice, potty seats, and children's movies.

Travel Warnings

As tempting as it may be to turn baby into a world traveler, you might want to hold off on major excursions until baby is a bit older. The reason? With the number of germs and illnesses in the outside world, you're putting baby at a significantly higher risk of getting sick. When you're miles away from your pediatrician, getting proper health care for a sick infant becomes all the more challenging, so do investigate emergency options in advance of a trip.

If you do decide a trip is something you want to experience with your new baby, or if a trip simply can't be avoided due to a family situation or need, you might consider packing your own travel playpen/crib. Many hotels, though well-meaning, are not childproofed and still use cribs that have been recalled.

Home, Sweet Home

What if you decide that for financial or other reasons the best place to go on vacation this year is home? For parents who work outside of the home a lot, this is the perfect option. After all, for these parents, being home for a week can be a real novelty.

But can it be fun for baby, too? Sure it can, if you plan it right. Start off with some quality time with baby, and then do some things that are out of your ordinary routine. For instance, pretend you're a tourist in your own area—visit the area zoo, museums, restaurants, specialty shops, and so forth. Sometimes people ignore great things just because they're in their own backyards.

Take a Day Off—Together

You might consider getting a babysitter for a day so that you and your partner can get reacquainted. This will also give you a little break from baby, which is necessary every once in a while. Or spend a night at a friend's house—or at Grandma's—with baby. Lots of people would love to have you (and especially baby) come for an overnight visit.

Spending an adventuresome day outside can be another great way to take some time off as a family. Pack a picnic and go to the park for a day of hiking and exploration. Parks are a perfect choice for a day-long excursion because babies love to see lots of people, animals, and nature. Most parks have walking trails, rest areas, and even swings and a play area for babies. Take baby to the duck pond to feed the ducks; baby will love it, and you'll get some terrific pictures—and memories—to share later.

Chapter 15

Dads Are Special Too

With all of the excitement over the baby, it's easy for everyone to forget all about dear old Dad. You're the guy who made the baby possible; yet you weren't invited to the baby shower, and no one asks you how *you're* feeling about the new baby. The trouble is, with everyone scurrying around in an effort to get both baby and mom-to-be ready for the "big event," it's hard to express your true feelings. So, what's a guy to do?

Adjusting to "Daddyhood"

If you are a new dad or dad-to-be, you may actually have a lot on *your* mind while others think that you're uninterested. That's why, as early as possible in the pregnancy, you should start trying to figure out what questions you would like to have answered. You can start by going to as many of the obstetrician visits as possible; even if you just sit in the waiting room, there are plenty of resources available that will spark your thought process and generate the kinds of questions that would've eventually come anyway. If you choose to go into the examining room for each visit, have some of your questions ready for the doctor (who's been through this experience hundreds of times and can probably give you lots of reassurance).

Typical Concerns

Understanding your role as a father can be confusing, to say the least. Who should get more of your attention, your wife or your helpless little one? How can you balance the care of your family with your job while keeping your own stress level to a minimum? Where will all of the money come from to raise this new life and put it through college? These are typical concerns of new fathers.

E-SSENTIAL

Talk about your feelings as openly and directly as possible. Ask your partner to listen without judging you or your feelings. Tell her that you simply need to express yourself and be heard. What you really need, after all, is the same thing that she does: reassurance that you can indeed be a good parent.

Communicate—with Everyone

The most important thing you can do as a new father is communicate with your mate, your baby, and the rest of your family. Read parenting magazines to familiarize yourself with all of the issues of parenthood. Ask your father how he coped before you were born. Or talk to other new fathers you know. Ask a lot of questions; you'll feel much more confident after you hear about what other fathers have experienced. And you might get some great ideas!

Relax and Enjoy!

Most of all, relax and enjoy this exciting new stage in your life. You are going to be a major influence in your child's life, and everything will work itself out in due time. You may not realize it, but it is likely that your own father grappled with the same dilemmas, worries, and concerns that you now face; he survived, and so will you.

Helping Before Baby

What does the mother of your child need most, and how can you anticipate those needs? There are actually lots of ways you can help—so many that it might at first glance seem overwhelming. Fortunately, there's still time to slow down and take things one trimester at a time.

First Trimester (Months One to Three)

In these first few months of pregnancy, your wife will need your emotional support as she adjusts to this exciting (yet sometimes frightening) time in her life. If she's having morning sickness, reassure her that this is only a temporary phase. If she's tired all the time, take on extra household duties and make sure she gets enough rest. What she really needs most of all is knowing that you are there for her, that you support her and love her for this beautiful, temporary sacrifice her body is making. Take an active role in reading about the baby's development, too. Go to those early doctor's appointments so that you can hear firsthand information.

Second Trimester (Months Four to Six)

As her body changes and the baby grows, a woman needs to know she is still attractive to you. Tell her how she looks: She's not fat—she's pregnant; she's got a healthier glow than you've ever seen before. Let her know you're proud of her and the baby. Be with her as much as you can, and enjoy the time you have left—it'll be a long time before you're "empty-nesters" again!

Third Trimester (Months Seven to Nine)

Mom-to-be may be a little uncomfortable—not to mention emotional—these last months of the pregnancy. Try to get her out of the house; go to dinner, a movie, or even for a short walk. You'll have to ask her what other things she'd like you to do, but she'll likely want to decorate the baby's room and stock it full of things for you to put together (you'll be very thankful for those handy instructions!). And—no doubt—good, strong back rubs are in order. Of course, if you're the labor coach, you'll have lots of other items of business to attend to during that last month, like creating a phone list, finishing up the baby's room, and packing the car for the big day!

After Baby Arrives

After the birth of your baby, believe it or not, you'll be needed even more. You can help your new family by calling everyone who needs to know about the birth (this includes shielding Mom from well-meaning folks who want to chat when she needs to rest); limiting visitors (they can make Mommy and baby very tired in the first few days); and doing housework and cooking for your family. Just knowing that you are there for her and willing to help at every stage is going to go a long way in terms of adjustment and the well-being of your new family.

Offer Breastfeeding Support

Some dads feel a bit left out when the mom gets extra bonding time with baby at breastfeeding time. If you feel like a third wheel, participate by holding baby's hand or even softly singing to baby. Sometimes just being in close proximity will help you feel just as important to baby—and your closeness is sure to be appreciated by Mom, too!

"C" Can Mean Extra Care

If the new mom has had a C-section, your help will be even more critical during the first six weeks home. Since most doctors won't let recovering moms drive or lift anything for four to six weeks, you may need to do everything from grocery shopping to cooking and housekeeping—all while maintaining your regular work schedule.

Ask Before Getting Help

You can keep stress to a minimum by allowing others in your circle of friends and family to help—after you get an okay from your wife or partner. Make sure she feels comfortable with others helping during those emotional first weeks home. Suddenly turning everything over to her least-favorite (but well-intentioned) Aunt Martha when she's on bed rest could be a very bad idea.

E-ALERT!

If the new mom has bouts of the "baby blues," you needn't worry—these low times are brought on by hormonal changes and are normal. But if she seems to grow more depressed over the next few weeks, she may have postpartum depression. Look for the signs, and don't be afraid to call the doctor if you're worried or unsure.

Staying Involved While Working

When the baby is finally born, you will relish those first few days home with your new family. But just as you were all feeling warm and comfortable in your newly populated nest, reality sets in: It's time for you to return to work.

Hard as it may be to separate yourself from your happy new home, someone usually has to keep working in order to pay the bills. If that someone is you, there are still some ways you can stay connected while you're toiling away at work:

- ✓ Visit Mommy and baby on your lunch break.
- ✓ Call in a few times per day to see how things are going—or if Mommy needs you to pick up anything (like dinner!) on your way home.
- ✓ Create a slideshow of baby photos to share with coworkers (if company policy allows).
- ✓ Form a "new dads" group at work and meet at lunch.

Be sure to follow all company policies at your workplace. Many companies don't allow employees to make personal phone calls or share photos on their computers. If you're unsure about such policies, ask your supervisor or the human resources manager. Better safe than sorry—especially now that you have an extra mouth to feed!

Connecting with Web Sites and Community Groups

If your work hours and family commitments don't leave time for much socializing with other new parents, consider joining an online parenting group or Listserv. Here, you can freely post any questions, answers, or comments you have about life in your baby's first few years. You'll find that there are many other parents out there who want to feel connected to others who face similar challenges and triumphs. Like you, their jobs may be demanding on their time, making it difficult to meet up with other parents in person.

Bookmark Solutions

If that's still too large a time commitment for you, a second option would be to surf the Internet for the best baby and parenting Web sites and bookmark them for easy, as-needed reference. You never know when you'll need a fast solution to a 3 A.M. problem!

Bringing Work Home

When the work-life balance seems to be too difficult, many new fathers are doing things their own fathers never dreamed possible: They're bringing work home with them, either through a flex-time arrangement with their employers, or with flat-out telecommuting one or more days per week. Discuss creative work arrangements with your supervisor or human resources manager; often, they will ask you to develop a work plan to show how you will manage all of your projects without interrupting the normal flow of business operations.

E-ALERT!

If you reach a point where you really want to work from home but your employer won't allow such an arrangement, consider transferring your skills to a home-based business of your own. Being your own boss can put you in better control of your time, and in many cases, you actually stand to earn more as head of your own company.

Don't Be Too Impulsive

Turning your back on an established career needn't be something you do impulsively. Take some time to consider all of your options, and create a solid business and marketing plan with at least six months of reserve funds to keep the bills paid as you embark on your new life. Keep baby's mom involved every step of the way, and let her help you build your dream. Together, you can create a wonderful (and hopefully prosperous) new life for your young family. Who knows? Maybe someday, you'll make baby your "junior partner!"

E-FACT

According to 2005 U.S. Census Bureau figures, there are 143,000 stay-at-home dads in the United States today. Twenty percent of fathers with employed wives are the primary caregiver for their preschooler. Thirty-two percent of fathers who regularly worked evening or night shifts were the primary source of care for their preschoolers during their children's mother's working hours.

Mr. Mom

Some nontraditional households have mothers back in the boardroom and fathers at home providing baby care after a baby is born. More and more fathers stay at home to raise their children, and although they don't provide *exactly* the same kind of care that a mother provides, they have proven that they can be equally effective parents. As surprising as it may seem, it's a growing trend—so much so that there are magazines, books, and Web sites dedicated to the "house dad."

E-SSENTIAL

Be sure to relish any free moments you get and take advantage of them without feeling guilty. After all, you're a new dad who's probably more involved in parenting than your own father was during your childhood. You've got an incredibly challenging job and deserve every break you can get.

If you should decide that you will be the primary parent to care for your new baby, there are lots of ways you can get through the experience as smoothly as possible.

✓ **Establish a routine.** Set regular times of the day for laundry, housework, and cooking. The baby will set the schedule for feedings and diaper changes, but you can choose a time for bathing the baby and for playing games.

✓ **Ask for help when you need it.** Don't be afraid to call Grandma or any other knowledgeable person when you're stuck. Read any parenting magazine or book you can get your hands on. What you don't know, find out.

✓ **Build connections.** Take your baby to playgroups and other functions where there are other babies and their caregivers. There are networks, meetups and support systems for stay-at-home dads; check the Internet or ask other parents in your community for meeting times and places.

✓ **Reserve time for yourself.** You need time on your own, too. To keep your sanity, do at least two things per day that are strictly for you: Watch a sports event on TV, go out for a while after the baby's mother comes home, or take a bath to unwind.

"Daddy and Me" Activities

You've seen other dads around town who look like they are having a ball with their kids. But how did such great relationships begin? Most likely, they started with "Daddy and Me" activities way back in baby's infancy.

The best kinds of activities for new dads and babies to share are the physically oriented variety. Take baby on a hike in the park or for a bike ride with a baby seat and helmet. Sign up for water baby classes and help your baby learn to swim at an early age. For times when the weather's less ideal, or when you just want to shoot the breeze with other new dads, find a "daddy meetup" in your area and meet for coffee with others who share your questions and concerns as a first-time parent. Hooking up shouldn't be very difficult—and even though you might at first feel uncomfortable, you'll soon be relieved to know that daddyhood is also new territory for the other meetup participants!

What Happens at a Daddy Meetup?

Daddy meetups can vary from town to town, but the basic premise is the same: They are safe places for dads to brag, ask questions, share advice, and watch their new babies socialize with one another. Generally, each meetup has a time limit of one to three hours, but the members who "meet up" can set any parameters that feel comfortable.

There are several different types of daddy meetups; in some areas, there are even subgroups divided by interests, hobbies, and whether the daddy is employed in a traditional work environment, a work-from-home dad, or a stay-at-home dad.

It's Time to Go to the YMCA

Many meetups are held at the YMCA so that the babies can play (while supervised by Daddy, of course) on floor mats or in the baby pool. Some meetups happen at coffee shops with play areas, or rotate at each member's house. Wherever and however they occur, these meetings are a great way for dads and babies to socialize together. For fathers as well as babies, meetups can lead to lifelong friendships. Forming such bonds can be a great way for your baby to learn the value of social interaction—a skill that will stay with the child as he or she grows into adulthood.

Are you looking for a new way to bond with baby?
Try learning baby sign language. It takes time and patience, but once your baby starts making the connections between hand movements and specific requests, you'll be amazed at how well you can communicate—and how well-bonded you will feel as a result.

More Ways to Bond with Baby

If you're still having a hard time thinking of ways to bond with your tiny new bundle of joy, here are a few more ideas to start the wheels turning in your head:

- ✓ Carry baby with you in a sling or backpack as you tend to chores.
- ✓ Go for walks with baby in a stroller, backpack, or sling.
- ✓ Take the night shift for bottles and rocking.
- ✓ Sing funny songs to baby.
- ✓ Watch the game together.
- ✓ Eat together—and share some food when baby is able to eat solids.
- ✓ Take naps together (safely).
- ✓ Be the keeper of snacks and goodies (like Cheerios or vegetable slices).
- ✓ Help baby learn new things by reading together.
- ✓ Make a video of baby and watch it together.

Psst: Don't Forget Mommy!

Now that you know all of the wonderful ways you can be an important part of your baby's life, there's one more thing to do: Make sure you leave some time for togetherness apart from your new baby. Keeping your primary relationship alive and well after you start adding children to the mix can be a challenge, so enlist the help of a good babysitter ("Hello, Grandma?") for as little as a few hours one day a week, just so the two of you can take a break. Time for reconnection is time well spent, as it will help the two of you stay young, fresh, and in love. What more could a kid ask for but parents who love each other like that?

Chapter 16

Going Back to Work

For most parents, the choice between staying at home as a full-time parent and returning to work after baby is born is a difficult one. It's a major decision that can cause inner turmoil. Still, many parents manage to adjust the particulars of their work life so that they can both work and still spend plenty of time with their baby. With the technology available today, you should have more choices than ever!

The Work-Guilt Paradigm

In today's society two incomes are the norm, and some parents have as many as two jobs each, not counting their important jobs as parents. People have all kinds of issues and concerns about whether they are good enough parents, or employees, or people. It's easy to get caught up in the belief that despite all the things you do you are simply not good enough. Magazines tell you that working parents don't feel they have enough time with their children and that stay-at-home parents don't feel fulfilled. Somewhere in-between is the truth: There is a balance; it just takes a lot of effort to find it.

Job Sharing and Flex-time

There are several ways your employer should be able to help you balance your work and home life. For instance, perhaps your employer would consider a job-sharing arrangement—one in which you would split a full-time job with another person who can do the same kind of work into two part-time jobs. This way, you and a fellow employee would have more time to spend with your families—and the job would still be accomplished for the company without skipping a beat.

E-QUESTION

Does your company permit use of a flex-time option?
If so, your forty-hour workweek could become four days per week at ten hours each—with one extra day off each week. If this sounds like it would be too grueling, ask if you can arrange a workday that begins earlier or ends later than usual.

Telecommuting

If your job is one that can easily be accomplished at home, ask if you can work from home—and come in only for important meetings, presentations, or the like. Working from home is every bit as challenging for a tele-commuter as it is for an entrepreneur, so be sure you're up to it. If you're the type who's distracted by the need to vacuum over the need to finish a report, think twice before considering the telecommuting option. And remember, just because you are at home you will probably still need child care in order to get anything done—however, your baby can be cared for in your own home in your presence.

Other Options

Hunt for a new part-time job. There may not be much part-time work available in your field, but you might consider branching out into a related field. You just might find work that you enjoy even more than your old job!

Or you could consider a job where you can work evenings while your partner works days (or vice versa). That way, one of you can be with the baby all the time. This option works best when one parent has a part-time job. If that's not possible, make sure to reserve some time each day when you are all together.

Financial Considerations

There are plenty of questions to ask yourself before making a decision as to whether or not to return to the work force. Weigh all factors before making a final decision. Your reasons for wanting to return to work may be for professional development purposes, but, for many people, it's a financial decision. If you don't feel comfortable analyzing your needs yourself, seek the help of a financial consultant.

Figure Out What You Need to Live On

Total up all of your monthly living expenses, and don't forget to prorate those items that you pay for once or twice per year (such as taxes and home or car insurance). Now analyze these expenses against your current and projected new incomes. Can you still meet your monthly obligations if you decide to start a business or stay at home as a full-time parent?

Things like lunches, gas or transportation, and daycare add up. Will you still be making any money after these expenses are taken into consideration, or will you simply be paying for time away from your child? If you aren't going to benefit enough financially, ask yourself what you really want from a work situation. If it's about self-esteem and career identity, that's okay—it just needs to be profitable for your family, too.

Determine Whether a Second Income Is Necessary

What does a second income bring to your family each year? Is it a substantial enough amount that its absence would be harshly felt by all? What would you have to give up in your current lifestyle to stay at home, yet still be comfortable? Downsizing your lifestyle may be an option, since it could help keep you at home with baby if that's what you most want to do.

Next, compare income compatibility with your personal goals. If your goal is to buy a new minivan, for instance, could you still accomplish this if your family is living on one income? What about taking family vacations? Take a good look at your long-term goals to see how they might be impacted by a decision to stay home for a few years.

Live Comfortably with Your Choice

Should you decide you can afford it, staying home is a wonderful option for both parent and baby. It's a beautiful choice that can lead to many terrific memories.

As a final note, remember that these days, it's not always the mommy who stays home with baby. More and more daddies are leaving the rat race to spend time as "house-dads," and they should be applauded for their efforts.

Work-Life Balance Programs

It's not easy to balance a professional life with the needs of a growing family. That's why many companies now offer "work-life balance" programs for employees whose needs depend on achieving that balance. Exceptional companies recognize that employees can be dedicated to both job and family. Some programs may include:

- ✓ **Flex-time and job sharing.** Flex-time allows parents to set their own schedules to accommodate the needs of their children and balance parenthood with work duties. Job sharing allows employees who choose it to work part-time, sharing their workload with other part-time employees.
- ✓ **On-site daycare.** Many employers now offer on-site daycare facilities, complete with an after-school program (with company-provided transportation from local schools) and two months' paid parental leave.
- ✓ **Financial support.** Many companies offer subsidies for parents who are adopting children, or flexible savings accounts (FSAs) for parents who want to set aside a percentage of their pretax salary to help offset health insurance and child-care costs.
- ✓ **Accommodations for breastfeeding moms.** Some innovative companies provide on-site services for breastfeeding moms, including rooms for breastfeeding and refrigerators for storing breast milk.

E-FACT

To cut down on sick days that parents take to care for children, some companies offer discounts on sick-child care at their local children's hospital—or if that's not available in the area, a bonus number of sick days for each employee to cover the necessary time off. For longer illnesses, talk to your human resources manager about the Family Medical Leave Act.

Finding a "Family-Friendly" Company

If you discover that you *do* need two incomes in order to maintain your current lifestyle (or grow into one that better accommodates all of you), you should first lay aside any guilt you might be feeling about leaving the baby to go back to work. Then dust off your resume, pull out that suit, and brush up on your interviewing skills.

Once you're at the interview, you should be familiar with the new "ground rules." A potential employer should never ask you very much about your family life. Questions like "Are you very involved in your child's activities?" or even "How many children do you have?" can be borderline illegal for a potential employer to ask, since these types of questions can often lead to discrimination. For instance, if they ask you how many children you have, and your answer is five, they may be weighing the costs of your medical benefits in relation to those of a single, nonparent job applicant. A company that makes its hiring decisions based on these kinds of criteria is in violation of the Equal Opportunity clause.

E-ALERT!

Not all companies operate in a discriminatory manner against parents, but you'd be surprised how many still do it subtly. Once employed, it's important to discuss any discrimination concerns with your human resources manager. The Family Medical Leave Act provides some protection for employees with at least one year of eligibility.

Because the "family friendliness" of any company is hard to judge from the outset, you might do well to ask a few questions at the interview stage:

✓ What kinds of policies do you have regarding family emergencies?
✓ Do you have on-site daycare available?
✓ Is flex-time an option?

Make a Visit

Take a look around at any company with which you interview. Ask for a tour, and make mental notes of how many folks have pictures of their children on their desks; whether there is a daycare room; and how many young, single people you see milling around. If you notice that most of the employees appear to be young and single—and travel frequently—you might do well to consider applying elsewhere (unless you're willing to travel frequently yourself and the child care is already in place).

Starting a Home-Based Business

Maybe you've decided that the best option for you is to work your own hours, at your own pace, and still have the luxury of keeping your time with your baby. You want it all, and if you have the right skills, maybe you can have it all. Never has there been a friendlier environment for those who wish to escape the rat race and particularly for those who want to leave the rat race for the things that matter in their lives: their children.

Can You Do It?

Once you've decided that you'd like to start a business, you should give some thought as to whether an entrepreneurial lifestyle really suits you. Can you work on your own? Have you been self-directed and able to set and accomplish your own goals? Can you perform several tasks at one time or at least switch gears in an adaptable, highly flexible manner? If you can answer yes to any of these questions, you could enter the entrepreneurial zone with little or no problem.

If you lack initiative and prefer to have others tell you what to do, you could find yourself in a stress-filled environment within your own walls. Don't take on an ambitious, time consuming project like launching a business if you aren't 100 percent certain you can handle it. Once you've made a commitment to running a business, it isn't easy to walk away from it.

E-QUESTION

Can you afford to pay self-employment taxes?
You will need to do this on a quarterly basis if you choose self-employment. If this is not feasible for you, it may be worth your while to work full- or part-time for someone else and let them worry about the paperwork and taxes.

Setting Up Shop at Home

If you've decided to take the plunge into becoming an entrepreneur, plan as much as you can about your new work situation before involving baby. Take time, for instance, to set up a baby-friendly office that takes baby's safety into account.

Position as much of the baby's things in your office as you can. If you should decide to go back to work soon after the baby is born, position the bassinet next to your desk.

If the baby is in another room, use a room monitor to keep track of what's happening with baby. When you're engulfed in your work, it's easy to forget there's a baby in your home.

Keep electrical cords out of the way of crawling babies. Remember to schedule more breaks for yourself than you would normally need. You could take at least one nap that coincides with baby's and get some much-needed rest. That's why answering machines, voice mail, pagers, and fax machines were invented—so that you can run your office without always being there.

The Home-Based, Working Parent

Working at home means that you'll sneak into your office to work early in the morning—or late at night—when the little one is asleep. You'll often work in your pajamas, with one ear cocked for sounds from the baby's room. Eventually, you'll see this way of working as "normal"—just don't forget to change into regular clothes when it's time to meet with a client!

I'm Really Working Now—Really!

Maybe you discover that you can seamlessly move from breastfeeding or bottle preparation to answering the telephone in a professional manner, and no one's the wiser.

Still, after the baby becomes more active, you might wind up feeling like a never-ending recording of things like: *"Even though I'm right here with you, I'm working. I can't play right now. I'm working. Pretend I'm not here. I'm working. Ask Daddy (or Mommy). I'm working. Really, I'm working."*

Developing New Skills

Learn to work with the skill of three people and the arms of an octopus. By developing a split-brain, work-life personality, you can negotiate a major deal on the phone while simultaneously encouraging your baby to smile again. You can train yourself to develop tremendous powers of concentration. Somehow you'll manage to produce good work, even when you hear a skirmish on the other side of the house between Daddy (or Mommy) and baby, or baby and babysitter. You'll keep your mind on your work despite loud wails and numerous interruptions ("Mama . . . hug?" "Dada, I'm hungry." "Playtime?").

Handling Stress

Stressful moments will be offset by a hug or smile that comes at a critical moment from the "junior partner," because you'll have a constant reminder of what really matters most in life—your special little someone. You'll enjoy unlimited access to an "assistant" who will basically work for hugs. From about the age of two or three, this assistant will pick up faxes (even before they're completed), use up all of your paper clips to make a chain, and illustrate your most important files in crayon. This inventive little one will also take all of the nicely sharpened pencils off your desk, cover your office floor with toys, and stand behind your right shoulder as you answer the phone. The crazy thing is, you'll still love your "assistant" anyway!

E-ALERT!

Being a home-based working parent means you must have a clear sense of priorities. Most likely your family already is a top priority, and work is a close second. However, there will be moments when this order must be reversed. A successful work-at-home parent is able to walk the daily tightrope, achieving this ever-changing balance.

Juggling Family and Work

The reality is, both raising a family and developing a business are full-time jobs. So, how can you give 100 percent to each and still maintain your sanity?

First of all, set aside a special time each day or week that is designated as "family time." During this time, don't accept phone calls, don't set appointments, and don't even think about your business. You might not even want to stay near your office. Consider going out to dinner and sharing the three best experiences had by each family member during that week.

If you feel you can incorporate your family into parts of your business, you might help family members to better understand your needs and constraints. It's one thing for your spouse or children to see you completely stressed out; it's quite another for them to be in your office when that high-volume order comes in on short notice. It would be a positive experience for your children to observe your commitment to your work.

Dealing with Challenges

You'll need to develop the skill to work around any obstacle or challenge, and the best way to accomplish a good balance between work and home life is to learn to follow a time-management program. Scheduling your time is the best way to make sure that everything gets done. The rest is just recognizing that it is possible to have two loves: your business and your family.

What should you do in the event that a client or customer wants to meet during one of your special family times? You can handle it one of two ways: You could rearrange your family time; or, better yet, you could simply say, "I already have a meeting at that time. Is there another time that works for you?" Others will respect your attention to commitments, and you never have to offer any further explanation as to whom you're meeting with. However you decide to work your children into your business life, one thing is for sure: There will never be a time without challenges or interruptions.

Five Steps to Better Time Management

Client calls. Meetings. Sales seminars. Well-baby appointments. How can you manage the ever-increasing details of your business and personal lives? Relax. Once you know how to do it, managing your time can become part of your daily routine.

✓ **Focus on goals and priorities.** Keep a running list of goals that you refer to each day. Give your tasks priority according to what must be done today and what can be done tomorrow. You can manage interruptions by using voice mail to prioritize your calls and by focusing on completing tasks by the end of each day.

✓ **Delegate wherever possible.** Find someone whom you can delegate specific tasks to when you need back-up assistance, or to maximize the time you spend on high-payoff activities. Invest the time at the outset to explain the task, the results you expect, and the deadline. You'll soon notice the benefit.

✓ **Clear your desk each day.** Clearing your desk will give you a sense of accomplishment, and will help prevent an overwhelming feeling the next day.

✓ **Make "wasted" time productive time.** This may call for an investment in a cellular phone or a laptop computer; however, much of the time you spend, for example, sitting in lobbies, will become more productive as a result. Even driving time can be more productive if you make calls along the way.

✓ **Give yourself creative time.** With all of the demands on your time, be sure you always reserve at least an hour each day as "creative" time. This is your special time to dream and plan for the future!

Choosing Your New Business

If you've decided to work at home, there's never been a better time to become an entrepreneur. Granted, it's a little more challenging with small children at home, but that's what makes it interesting, right? Following is a brief list of potential businesses you can start on your own with little or no seed money. (For more options, check out *The 200 Best Home Businesses: Easy to Start, Fun to Run, Highly Profitable.*)

✓ Bookkeeper
✓ Virtual assistant
✓ Writer/editor
✓ Graphic artist/illustrator

- ✓ Genealogical service/family history writer
- ✓ Jewelry designer or reseller
- ✓ Makeup artist/cosmetics representative
- ✓ Party planner
- ✓ Web site developer/layout specialist
- ✓ Babysitter
- ✓ Fund-raising specialist
- ✓ Dog walker/pet sitter
- ✓ Medical claims processor or transcriptionist

Where All Ends Meet

In the end, only you and your husband or partner can know what's best for your family in terms of a work arrangement outside of the home. Finding a job (or business) that pays well enough to make a profit despite the potential offset of daycare costs is a challenge for all parents, every day of the year. What works in the beginning may need to be tweaked later on down the road, as your career grows and changes perhaps as often as your child does. The important thing is to stay focused on the ultimate goal: Providing the best lifestyle for your family every step of the way.

Chapter 17

Getting Social

After you've figured out your baby's feeding and napping preferences, it's finally time to take the show on the road. Introducing baby to the rest of the world will give you both some well-deserved change of scenery and social time. Once the diaper bag is stocked and the stroller packed, you'll find it isn't so difficult to share all of your previous favorite places, people, and activities with your baby. More than likely, you'll both discover new friends and places on your exciting new social outings.

So Happy Together

Zoos, natural history museums, and aquariums offer great escapes—and social opportunities—for cooped-up parents. These options are particularly fun if you have other preschool-aged children. Not only do they offer clean family-oriented bathrooms, good parking, and snack bars, they also offer annual family memberships that cost less than $50 and allow unlimited repeated visits. Baby will enjoy the movement of fish in aquariums, the low lights, and watching other kids play and run around. You will enjoy the chance to get out and maybe even talk to other parents with new babies.

E-QUESTION

How do I get to the aquarium when I can barely get a shower?
Start small! Don't try to spend an entire day out with baby. If you do too much, you'll both be exhausted by day's end and reluctant to go again. Choose the time of day your baby seems most relaxed and happy, or stay close to home.

Spread the Joy—Not the Germs

Of course, getting too social too early can be risky, as the more you are around other kids, the more likely that your child will get sick. Even if your child isn't in daycare, a few weekly trips to a playgroup and the library might get her a regular cold or ear infection. This might be a good reason to delay getting social until baby is at least two to three months old (or even older)—especially during cold and flu season.

Start Simple—and Easy

Once you're ready to roll, you can keep the outings simple at first by just going on errands together. If you live close enough to town, you can take a walk to return those videos or to get an ice cream cone. The fresh air and scenery is good for baby and the walk is great for you. As you run through the grocery, show baby the things you are picking out and describe the colors. Babies love to be talked to and conversation is how they learn to be able to talk with you; it doesn't matter that they don't know what spaghetti marinara or an eggplant is, just the tone of your voice and engaging with you is important.

Time for "Mommy and Me"

If you're at a loss for ideas on what to do with your baby socially, check out "Mommy and Me" (*www.mommyandme.com*), a national playgroup directory and free online resource full of great ideas for activities with little ones. On the site, you can quickly and easily find playgroups, classes, and clubs in your area. Become a member (also free) and gain access to an idea-packed daily activity calendar, or sign up for the e-newsletter and receive tips, product reviews, and more, delivered to your e-mail box on a monthly basis.

Classes for You and Baby

Once you have a better sense of your baby's biorhythms and schedule, you may want to try signing up for a class together. Learn some great new tunes by taking musical classes at Music Together, Musical Munchkins, or Kindermusik. These are great ways to engage with your baby as well as meeting places for other parents. The classes are usually short, sweet, and in a place set up for easy access for parents. They may be in someone's home or at a church or community center. You may even make some new friends while learning songs and activities you can do with baby.

Mommy Meetups

As you have probably noticed, you aren't the first person in the world to have a baby (although yours is definitely the cutest ever!). There are vast resources for new parents; all you need to do is ask other parents in your neighborhood. Once connected, you'll have many opportunities to socialize, as well as to compare notes when you're having "one of those nights." Maybe you'll just need a referral, or simply want to know which brand of diaper works best—but regardless, all you need to do is reach out for help, and you'll find it's just a phone call or e-mail away.

Mommy meetups are a great way to get connected with other parents in your community—or online. To find a meetup near you, try using a search engine with the keywords "mom," "meetup," and "[your city name]."

Mother's Clubs

Mother's Clubs are part of a national organization offering playgroups, lectures, and presentations (usually with babysitting available), outings, and other resources for parents. Offerings vary regionally, but you can check Web sites and a local phone book or contact your chamber of commerce for information. Those free flyers at the grocery store are also a great source for information on other parenting groups active in your area.

E-SSENTIAL

If you strike out with civic groups, check your church bulletin board or other professional organizations to which you may already belong. If you still come up dry, post a bulletin in an alumni or sorority association newsletter offering to start your own playgroup for members.

Other Meeting Places

Once you have a group, what do you do and where do you meet? Parks, malls, and people's homes are logical gathering places for new parents. When babies are less than six months old, they won't interact much or have the need for running space. The gathering will be mainly for your benefit, but that's okay. When Mom and Dad are happy, baby is bound to be happier, too! After six months or so, a friend's living room is a logical choice for a meeting place. Share the load; rotate weeks and have someone else bring a snack so that the host only has to clean the floor of their living room and not make muffins, too.

Water Babies Class

Since your baby spent nine months swimming around in your abdomen, it's only natural that he would feel comfortable being back in the water.

That's why Water Babies classes are so popular—babies generally take to it quickly and easily, as long as you're there for support (both moral and physical).

Through songs, games, and positive word associations, classes emphasize bonding between parent and baby, building communication skills, and getting adjusted to the water. Techniques typically taught for babies in the four- to nine-month range include back floating, submersion, and water safety. Instructors work with parents to help them become comfortable handling their baby in the water—facilitating the deepening bond between parents and their babies.

Parents' Night Out

As much as you love your new baby, it'll be a happy day when you realize that you don't have to spend every waking and sleeping moment together. It can be quite a shock to realize that lately, all of your conversations with your partner (or family members) seem to center around feeding schedules, naptimes, and diaper changes. Help is not far away, because every other parent of a newborn is in the same boat. Here, there is empathy in numbers. So, get organized—swap a good night out with other parents and get free babysitting plus the benefit of knowing another parent is watching your precious baby (and not the fourteen-year-old down the street with a new boyfriend and a cell phone).

E-ALERT!

Be assertive and ask tough questions before leaving baby with new friends. For instance, do they have guns in the house? Will they follow your schedule for baby? Remember, any deviations from your established routine might be disruptive to your parenting patterns.

Some Parent's Night Out groups are well established and organized with point systems so that one family doesn't end up sitting for everyone else all the time. Others are loosely arranged. If you have older children, they will definitely enjoy a playdate with other kids their age. Pack the pajamas before you send them off so all you have to do is bring them home and put them to bed.

Start Your Own Group

Look around your neighborhood and group of friends to see if there are any other parents interested in starting a group or already have one established. Single parents will especially appreciate the break—just make them promise to do something nice for themselves if they don't have a date—and don't let them go home to do laundry! Also, when taking a well-deserved night out, don't forget to leave the name and number of your pediatrician and contact details for where you will be. You may also want to leave the name and number of a relative in the area that might know baby's favorite bedtime song in case you forget to tell them.

Know Thy Neighbor

Before your baby comes along, it might be a really good idea to get to know your neighbors better. Host an ice cream social, or just invite your neighbors over for a cookout. Watch how they interact with their own kids, and spend time asking them for parenting advice (even if you really don't want any right now!). Making these kinds of inquiries will give you lots of great insight into their parenting philosophies, and they won't need to know that you are, in fact, screening them as potential babysitters or as friends you'd like to socialize with more after your baby is born.

Staying Social

Now that you know you are allowed a social life outside the "baby bubble," don't forget that you can also take your baby with you on various social outings. If you belong to a book group or card-playing group that meets regularly, chances are there are many moms and grandmothers longing for the chance to hold and snuggle a new baby. The holding and snuggling desire may decline rapidly when baby has a record-making blowout diaper or a colicky crying jag, so you need to be aware when it is time to leave.

Be prepared to adjust your expectations—if you were the last one to close down the party before baby, you'll need to prepare yourself that now you'll probably be the first to leave. Get there early and bring all the changes of clothes and bottles you might possibly need to avoid the disappointment of having to leave just because you need something at home.

Tote Baby Around with You

Many young babies sleep soundly in their carriers, so you can tote them to a movie or the concert series you bought tickets for long before baby got here. Just be aware of others around you; they also paid a lot for their tickets and may be on a date night away from their own babies, so they won't necessarily want to hear your rendition of "Itsy Bitsy Spider" during a Yo Yo Ma concert.

Story Hours

You're never too young—or old—to hear a good story. For another fun (and free) outing in your community, take baby to story hour at your local library. Many are tailored to audiences with babies and small children, and several feature puppets as well. Baby will enjoy the sights and sounds, but will also benefit from hearing stories read aloud. Encouraging this kind of social event as early as possible will help foster a love of books and reading later on—so this is definitely an activity worth participating in together!

Pack a diaper bag the night before a big outing, or during baby's naptime. Never raid the diaper bag for diapers at home, or you may get caught diaper-less while you're out and about. Keep special toys (plastic mirrors, rattles, teethers or soft books) that only appear on outings so they will always seem fresh and new.

Playgroups

If you are lucky enough to have friends with babies the same age, then you have a built-in playgroup. As babies grow, they will need the chance to socialize and learn all the ins and outs about playing together. You can chat with your friends while your baby gets to play with "new" toys and experience a different home environment. If you see each other often, then your friend's home will become a "home away from home" as your baby grows, where he will be comfortable with your friends and their different routines. It is a lifesaver to have a place for your child in a pinch when you have an unexpected doctor appointment or trip to the garage with your car.

Do a Swap

You might even consider a "toy swap" or "book swap" with friends so babies get to experience new toys that you don't have to buy. Just make sure it isn't someone's favorite before borrowing that squeaky bug toy for a while. When the toys and books return to their original owners, they will be new all over again, if slightly more well-loved. Be a good friend and try to keep toys and books in good condition; wash them, if possible, before returning them. Don't loan out super favorite irreplaceable toys that came from Grandma's once-in-a-lifetime trip to China; it sets up both you and your friend for an uncomfortable situation if and when they get damaged during what was supposed to be baby's fun time.

For Playgroups, Etiquette Is Key

When participating in a playgroup with other parents (and their babies, of course!), having fun is the main objective. You'll want as diverse a group as possible, so that the conversation is always interesting. Even though you won't likely hear or see specific signs, babies do pick up on how well their grown-ups get along and often mimic behavior they see, whether it's for good or ill.

Limit group size to no more than a dozen participants (babies included). That way, the group will be more manageable, and everyone can take a turn as host or playgroup leader. Ideally, the babies should be close in age to better form a peer-based learning environment. Toddlers and older kids can play in another room during playgroup times for babies.

Playgroup participants should let others know in advance whether they have any pets, as some participants may be allergic to animals. It's a good idea to have all participants list any pet or food allergies on a form before the first meeting, to avoid any possible allergic reactions.

Set Ground Rules

It might help your playgroup to develop some "ground rules" or behavioral guidelines for participants. This way, no one will be likely to upset other members with inappropriate comments, "baby boasting" or unfair comparisons. One of the primary reasons people leave groups is that they feel uncomfortable with the comments of other group participants, so head this off at the pass. Here are some good starting points for setting ground rules:

- ✓ Set meeting times, dates, and places on at least a quarterly basis.
- ✓ Call your host if you're unable to attend or if baby's sick.
- ✓ If hosting, clean your house and remove all temptations that could cause safety problems.
- ✓ Promptly address your own child's bad behavior—but don't discipline another parent's child.
- ✓ Don't change playgroup dates very often, as this will create group instability.
- ✓ Always help clean up when playtime is over.
- ✓ Suggest other activities that your group's members may want to participate in together (i.e., a Chinese New Year party at a local restaurant, or puppet show at your local library).

Some playgroups designate two parents to supervise the babies while the other parents have a meeting, complete with an informative speaker on various parenting topics. Consider surveying your group to determine their interest level in

having such an arrangement. If half of the members would like to have meetings with speakers and the other half only wants playtime, consider breaking into two groups that rotate their meeting times. This way, you can maximize their interests—and keep membership at worthwhile levels.

Family-Friendly Baby Stuff

There are so many places catering to families, it's easier than ever before to choose a family outing that everyone can enjoy. With conveniences like family restrooms and breastfeeding rooms, many of the hassles of traveling in a pack are minimized. That's why museums and zoos are such great places for everyone in the family; each family member can appreciate things at his or her own level and pace, and there are plenty of places to take a break if anyone gets tired.

Head for the Great Outdoors

Local parks are great, too, particularly if they have hiking and biking trails. Baby can ride snuggly in a bike trailer behind a parent while brother and sister master training wheels, roller blades, or their scooter. Many parks offer free concerts in the summer; that's a great time to spread out a blanket and let baby look up in the trees while listening to music or take a nap while siblings dance and play in the playground. There is also the added advantage of being outside with other families, where no one expects children (or adults) to sit quietly. In settings like these, it's much easier to relax and not worry about noise levels.

E-SSENTIAL

Don't forget to pack sunscreen (at your pediatrician's recommendation) or a hat in summer and winter for baby, as well as all the weather gear appropriate for the season whenever you go out. A bit of planning can make the day so much smoother for you and baby.

The Great Big Indoors

The shopping mall beckons again in bad weather, offering rental car- and train-shaped strollers. Some malls even have miniature golf and merry-go-rounds for older kids. Most cities and towns have indoor "play places" geared at the toddler set: a large, open space similar to a great kindergarten classroom, complete with dress-up, tricycles, games, and even play structures. Kids can play safely without you having to watch every move like a hawk, so you, your partner, and baby can enjoy watching the fun.

Seasonally, art, church, and music festivals abound in the summer, and if you live near a lake or beach, you've got a built-in destination for fun in the sun.

Just Have Fun!

Whether it's at the store, in a special class, or with family or friends, you should relax, have fun, and enjoy your time together with baby. After all, you're making memories together that baby will enjoy hearing about much later on. Enjoy your many explorations of the world, and realize that what's fun for you is often just as fun for baby. If you aren't having fun, neither is baby, but try to laugh it off and do something else another time. When it comes to baby's first social escapades, sometimes false starts and disastrous playdates make the best stories!

Chapter 18

Playtime with Baby

You'll probably want to learn a few nursery rhymes and games to play with baby. Both have a long-standing history of helping babies to develop. And some stay forever etched in your memories, sending you on a sentimental journey every time you hear them. Even though at first you may feel self-conscious about tugging at baby's toes and playing peek-a-boo over and over again, nursery rhymes and games can be a good way to bond with your child. Playtime can be special time together!

New Baby Games

With myriad choices in the stores today, it's easy to forget that some of the best games for you and baby are the ones where you are playing age-appropriate games together. But where do you start? The easiest way to look at the new games you can create on your own is to match them to specific time frames in baby's development. As you'll see, much of game-appropriateness is determined by baby's cognitive development.

E-ALERT!

Don't inundate your baby with lots of toys and games—and don't expect to fill every quiet moment with giggles or smiles. Babies need some downtime just as much as adults do. An overstimulated baby will have difficulty staying on a good sleep schedule and may be more colicky than babies who have more periods of rest.

Zero to Three Months

Most of the games you play in the first three months of baby's development are going to be the kind that you create yourself, since baby has no idea what fun really is at the moment. For some babies, being rocked is one of the best early playtimes they can share with their parents; however, for others, there needs to be more entertainment. These little ones are all about their basic senses—especially sight and sound. They respond best to being held and danced with, having a private music festival with you in your living room, and watching a "light show" with a flashlight or a "baby planetarium" that flashes stars across their heavenly little bedroom ceiling. Keep it simple at this stage, and you'll have a peaceful, appreciative little child.

Four to Six Months

Your baby is bound to be a little more active now, so entertainment can be more physical (i.e., tactile or mouth-based). There's nothing a four- to six-month-old loves more than to explore the wonders of his own mouth, so have lots of clean teething toys around. You can also garner some giggles with tickle games, bubble blowing (outside or in the tub, which is probably the best place to play!) or playing "baby airplane" by holding baby up in the air, and pretending baby can fly.

Seven to Nine Months

Motor skill development, as well as crawling, can lead to some interesting places for baby to explore. While this can be a fun time, it can also be a dangerous one, so keep your eyes on baby at all times! Fun games for the seven- to nine-month set can include "Scavenger Hunt," where you place favorite toys a foot or so away from baby and encourage baby to crawl to retrieve it; "Bang and Clatter," a musical game using kitchen pans and wooden spoons (a timeless game!) and "Play Ball," where you glide a small ball across the floor and watch baby learn how to play over time. Soon, your little one will be an old pro at motor skill games!

Ten to Twelve Months

Now that baby is likely to be holding on to tables and chairs and taking steps, it's time to start making play more interesting. Now is a good time to play with finger puppets or do a story time featuring short, simple-concept books that appeal to baby's sense of rhythm, sound, sight, and touch. Books that make animal sounds or that feature furry creatures are often favorites of babies close to one year old.

E-SSENTIAL

You can learn traditional rhymes and games, or you can purchase state-of-the-art stimulators, such as flash cards that come in black, red, and white and feature very simple shapes for baby to stare at. Or try videos featuring the faces of other babies or animated characters, CDs with funny songs for babies, or simple computer games for babies.

Nursery Rhymes

For the more traditional minded, here are some tried-and-true nursery rhyme games you can play with your baby. If you start to get bored with these, try some adaptations of your own.

This Little Pig Went to Market
(Traditional, North American)

> *This little pig went to market.*
> *This little pig stayed home.*
> *This little pig ate roast beef.*
> *This little pig had none.*
> *This little pig cried, "Wee, wee, wee"—all the way home!*

Hush, Little Baby
(Traditional, United States)

> *Hush, little baby, don't say a word,*
> *Papa's gonna buy you a mockingbird.*
> *If that mockingbird don't sing,*
> *Papa's gonna buy you a diamond ring.*
> *If that diamond ring turns brass,*
> *Papa's gonna buy you a looking glass.*
> *If that looking glass gets broke,*
> *Papa's gonna buy you a billy goat.*
> *If that billy goat don't pull,*
> *Papa's gonna buy you a cart and bull.*
> *If that cart and bull turn over,*
> *Papa's gonna buy you a dog named Rover.*
> *If that dog named Rover don't bark,*
> *Papa's gonna buy you a horse and cart.*
> *If that horse and cart fall down,*
> *You'll still be the sweetest baby in town.*

Hey Diddle Diddle, the Cat and the Fiddle
(Traditional, English)

Hey diddle diddle, the cat and the fiddle,
The cow jumped over the moon.
The little dog laughed to see such sport
And the dish ran away with the spoon.

Sleep, Baby Sleep
(Traditional, English)

Sleep, baby sleep,
Your father tends the sheep.
Your mother shakes the dreamland tree,
Down falls a dream for thee.
Sleep, baby sleep.

To Market, to Market
(Traditional, English)

To market, to market, to buy a fat pig,
Home again, home again, jiggety-jig.
To market, to market, to buy a fat hog,
Home again, home again, jiggety-jog.
To market, to market, to buy a plum bun,
Home again, home again, marketing's done.

Rub-a-Dub-Dub
(Traditional, English)

Rub-a-dub-dub,
Three men in a tub.
And who do you think they be?
The butcher, the baker, and
The candlestick maker.
Turn 'em out,
Knaves all three!

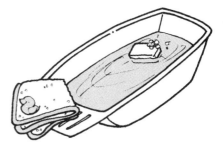

Ring Around a Rosy
(Traditional, English/American)

Ring around a rosy,
A pocket full of posies,
Ashes, ashes
We all fall down!

E-FACT

Many nursery rhymes are about sleep, because their object is to help baby to relax and get some rest. Particularly in your first few months home, baby will sleep way more often than she will engage in play-time with you. Don't worry—that will all change soon enough!

The Itsy, Bitsy Spider
(Traditional, English/American)

The itsy, bitsy spider
Climbed up the waterspout.
Down came the rain and
Washed the spider out.
Out came the sun and
Dried up all the rain.
And the itsy, bitsy spider
Climbed up the spout again.

There Was a Crooked Man
(Traditional, English)

There was a crooked man, and he walked a crooked mile,
He found a crooked sixpence against a crooked stile;
He bought a crooked cat, which caught a crooked mouse,
And they all lived together in a little crooked house.

Old King Cole
(Traditional, English)

Old King Cole was a merry old soul,
And a merry old soul was he.
He called for his pipe and
He called for his bowl and
He called for his fiddlers three.

Pat-a-Cake
(Traditional, English/American)

Pat-a-cake, pat-a-cake, baker's man.
Bake me a cake as fast as you can.
Pat it and roll it, and mark it with a "B,"
And put it in the oven for baby and me.

Row, Row, Row Your Boat
(Traditional, English/American)

Row, row, row your boat
Gently down the stream,
Merrily, merrily, merrily, merrily,
Life is but a dream.

Old MacDonald
(Traditional, American)

Old MacDonald had a farm,
E-i-e-i-o!
And on that farm he had a (pig, cat, cow, chick, etc.)
E-i-e-i-o!
With an oink, oink here, and an oink, oink there
Here an oink, there an oink
Everywhere an oink, oink
Old MacDonald had a farm,
E-i-e-i-o!

The Wheels on the Bus
(Traditional, English/American)

The wheels on the bus go round and round
Round and round, round and round
Wheels on the bus go round and round
All through the town.
The people on the bus go up and down . . .
The wipers on the bus go swish, swish, swish . . .
The babies on the bus go "Wah, wah, wah!" . . .
The mommies on the bus go "Sh-sh-shh!" . . .

London Bridge
(Traditional, English)

London Bridge is falling down,
Falling down, falling down.
London Bridge is falling down,
My fair lady.
Build it up with iron bars,
Iron bars, iron bars.
Build it up with iron bars,
My fair lady.

E-SSENTIAL

The more physically expressive you are for nursery rhymes, the more both you and your baby will enjoy playing together. If you're very expressive, baby will grow to be more expressive back, and expressive babies are also generally better communicators later on in life.

Classic Fun

Of course, there are still plenty of tried-and-true baby games you can share. These are the ones that you grew up with, and you turned out alright, didn't you? Regardless of how you might answer, following are some classic gems baby's sure to enjoy.

Peek-a-Boo

Put your hands over your face for a few seconds, and then remove them quickly and say, "Peek-a-boo." You can also try this game using a blanket covering your face.

I'm Gonna Get You

While the "got-your-nose" game seems a bit on the gory side, small babies don't seem to think so. They laugh at this game until they are at least two or three years old—so it must be worth something. Put your thumb between your first two fingers and say, "Got-your-nose!" Make your own variations. Creep up baby's stomach with your fingers, like a spider, while saying, "I'm gonna get you!" It's scary, but a fun kind of scary.

Where Is It?

The object is for you to show baby a brightly colored object or toy, and then hide it under a blanket or pillow. Ask baby, "Where did it go?" and baby will probably respond with smiles or giggles. Because they don't understand the concept of object permanence yet, babies find this one highly entertaining.

Babycise

Baby exercises might include sit-ups, knee bends, tug-of-war, and so forth. These games are a little more physical, with baby relying on you to move his legs. Or you can give baby a blanket or toy to hold on to while you pull him up. If you have a padded surface below, you can pull baby up a bit and let him fall gently back down on it, saying the word boom each time. Babies also think this one is really funny.

Funny Sounds

Babies love to learn the sounds that other creatures make, and it helps them learn how to make sounds, too. Don't be surprised if one of baby's first words is "kitty" or "moo."

E-ALERT!

If your baby is still having difficulty with object permanence, you might hold off for a while on games where you or Daddy disappear. Wait until baby is a bit older, or make sure you pop around the corner way faster than you would for an older child. This way, baby will see you leave and come sooner, lessening stress.

Where's Mommy?

Hide around the corner, and ask, "Where's Mommy?" or "Where's Daddy?" (Depending on who or what you have in the room, you could use variations from kitty to Grandma.) If the baby starts to cry when you disappear, she might still be too young for this one. Generally, the three- to eight-month crowd finds this one most entertaining.

Music Making

If you have an instrument such as a piano or drums, let baby tap out a few notes occasionally. You don't have to start with formal classes, unless your child appears to be a prodigy. For most of us, it's just a lot of meaningless (yet fun) noise that baby gets to make. It does, however, teach baby a little about cause and effect. If you don't have musical instruments, give baby a pot or pan and a wooden spoon—many babies enjoy these even more than the real thing.

Art Time

Give baby a big, fat crayon and paper or a bowl of colored Jell-O for finger painting. This activity should be closely supervised and is expressly for those babies who are six to eight months or older. Any younger and they're just not interested; the advantage to the Jell-O is that it's completely edible, should your child decide that he is not Picasso.

E-FACT

Until they are at least three months old, babies generally tend to respond better to black and white toys versus colorful ones. Once their eyes get used to contrasts, they can process more colors—and then they'll soon find themselves attracted to the brightest, prettiest colors.

Baby Toys

The big world of baby toys beckons. There are so many toys out there—where do you start? First of all, the most important aspect of play with your baby is your time together. Interacting with baby teaches him so much about you and how to manage his expanding world. So look for toys you can enjoy together and that are age appropriate, Most toys are labeled well to show you which toy to choose according to age.

Crib, Car Seat, and Stroller Toys

One of the best toys for baby is one that can be secured with Velcro and hung on cribs, car seats, and strollers. The same toy can be fastened to a shopping cart seat, covering the icky bar that everyone has sneezed on and providing baby with a virtual command center of activities to make that trip through the store so much easier.

Wooden ABC Blocks

For centuries, wooden blocks have been favorite toys for little ones. They are easy to grasp, fun to build with, and generally quite safe for baby to use for play. Stacking them—and watching them fall—can teach baby about cause and effect, which is good for cognitive development.

Shopping Cart

Playing "store" is a fun way to get little legs up and running, so get baby her own shopping cart and enjoy watching her pick up toys and cart them all over the playroom. Use the cart to help clean up when it's time for a nap.

Baby Yoga and Massage

It isn't hard to believe that two things you like to do, baby likes as well. Books, DVDs, and classes abound on bonding with baby through touch. Yoga and massage help the body function to its fullest potential, and what could be a better gift for your new and growing baby? Explore the offerings out there and see what fits with your personal style. Babies can't do all the yoga poses you can, so get instruction before trying out any poses on baby.

Many yoga DVDs and videos for Mom and baby include breathing and stretching as well as poses that cuddle baby on Mom's tummy, and some use babies as weights. Moms even do push-ups over their new little ones. Baby gets to do some stretches as well and finally end up in relaxation poses with Mom. What a great way to tighten up those postpregnancy abs and bond with baby!

E-QUESTION

What are the benefits of baby yoga?
People who practice yoga with their toddlers maintain that their child sleeps better, digests food better, has better muscular control and coordination, and develops a unique sense of confidence.

TV Time with Baby

Can you remember the first thing you saw on television when you were young? Most likely, it was *Sesame Street* or *Mister Roger's Neighborhood*. That was before cable TV could give pay-per-view options—and long before satellite TV could bounce more channels than you can count.

So, now that you have more choices than ever, what should you watch with baby, and how long should you watch it? Though there are several high-quality shows on cable TV (notably, on Nickelodeon's Nick Jr. and The Disney Channel), many parents still prefer the learning focus of *Sesame Street*. There's even BabyFirstTV, a new channel just for babies featuring lots of short, animated shows with plenty of learning opportunities. Check out lots of different shows for kids, and then pick out your own favorites. Baby will enjoy whatever you enjoy, because you are the one who will make it all a fun experience for baby! So clap, sing along, and learn new things together—just keep it age appropriate for baby's developing brain.

E-ALERT!

Experts still disagree on exactly how much television babies should watch—and even whether they should watch at all. Try to be a responsible parent: if baby is watching TV, you should be watching with baby, singing and playing along to make it an interactive experience. Don't use the TV as a babysitter.

Enjoy Yourselves!

The most fun you will have in your playtime with baby is when you are a barrel of laughs yourself. That's why it's so important that you get the proper amounts of food and rest—you'll want to be in rare form for your adoring little audience. Since playtime can be both a performance and a collaborative effort at times, keeping the rest of your life in balance is pivotal to your success as an entertainer. You have a show to put on, indeed, but the best part is, you'll have full participation from a completely nonjudgmental audience. What could be more fun than that?

Chapter 19

Capturing Baby's First Year

Making a permanent record of your baby's important milestones can be an incredibly daunting task. You may be unsure about what to put in and what to leave out. And you may be afraid to miss something that will later be of significance to your baby. No matter how you decide to do it, putting all of your baby's special moments into one space will undoubtedly help you when baby grows up and asks you that age-old question, "What was I like when I was a baby?"

Putting It All Together

There are many resources available to help you in this endeavor. You can ask other parents how they preserved their babies' collections of "favorite things," or you can surf the Internet for a wider range of ideas. Some of you artsy, nontraditional types may choose to capture your baby's precious memories in your own personal style.

E-ALERT!

Be careful to store your book or box of memories in a dry place. Excessive heat or cold could damage your materials, making them musty or unsalvageable. Taking the time to store your memories properly now can save you both time and tears later.

One popular method is to dry mount all of the items in a large binder with plastic page protectors. This method will keep all of your papers neatly preserved for many years. You can add pages when necessary or remove some for show. Or you could preserve each item in a clear plastic bag (the ones that are self-sealing work best), placing the bags on top of one another in a large decorated box.

Memories to Keep

After you've made the commitment to collect as many memories of your baby as humanly possible (between diapers and feedings, of course!), the next step is to decide what to include in baby's keepsake. Here are some suggestions:

- ✓ Early photos
- ✓ Baby's birth statistics and other details about the birth experience
- ✓ Baby's first gifts and well-wishers (and perhaps a collection of greeting card wishes sent to baby upon arrival)
- ✓ Information about baby's looks: What color hair and eyes did baby have? Whom did you think baby looked most like? Whom did other people think baby looked most like?

- ✓ Details about baby's ride home: What kind of car did you bring baby home in? Did you stop anywhere first? Did baby seem to enjoy his or her first ride?
- ✓ Photo and address of baby's first home
- ✓ First visitors
- ✓ Copy of baby's first footprints and birth certificate
- ✓ Newspaper clippings announcing baby's arrival
- ✓ Printout of baby's Web page (if applicable)
- ✓ One birth announcement (whether you had some professionally made, or created them yourself)
- ✓ Brief stories about baby's favorite things: songs, toys, people, stories, and activities
- ✓ Favorite (and not-so-favorite) foods
- ✓ The time, date, and place of baby's first steps
- ✓ Baby's first words and nicknames for siblings (especially if the sibling has a hard-to-pronounce first name)
- ✓ Items related to baby's first holidays (Halloween costume, Christmas photos, Hanukkah celebration, or other event)
- ✓ Special trips baby took (to Grandma's, to Walt Disney World, etc.)
- ✓ Handmade items from siblings or relatives that carry a special significance

Durability Keeps Memories Better

Whatever form in which you choose to house your child's earliest memories, keep in mind that it should be something fairly durable. In just a few years, this will be baby's favorite thing to look at again and again, and you'll want it to be able to stand the test of time. Some parents even keep an online photo gallery, CD-ROM, or DVD backup of everything in their baby's memory box, just in case baby (or baby's canine friend) wears out the original.

Baby's Firsts—in Real Time

Some cyber-savvy parents post all of the important updates about their baby's "firsts" on a Web site designed especially for baby. All you have to do is find a host (America Online, Yahoo Groups, or your own Web hosting service) and use a template to design the Web site. Then, be sure to update baby's site regularly, keeping the memories fresh for everyone you invite to visit often.

You can accomplish a beautiful, near-professional quality Web page in a matter of minutes from good templates, and literally thousands of these are available on various Web design sites that you can find using a simple search engine. If you don't feel comfortable designing a Web site yourself, there are plenty of Web-based businesses or local Web site developers that can help you design a Web site for your baby. Use a search engine or a local phone book.

E-QUESTION

How can I add audio and/or video to my baby's Web site?
Capture coos with a digital recorder, convert the file to an mp3 format, and then upload to your site. Adding video to your site can be easily accomplished using Macromedia Dreamweaver and Flash. If you have a Mac-based system, use iLife or iMovie. You can also upload to Google Video or YouTube—or narrate a slideshow of photos on SnapFish.

Baby's First Blog

Creating an online diary, or blog, can be a great way to keep people posted on baby's daily milestones. Blogs are a particularly good way to communicate in near real time when you have lots of faraway friends and family, since they can create an RSS feed that populates their computer with up-to-the-minute news about all of the happenings in baby's life. Subscribers to your blog can also post their own comments, which will create even more great memories for baby once he is older.

Finding a Blogsite

You can build a blog for free using any one of several providers. The most popular at the moment are Blogger, Live Journal, and Word Press, though there are now literally hundreds of places where you can post a blog for free. Just use a good search engine and check out all of the great possibilities!

Making a "Baby's First Year" Scrapbook

One of the best (and most fun) ways to keep memories from baby's first year is to make a fun-filled, spirited scrapbook. This option offers you lots of three-dimensional creative opportunities, such as including stamp art, ribbons, and glitter, or highlighting special memories with glued-on mementos like baby's hospital bracelet. You can be as bold or conservative as you want, and you can even host a scrapbook night for other new moms in your circle of family and friends. The most important thing is to have fun!

Here's what you will need to make a homemade scrapbook full of baby's "firsts":

- ✔ Scissors, tape, and glue
- ✔ A computer and printer (there are great software programs available for keeping family records and milestones)
- ✔ Wrapping paper, tissue, and stickers
- ✔ Mounting spray
- ✔ Photo holders
- ✔ Labels (for photo captions)
- ✔ Plastic page covers
- ✔ A notebook (for scribbling ideas)
- ✔ A storage box (a shoe box will do to start)
- ✔ An X-Acto knife (for trimming edges of photos neatly)
- ✔ A binder with extra filler pages (large photo albums work best)
- ✔ Colored pens (to add narrative throughout the scrapbook)

E-ALERT!

Don't forget to leave some room in your scrapbook for notes, personal commentary, and other stray (yet important) memories. You'll want to create a memory book that's sure to make baby smile later in life when sharing these special moments with family and friends.

Other Creative Ways to Immortalize Baby

Whether you choose to bronze baby's first shoes (as was so popular in the 1950s and '60s) or to mount a small collection of baby things to hang in your living room, you will want to find some unusual ways to remember those beautiful and loving early days. These are keepsakes you will cherish while you have them, and that your children will appreciate taking with them, especially when they're ready to start families of their own. Whatever form you choose to immortalize baby, know that you are preserving memories for future generations, too!

A Painted Portrait

Have a local artist paint your baby's portrait. It doesn't have to be the standard, run-of-the-mill pastel (unless that's what you want); it can even be an abstract or computer graphic.

Photo Portraits

Once you have a baby, you'll find that there's no shortage of direct-mail advertising encouraging you to have your baby's portrait taken at one of several dozen photography studios. Pick one that's not only a good deal, but that also seems to have the style of photos you'd most like to keep and share with friends and family. Shop around, and ask other new parents where they went for baby portraits—or where they got their plates with the mold of baby's hand and foot prints. Some photo shops offer newer digital technology called Magic Portraits that allows you to take a photo of baby in a particular pose, then merge that image with a fantasy background that makes baby appear to be sitting in a flower, in front of a castle, or even on a unicorn. These are beautiful pictures to frame and give as gifts!

E-SSENTIAL

Have a professional photographer shoot black-and-white photos of baby dressed as an angel, or wearing an unusual hat, or with a puppy. The best black-and-white photos of babies are the ones when the photographer catches baby in a candid moment.

Mounted Mementos

Collect a few items that are of sentimental value to you from baby's first days. Have them mounted and framed in a Plexiglas frame, with a printed note card explaining the significance of each item and giving the date. Suggestions include a favorite photo, baby's birth certificate, baby's hospital cap, dad's hospital shirt from the delivery room (some even have the baby's footprints on them), baby's first rattle, and a christening gown with the invitation next to it.

How to Write Your Baby's Story

Every person on this planet is entitled to their story—and who better to write a baby's story than the parents? If you decide to chronicle your baby's earliest days in written form of any kind, you should start yourself off with a few ground rules.

First, choose a tense, and stay in it. If you choose to write everything in active, present tense, you should be consistent throughout the diary. If you choose past tense, keep it in the past.

E-ALERT!

Just because your baby is small doesn't mean you have to write in baby talk. Remember, she'll likely read this with you when she is much older.

Next, include the daily, mundane activities along with the interesting or funny episodes you have with baby. You'd be surprised how important those seemingly insignificant little details will become after your baby has grown.

Finally, write like you speak. Pretend you're narrating this story to your child as an adult, looking back on fond memories. Relax, and enjoy telling your child the one story she will want to revisit many times throughout her life.

Add Images and Captions

Illustrate your diary with plenty of pictures, and write lively, interesting captions for them. Some parents do thought-clouds (as in cartoons), in which they provide baby's imagined dialogue, which can be extremely entertaining for others who read the diary.

You can also weave in some of the news of the day, including world events, entertainment, sports, and popular culture. If you're feeling particularly creative, you can put some of these items into a tube with a label that says, "Time Capsule." This way, years from now, the grown-up child can find out what was happening in the rest of the world at the time when she was born. Time capsules also make great baby shower gift ideas!

E-SSENTIAL

Set aside a regular time at least once per month to update your baby's diary. If you let a few months' worth of writing pile up, you may forget some precious little memories; and it's hard to remember tiny details for long periods of time. Make diary time a habit, and you'll be happier with the results.

Baby's Growth Stages: What Happens When

Part of being successful at capturing your baby's milestones is knowing when these incredible moments are most likely to occur. If you're thinking baby's first tooth is more than six months away, you'll be caught off-guard when it shows up a month or so earlier! For at least the first year of baby's life, there is bound to be a new photo opportunity each month—and you'll want to be poised to capture everything you want to remember for years to come. Just keep in mind that development varies widely from child to child. Some milestones may come late, others early, but following are some general guidelines.

One Month

Babies still sleep more than they are awake at this stage. They should be able to lie on their stomachs and lift their heads for brief moments. A one-month-old can usually recognize the voices of his or her parents and perhaps a sibling or two. Babies at this early stage are good listeners, since they are just beginning to learn the language.

Two Months

Two-month-olds can often roll from a side position to their backs. They are beginning to make simple vowel sounds, most often after watching their parents' lips and mimicking them. Smiles begin this month— so get your camera ready to catch as many as you can!

Three Months

Babies get more of a personality and seem to smile at more specific things (such as a parent's smile, a toy, or a sibling). Now is a good time to start playing more music or to sing around your baby, if you haven't already. Babies react more to music at three months.

Four Months

A four-month-old is much more lively and will likely have longer awake periods than younger babies. At four months, a baby can usually roll from stomach to back on his or her own. Laughter begins, and sounds begin to be more refined than in the previous month.

Five Months

Many babies begin to sleep through the night at five months, and their sleep patterns become more regular. With some support from you, baby should stand on his or her feet and bounce for a few minutes at a time. Five-month-olds should also be able to lie on their back and raise their heads and shoulders a little. Teeth may begin to sprout this month, as infants start teething anytime between the ages of three and fifteen months.

Six Months

Six months is a real turning point for babies, since they begin to sit briefly by themselves. Babies' noises begin to sound a little more like complete sentences, even though the sounds still don't amount to much more than cooing or simple words (dada or mama). Six-month-olds can reach for toys or other objects that they find interesting (such as earrings). Watch out!

Seven Months

Your seven-month-old is becoming more mobile, with rocking motions, more grasping with hands, and the ability to sit up all by himself. If you have gone back to work or even just leave the room for a spell, you may notice that baby isn't very thrilled about it. This is when separation anxiety starts.

Eight Months

Eight-month-olds sit up for longer periods of time by themselves and can even pull themselves up to a standing position, although they don't typically hold this position too long. They show more interest in learning to walk and may even start crawling. Also, a new study suggests that babies can remember things you say from this point on—so watch your language!

Nine Months

Your nine-month-old can crawl into the most unusual places, such as up a small staircase or under furniture. Some babies at this stage can even walk while holding on to a parent or some furniture. There is even growing evidence that baby actually understands many of the words you use.

Ten Months

At ten months, your baby can wave (and possibly even say) bye-bye; crawl nearly everywhere in the house; and form simple sounds and words like "mama" or "dada." The baby can pull himself into sitting position, sometimes by rolling up.

Eleven Months

Baby can walk with you, as long as you hold his hand. He can also call for "Mama" and "Dada," play simple hand-clapping games, and sometimes stand by himself for longer than one minute. Walking, of course, is still another matter. Expect baby to collapse back to the ground easily or to wind up in a squatting position.

One Year

Baby is one year old! Now, you need to get those video cameras rolling, since baby may be able to walk for three to ten minutes at a time. Of course, some babies don't walk on their own until they are about fifteen months old.

E-ALERT!

Just so you don't accidentally tape over some precious moments you'll never see again, it would be a good idea to transfer your videos to files on your computer, then burn a DVD once you've got several tapes together in one file. At the very least, you should label each videotape with the event and date immediately after filming.

The Journey That Lies Ahead

It may be hard to believe right now that your baby is actually going to grow up. In all honesty, your days with baby will pass too quickly. Someday, in the not-too-distant future, those tiny hands will be grasping for your car keys instead of the baby rattle. Those tiny feet will walk down the aisle on the arm of another. That tiny mouth will tell you incredible stories, and maybe pass yours on to another tiny little soul.

Listen to the parents who tell you that this time is precious and short lived. It absolutely is. Enjoy the moments you share with your new baby, and remember to reflect back on those moments at times when you are feeling overwhelmed or in despair.

Good luck as you embark on a journey that is beyond words and beyond any experience you've ever known before. May you live to see your grand-children's children, and may you share your own stories with them as life goes on and as they grow!

Chapter 20

Cyber Babies

The times, they are a-changin'. In the past, parents scanned bookshelves at the library looking for the latest information about babies. Most of it was written by doctors, and much of it was written by Dr. Benjamin Spock. Today, in the Information Age, you don't even have to leave home to access thousands of words of advice. You can surf the Net in your pajamas and ask for online help whenever you need it—even with baby fast asleep in your arms.

Help That's 24/7

It used to be that when you had one of those middle-of-the-night questions, you had to call your mother (or, gulp, mother-in-law) for advice. Now, you can surf the hundreds of Web sites and hyperlinks related to pregnancy, newborns, and infants and find information on everything from what to eat during pregnancy to how to ease your baby into toddlerhood to how to baby-proof your house. There's an interesting and useful baby-related Web site or blog on just about every topic imaginable; the hard part is figuring out how to narrow down your choices so that you're not connected to both baby and the Internet all day long!

Goin' Searchin'

Whether you're a "newbie" or cyber savvy, the most important tool you can have at your disposal when you need information right away is a good search engine. Of course, Google.com is the most popular, but there's also Yahoo.com, MSN Search, AltaVista, and even Dogpile.com. For the best results, choose specific keywords—and for the highest trust level, choose sites that are affiliated with larger, more reputable partners. Or visit only major sites produced by trusted brand names such as Pampers.com.

E-SSENTIAL

You can use your Internet provider's or search engine's blocking function to filter out any inappropriate sites with adult-oriented material. Unfortunately, there are many adult sites that "spoof" topics that would normally be of interest to new parents. Better to cut those off from your view by using an online filter—especially in your emotional state!

Pregnancy-Related Sites

Pregnancy can be one of the great mysteries of life, but with the Web, a lot of the mystery can be quickly and easily solved. Finding out as much as you can ahead of time will go a long way toward reducing any anxiety and stress you might be feeling about the impending birth experience. The following sites are dedicated mostly, if not entirely, to the pregnancy and birthing processes:

✓ **Childbirth.org** (*www.childbirth.org*)

This fabulous resource offers a home page with a library link and plenty of opportunity for discussion. It covers virtually every aspect of giving birth.

✓ **Babyonline** (*www.babyonline.com*)

This site is packed with articles (and an extensive archive) related to everything from getting pregnant to baby safety and the latest on postpartum issues for new mothers. There are even items geared especially for the new dad.

✓ **Interactive Pregnancy Calendar** (*www.pregnancy.org/pregnancycalendar*)

This innovative site allows you to enter your due date for a more personalized pregnancy calendar. You get a detailed, day-to-day account of your baby's development that you can print out each month as a keepsake or launch pad for your pregnancy journal.

✓ **Lamaze International** (*www.lamaze.org*)

This site has everything you need to know about the Lamaze method of childbirth. It's educational and useful to those still trying to decide on a method, too.

✓ **Pregnancy Basics** (*http://obgyn.health.ivillage.com/pregnancybasics/*)

This fun, interactive site features everything from baby's horoscope to information on postpartum depression; and it links to an interactive, personalized pregnancy calendar. It's a fun way to learn about your body's nine-month adventure.

✓ **Obstetric Ultrasound** (*www.ob-ultrasound.net*)

Ever wonder how the doctors can make heads or tails of those ultrasound pictures? Here, a doctor explains it to you; and he uses some fascinating pictures.

✓ **The Planned Parenthood National Site** (*www.plannedparenthood.org*)

This site offers a special section on pregnancy and related issues.

✓ **Online Birth Center** (*http://moonlily.com/obc/default.htm*)

This site is dedicated largely to the cause of international midwifery; yet it provides plenty of good information and is highly searchable.

✓ **Baby Names** (*www.babynames.com*)

Find out the meaning of your baby's name—or browse through hundreds in order to choose the ones you like the best.

E-QUESTION

How can you be sure you have the correct meaning of baby's name?
Since many sites offer slight variations of meanings for baby's name, your best bet is to check several resources and then synthesize the most common meaning to arrive at the most accurate one. Be sure you're using the exact same spelling of the name.

Birth Story Sites

There's never been an easier—and more visible—way to share the story of your baby's life from conception to present than a good birth story site on the Internet. While you're still pregnant, you can read the exciting (and typically very emotional) stories of other new parents and get an idea of what you might expect on your own "D-Day." Or post your own story from beginning to baby's latest milestone. The choice is yours!

Don't forget to create a good backup of your birth stories and blog posts. A good way to do this is to burn your files onto a CD or store them on a zip drive. It would be a tragedy to lose your musings about baby's first smile, or photos of baby's first steps.

✓ **Birth Stories** (*www.plomp.com/birth*)

Read the birth stories of other parents, or post your own birth story (once you've had the baby, of course!).

✓ **Baby Bag Online** (*www.babybag.com*)

This site includes product reviews, shopping links, a section for birth announcements, tips on safety, surveys and articles, and, of course, a place to share your birth story.

Newborn and Beyond

Once the baby's been born, there will be a whole new ocean of information for you to discover. For instance, you'll want to know what cradle cap is, or how to deal with croup. Perhaps you just want to know how to cook natural foods for your baby, or where to find environmentally safe diaper products. These sites cover general parenting issues, from baby care to teen years:

✓ **Parent Soup** (*http://l.webring.com/hub?ring=psring*)

This is a collection of home pages of parents with children of all ages. Here you'll find discussion groups, chat rooms, and expert advice. This site covers everything from pregnancy to baby naming to discipline tactics.

✓ **The American Academy of Pediatrics (AAP)** (*www.aap.org*)

The definitive source for all of your baby's health care needs. Bookmark this site and visit it often—you'll value it as a knowledgeable resource.

✓ **About—Parenting & Family** (*www.about.com/parenting*)

Another great resource with links to several other informative Web sites on a wide variety of parenting topics, from family life to product recalls.

✓ **BabyCenter** (*www.babycenter.com*)

This site is cool, interesting, and informative, with plenty of links to related sites. It contains health and general parenting tips, community, ovulation and pregnancy calendars, and so much more.

✓ **ClubMom** (*www.clubmom.com*)

A virtual community and supportive site for moms, this site includes helpful tips from other moms, a cyber shop, and coupons.

E-SSENTIAL

Many sites offer coupons and discounts for their registered site members. Join the online "club" for all of the products you most prefer, and reap your rewards with printable coupons or free downloadable products such as calendars, journals, or publications.

✓ **FamilyFun** (*http://familyfun.go.com*)

Great ideas for fun activities, from *FamilyFun* magazine.

✓ **Zero to Three** (*www.zerotothree.org*)

Run by a child advocacy group, this site has much in the way of research and information related to child development.

✓ **Parenting Twins or Other Multiples** (*www.nomotc.org*)

This is one of the most comprehensive sites so far on the challenging role of parenting more than one baby at a time.

✓ **Parenthood.com** (*www.parenthood.com*)

Here you can find good advice for new parents, offered by a panel of experts. You can also access local information specific to most metropolitan areas nationwide.

✓ **Parenting** (*http://parenting.ivillage.com*)

This site was launched by parents who wanted to offer others the advice they wish they had gotten. Now located at iVillage.com, the site has become a great resource for beleaguered parents who are hungry for information and tips on everything from what to feed their kids to teething and health issues.

✓ **Stay-at-Home Parents** (*http://homeparents.about.com*)

The emphasis here is on at-home parenting as a positive choice (although employed parents are also welcome). This site offers useful information, especially about finances.

✓ **Work-at-Home Moms** (*www.wahm.com*)

This site is geared toward the growing number of mothers for whom every day is "Take Your Child to Work Day." You'll find lots of good advice from other moms in similar situations; it also has a classified section and profiles area to promote your business. The encouraging, networking environment is a plus.

✓ **Fathers.com** (*www.fathers.com*)

This site created by the National Center for Fathering offers advice and detailed information for fathers who consider their roles in their babies' lives to be critical. You'll also find podcasts from their *Today's Father* radio program.

✓ **La Leche League International** (*www.lalecheleague.org*)

Anything you ever wanted to know about breastfeeding is on this site. It also contains valuable links to other baby-related sites.

For More Information . . .

Knowing where to look for information and ideas is key to good parenting. Many very informative sites offer the latest product safety recommendations as well as the option to subscribe to regular news updates via e-newsletter or RSS feeds. Here are some starting points on the Internet:

✓ **Amazon** (*www.amazon.com*)

Your best bet for good new and used books about everything from how to conceive to raising your toddler. Check out lists of recommended books from other parents who've posted their favorites on the mega-bookstore site.

✓ **U.S. Consumer Product Safety Commission** (*www.cpsc.gov*)

Before purchasing toys and furniture for baby, check out this site for the latest in safety information and product recalls. It's a definitive source.

✓ *American Baby* **magazine** (*www.americanbaby.com*)

Subscribe to this highly regarded magazine for parents and parents-to-be, or access articles through the archives.

E-ALERT!

Don't trust every piece of information you read online. Just because it appears on a Web site doesn't mean the information has been thoroughly checked out or verified. If you want the most accurate information, visit hospital, association, or brand name Web sites as authorities on the subject.

✓ **Depression after Delivery** (*www.depressionafterdelivery.com*)

This site is dedicated to the 20 percent of new moms who experience postpartum depression—the condition beyond the "baby blues." It's a valuable resource for you or any other new mother you know who's feeling like her depression is insurmountable. Here you find local chapters of support groups that can be extremely helpful.

✓ **Busy Mom** (*www.busymom.net*)

For stressed-out moms, here's a Web site that aims to preserve your sanity while informing you at the same time. It's a welcome (and sometimes comic!) relief.

✓ **The National Parenting Center** (*www.tnpc.com*)

Here is a terrific resource for parenting questions of all kinds, from newborn concerns to teen issues. It offers an extensive library, too.

✓ *Fathering* **magazine** (*www.fathermag.com*)

This publication is expressly for actively involved dads. After you've visited it, you'll see why these great dads don't want to be known as "Mr. Moms." After all, they are parents, too, and every bit as competent as moms!

✓ **Positive Parenting.com** (*www.positiveparenting.com*)

This site contains resources and plenty of information in the form of a newsletter; you'll also find a bulletin board, a chat room, articles, and a list of experts on a variety of subjects.

✓ **Nanny Network.com** (*www.nannynetwork.com*)

This site helps you locate child-care professionals in your area.

✓ **Childcare Directory** (*www.childcare-directory.com*)

This directory receives more than 20,000 searches a month from parents seeking child-care providers. A Child Care Parent Provider Information Network Web site.

✓ **eNanny Source** (*www.enannysource.com*)

If you're looking for the right nanny, this resource (constantly updated) is an excellent place to start.

E-ALERT!

Most online shopping experiences, especially with larger, more recognized sites such as Amazon.com or eBay.com, are safe places for credit card transactions since they use secure servers. Always look for the "https" to appear, with a warning box that you will be connected to a secure server, before entering your credit card information at any site.

Cyber Shopping

What if there was a mall that was always open, whenever you needed anything? With the Internet, the shopping never stops! Shopping online has the advantage of saving time and sometimes money. The only disadvantage is that you're buying an item you can see but can't touch; so be careful about your purchases and make sure there's a clear return policy, just in case the product doesn't meet your expectations. Always use a credit card so you can dispute any invalid transactions. Also, read the fine print to be sure of the online store's return policy. If you don't see one posted anywhere on the site, e-mail the site administrator (a.k.a. Webmaster) or move on to another, more reputable site.

✓ **eBay** (*www.ebay.com*)
Here, of course, you can find just about anything you need—from good, used baby clothing to unique shower gifts and designer baby furniture.

✓ **E-toys** (*www.etoys.com*)
Choose from hundreds of quality toys. Selections are organized by age group.

✓ **Little Tikes** (*www.littletikes.com*)
Order a catalog online, or make a purchase directly from the site. You can also access a list of stores nearest you that carry Little Tikes products.

✓ **Baby Depot** (*www.coat.com/babydepot*)
Order products online; or locate the store nearest you. This site features clothes, furniture, and accessories for baby.

✓ **Pampers.com** (*www.pampers.com*)
A great (and trusted) resource where you'll find some good general baby care advice from experts, as well as e-cards, product recommendations and a parent's forum.

✓ **Stork Avenue** (*www.storkavenue.com*)
Order birth announcements from this site.

✓ **H&F Announcements** (*www.hfproducts.com*)
Here's another source for birth announcements.

Stay Safe!

We'd all like to think that each baby announcement or posting on the Internet will be appreciated by everyone who visits our Web site or blog. But recent news stories tell a much different story.

Sadly, there are some unstable folks who actively search the Internet in hopes of finding a baby they can abduct and call their own. The best way to avoid such a tragedy is to limit the amount of identifying information you use in public places on the Web such as message forums, blogs, and even your own Web site. If you want to write about your pregnancy journey and share all of your good news with others, consider using only your first names, or use your full name without supplying any information about where you live.

Fortunately, many online groups and parenting forums require memberships, either through registration or by invitation. Most of the time, you can easily limit who joins your own online group or blog discussions. So, although you should keep a watchful eye out for online predators, you can relax and enjoy your experience in the places where the site is moderated, or where people have signed up for membership. On these kinds of sites, your own membership will be rewarded with a treasure trove of invaluable advice, guidance and support from others who have great experiences to share. You'll soon discover that your circle of friends is much wider than you ever thought!

Appendix A

Additional Resources

Expectant and New Parents

The following sites were created especially with pregnant couples and new parents in mind.

About—Pregnancy & Childbirth *http://pregnancy.about.com*

This highly informative site includes information on everything from conception to postpartum issues. Other very cool features include an ultrasound gallery and a week-by-week pregnancy calendar to guide you through each phase of your pregnancy.

Baby Bag Online *www.babybag.com*

A plethora of pregnancy, childbirth and parenting tips—plus recipes, product and book reviews, and message boards created for specific subgroups. There's also an online store.

BabyCenter *www.babycenter.com*

This site features lots of great articles on a variety of topics for expectant and new parents. Check out the due date calculator, as well as the pregnancy calendar designed for tracking your baby's growth throughout and beyond your pregnancy—week by precious week.

Pampers.com *www.pampers.com*

Expert information, product features and lots of great tips for new parents.

Parenting

The following sites contain broad, general parenting tips and advice – mostly from other parents, though some carry articles written by experts.

About—Parenting & Family *www.about.com/parenting*

Everything you want to know about parenting, family life, baby products, fatherhood, special needs, and stay-at-home parenting – plus the latest information on product recalls.

iVillage Parenting *http://parenting.ivillage.com/*

Full of great parenting tips from experts as well as other parents, this popular site includes an online community for more interactivity with others who've been there and lived to tell.

KidSource OnLine *www.kidsource.com*

Lots of information for parents of children from newbies to school-aged. Find what you're looking for by choosing sections of specific interest and then perusing the many articles contained in each section.

Parenthood.com *www.parenthood.com*

Subscribe to this free e-newsletter and you'll have instant access to hundreds of articles written by experts. You can add your own comments, or simply read others' comments in the reader's forum. If you want, you can also participate in surveys or in live chats.

Urbanbaby.com *www.urbanbaby.com*

Comprehensive resource guides and interactive communities in seven major metropolitan areas, including Austin, Boston, Chicago, Los Angeles, New York, San Francisco, and Seattle. Sign up for the Urban Baby Daily to receive regular tips, new product information, and more.

Zero to Three *www.zerotothree.com*

This site offers both professional and parents' sections, and provides insights into child development. If you're wondering whether your baby's on track, this will be a valuable resource for you.

Parent's Resource Center

The National Parenting Center *www.tnpc.com*
Get age-specific advice from the experts, who focus on distinct stages of child development.

Sesame Street Parents *www.ctw.org/parents*
Produced by the Children's Television Workshop (the same great folks who bring you TV's *Sesame Street*), this informative site offers content on everything from health and safety tips to education and community. One added bonus is an activities area featuring fun, yet educational, things to do together.

Parent News *www.parent.net*
Here you'll find lots of articles, tips and news-related content on a wide variety of issues and topics of importance to you as a new (or even experienced) parent.

Especially for Moms

Working Mother *www.workingmother.com*
If you work outside of your home, this site offers lots of great content for you. You'll appreciate advice on career strategies and finding balance, as well as the links.

Moms on the Move *www.momsonthemove.com*
An uplifting site for moms who seek reassurance that their lives are larger than their families. Visit this site to read inspiring stories of other moms who have somehow managed to have it all.

Especially for Dads

National Fatherhood Initiative *www.fatherhood.org*
This established group for fathers offers dads terrific support through events, programs, online resources, and a national educational campaign. But you can also find great tools for rating companies and local programs for "dad-friendliness."

Fathers.com *www.fathers.com*
This site was created by the National Center for Fathering, and is a fantastic resource for dads who want to be very involved in their kids' lives. Check out all of the tips and training-related content.

Health Care

Mayo Clinic *www.mayoclinic.com*
The world-renowned Mayo Clinic is your expert source for health information on everything from pregnancy to child and family health. Go to the "Healthy Living Center" for informative articles on several topics.

KidsHealth.org *www.kidshealth.org/index.html*
Sponsored by the Nemours Foundation, this site offers a section for parents as well as kids and includes a search engine to make finding your topic that much easier.

Healthfinder *www.healthfinder.gov*
Free health information from the U.S. government is at your fingertips through this consumer-oriented gateway site. Quickly and easily find links to the latest health news, events and press releases, as well as online journals. You can also locate toll-free numbers and self-help and support group information here.

WomensHealth.gov *www.4women.gov/pregnancy*
Here, you'll find Getting Ready for Baby fact sheets and links to other free, informative government resources.

Appendix B

Bibliography

Acredolo, Linda, Susan Goodwyn, and Douglas Abrams. *Baby Signs: How to Talk with Your Baby Before Your Baby Can Talk.* New York: McGraw-Hill, 2002.

Bernstein, Sara. *Hand Clap! "Miss Mary Mack" and 42 Other Hand-Clapping Games for Kids.* Holbrook, MA: Adams Media Corporation, 1994.

Bigner, Jerry J. *Parent-Child Relations: An Introduction to Parenting.* New York: Prentice-Hall, 2005.

Boates, Karen Scott. *Letters to a Child Being Born.* Philadelphia: Running Press, 1991.

Brazelton, T. Berry. *Touchpoints: Birth to 3: Your Child's Emotional and Behavioral Development.* New York: Da Capo Lifelong Books, 2006.

Brott, Armin A. *The Expectant Father: Facts, Tips and Advice for Dads-to-Be.* New York: Abbeville Press, 2001.

Carpenter, Humphrey, and Mari Prichard. *The Oxford Companion to Children's Literature.* London: Oxford University Press, 1999.

Davis, Laura, and Janis Keyser. *Becoming the Parent You Want to Be: A Sourcebook of Strategies for the First Five Years.* New York: Broadway Books, 1997.

DeFrancis, Beth. *The Parents' Resource Almanac.* Holbrook, MA: Adams Media Corporation, 1994.

Eisenberg, Arlene, Heidi Eisenberg Murkoff, and Sandee Eisenberg Hathaway. *What to Expect During the First Year.* New York: Simon & Schuster, 2004.

Eisenberg, Arlene, Heidi Eisenberg Murkoff, and Sandee Eisenberg Hathaway. *What to Expect When You're Expecting.* New York: Simon & Schuster, 2002.

Engber, Andrea, and Leah Klungness. *The Complete Single Mother: Reassuring Answers to Your Most Challenging Concerns.* Avon, MA: Adams Media Corporation, 2002.

Ferber, Richard. *Solve Your Child's Sleep Problems.* New York: Fireside, 2006.

Ford-Martin, Paula, with Elisabeth A. Aron. *The Everything Pregnancy Book*. Avon, MA: Adams Media Corporation, 2003.

Geddes, Anne, and Celine Dion. *Miracle: A Celebration of New Life*. New York: Andrews McMeel Publishing, 2004.

Harris, A. Christine. *The Pregnancy Journal: A Day-to-Day Guide to a Healthy and Happy Pregnancy*. San Francisco: Chronicle Books, 2005.

Hogg, Tracy, and Melinda Blau. *Secrets of the Baby Whisperer: How to Calm, Connect, and Communicate with Your Baby*. New York: Ballantine Books, 2005.

Huggins, Kathleen. *The Nursing Mother's Companion* (Boston: Harvard Common Press, 1995).

Iovine, Vicki. *The Girlfriends' Guide to Pregnancy: Or Everything Your Doctor Won't Tell You*. New York: Pocket Books, 1995.

Jacob, S. H. *Your Baby's Mind*. Holbrook, MA: Adams Media Corporation, 1992.

Kiester, Edwin Jr., Sally Valente Kiester, et al. *New Baby Book*. Des Moines, IA: Meredith Corporation, 1979.

Kiley, Susan. *Baby Love: A Treasury for New Mothers*. New York: Andrews & McMeel, 1994.

Kopp, Claire B., and Donna L. Bean. *Baby Steps: The "Whys" of Your Child's Behavior in the First Two Years*. New York: W. H. Freeman, 1993.

La Leche League International. *The Womanly Art of Breastfeeding*. New York: Plume, 2004.

Lansky, Bruce. *The Very Best Baby Name Book*. Deephaven, MN: Meadowbrook, Inc., 2006.

Lansky, Vicki, and Kathy Rogers. *Feed Me—I'm Yours*. Deephaven, MN: Meadowbrook Inc., 2004.

Leach, Penelope. *Your Baby and Child: From Birth to Age Five*. New York: Alfred A. Knopf, 1989.

Lipper, Ari, and Joanna Lipper. *Baby Stuff: A No-Nonsense Shopping Guide for Every Parent's Lifestyle*. New York: Marlowe & Company, 2002.

MacGregor, Cynthia. *Free Family Fun: And Super-Cheap*. New York: Replica Books, 2001.

McCarthy, Jenny. *Belly Laughs: The Naked Truth about Pregnancy and Childbirth*. New York: Da Capo Press, 2004.

Martin, Elaine. *Baby Games: The Joyful Guide to Child's Play from Birth to Three Years*. Philadelphia: Running Press, 1988.

Morris, Desmond. *Babywatching*. New York: Jonathan Cape, 1999.

Neifert, Marianne. *Dr. Mom's Parenting Guide: Commonsense Guidance for the Life of Your Child*. New York: Plume, 1996.

Podell, Susan Kagen. *Checklist for Your First Baby*. New York: Main Street Books/Doubleday, 1997.

Rifkin, June. *The Everything Baby Names Book*. Avon, MA: Adams Media Corporation, 2006.

Riverside Mothers Group. *Entertain Me!* New York: Pocket Books, 1993.

Saltman, Judith. *The Riverside Anthology of Children's Literature*. Boston: Houghton Mifflin Company, 1985.

Satran, Pamela Redmond, and Linda Rosenkrantz. *Cool Names for Babies*. New York: St. Martin's Griffin, 2003.

Sears, William, and Martha Sears. *The Baby Book*. New York: Little, Brown and Company, 2003.

Spock, Benjamin, and Michael B. Rothenberg. *Dr. Spock's Baby and Child Care*. New York: Pocket Books, 2004.

Tamaro, Janet. *So That's What They're For: Breastfeeding Basics*. Avon, MA: Adams Media Corporation, 2005.

Verny, Thomas, with John Kelly. *The Secret Life of the Unborn Child*. New York: Dell, 1982.

Verrilli, George E., and Anne Marie Mueser. *While Waiting: A Prenatal Guidebook*. New York: St. Martin's Press, 1987.

Appendix C

The Practical Side of Pregnancy—
A Nine-Month Checklist

MONTH ONE CHECKLIST

○ Evaluate your doctor, midwife, or group practice and decide if it's right for you and your pregnancy.

○ Discuss any possible on-the-job hazards with your doctor or midwife.

○ Evaluate your diet and begin taking prenatal vitamins if recommended by your doctor or midwife.

○ Get up to speed on your health insurance coverage for prenatal visits, delivery, and the care of your child.

○ If you smoke or drink, quit now.

MONTH TWO CHECKLIST

○ Start developing a maternity wardrobe.

○ Make room for your baby.

○ Create a baby-safe car environment.

○ Share the good news with your other kids.

MONTH THREE CHECKLIST

- ○ Prepare a budget to save for when your baby arrives.
- ○ Make sleep a priority; set a new early bedtime and stick to it.
- ○ Inform your employer.
- ○ Get details on your maternity benefits.
- ○ Look into a prenatal exercise class.
- ○ Decide where the baby's room or space will be.

MONTH FOUR CHECKLIST

- ○ Treat yourself to a special day out.
- ○ Begin keeping a food log.
- ○ If you don't have one, shop for a crib that meets current safety standards.
- ○ Create a prenatal exercise routine.
- ○ Find out how and when to add your new baby to your insurance coverage.
- ○ Do some basic baby-proofing.

MONTH FIVE CHECKLIST

- ○ Plan a special night out with your partner.
- ○ Choose a method of childbirth instruction.
- ○ Tour childbirth centers.
- ○ Perform a pre-baby car check.
- ○ Ensure that your vehicle is child-seat friendly.
- ○ Purchase a rear-facing infant seat for your child.
- ○ Try your hand at properly installing it in your vehicle.
- ○ Explore child-care options for your new baby.

MONTH SIX CHECKLIST

- ○ Take a day off and pamper yourself.
- ○ Start putting together your birth plan.
- ○ Think about whom you want in the delivery room.
- ○ Begin listing baby names.
- ○ Discuss your maternity leave plans with your employer.

MONTH SEVEN CHECKLIST

- ○ Make a date with yourself to relax, read, or just catch up on sleep.
- ○ Interview pediatricians.
- ○ Sign up for childbirth classes.
- ○ Sign your child up for sibling classes.
- ○ Contemplate the breast-versus-bottle decision.
- ○ Set up an appointment to discuss your birth plan with your provider.
- ○ Arrange for care for your other children during your hospital stay.

MONTH EIGHT CHECKLIST

- ○ Take five and de-stress; it's good for you and baby.
- ○ Lay out your baby's essentials.
- ○ Compare and decide on cloth versus disposal diapers.
- ○ Discuss circumcision with your pediatrician and your partner.
- ○ Start wrapping up projects at work.
- ○ Finalize your child-care plans for after maternity leave.
- ○ Preregister at your hospital or birthing center.

MONTH NINE CHECKLIST

○ Make sure that your other children's teachers and care providers are aware of your impending hospital stay.

○ Pack your bag and compile a call list for your partner.

○ Line up postpartum assistance.

○ Stock up the freezer with heat-and-eat meals or recruit postpartum kitchen help.

○ Make a plan and a backup plan for getting to the hospital.

○ Put your feet up, relax, and take a deep breath. The rest is up to your baby!

Appendix D

Baby Names
Baby Names Throughout the Ages

Top Ten Names of the 1880s

Boys:

1. John
2. William
3. Charles
4. George
5. James
6. Joseph
7. Frank
8. Henry
9. Thomas
10. Harry

Girls:

1. Mary
2. Anna
3. Elizabeth
4. Margaret
5. Minnie
6. Emma
7. Martha
8. Alice
9. Marie
10. Annie, Sarah (tie)

Top Ten Names of the 1890s

Boys:

1. John
2. William
3. James
4. George
5. Charles
6. Joseph
7. Frank
8. Harry
9. Henry
10. Edward

Girls:

1. Mary
2. Anna
3. Elizabeth
4. Emma
5. Margaret
6. Rose
7. Ethel
8. Florence
9. Ida
10. Bertha, Helen (tie)

Top Names of the 1900s

Boys:

1. John
2. William
3. James
4. George
5. Joseph
6. Charles
7. Robert
8. Frank
9. Edward
10. Henry

Girls:

1. Mary
2. Helen
3. Margaret
4. Anna
5. Ruth
6. Elizabeth
7. Dorothy
8. Marie
9. Mildred
10. Alice

Top Ten Names of the 1910s

Boys:

1. John
2. William
3. James
4. Robert
5. Joseph
6. George
7. Charles
8. Edward
9. Frank
10. Thomas

Girls:

1. Mary
2. Helen
3. Dorothy
4. Margaret
5. Ruth
6. Mildred
7. Anna
8. Elizabeth
9. Frances
10. Virginia

Top Ten Names of the 1920s

Boys:

1. Robert
2. John
3. James
4. William
5. Charles
6. George
7. Joseph
8. Richard
9. Edward
10. Donald

Girls:

1. Mary
2. Dorothy
3. Helen
4. Betty
5. Margaret
6. Ruth
7. Virginia
8. Doris
9. Mildred
10. Elizabeth

Top Ten Names of the 1930s

Boys:

1. Robert
2. James
3. John
4. William
5. Richard
6. Charles
7. Donald
8. George
9. Thomas
10. Joseph

Girls:

1. Mary
2. Betty
3. Barbara
4. Shirley
5. Patricia
6. Dorothy
7. Joan
8. Margaret
9. Nancy
10. Helen

Top Ten Names of the 1940s

Boys:

1. James
2. Robert
3. John
4. William
5. Richard
6. David
7. Charles
8. Thomas
9. Michael
10. Ronald

Girls:

1. Mary
2. Linda
3. Barbara
4. Patricia
5. Carol
6. Sandra
7. Nancy
8. Judith
9. Sharon
10. Susan

Top Ten Names of the 1950s

Boys:

1. Michael
2. James
3. Robert
4. John
5. David
6. William
7. Richard
8. Thomas
9. Mark
10. Charles

Girls:

1. Mary
2. Linda
3. Patricia
4. Susan
5. Deborah
6. Barbara
7. Debra
8. Karen
9. Nancy
10. Donna

Top Ten Names of the 1960s

Boys:

1. Michael
2. David
3. John
4. James
5. Robert
6. Mark
7. William
8. Richard
9. Thomas
10. Jeffrey

Girls:

1. Lisa
2. Mary
3. Karen
4. Susan
5. Kimberly
6. Patricia
7. Linda
8. Donna
9. Michelle
10. Cynthia

Top Ten Names of the 1970s

Boys:

1. Michael
2. Christopher
3. Jason
4. David
5. James
6. John
7. Robert
8. Brian
9. William
10. Matthew

Girls:

1. Jennifer
2. Amy
3. Melissa
4. Michelle
5. Kimberly
6. Lisa
7. Angela
8. Heather
9. Stephanie
10. Jessica

Top Ten Names of the 1980s

Boys:

1. Michael
2. Christopher
3. Matthew
4. Joshua
5. David
6. Daniel
7. James
8. Robert
9. John
10. Joseph

Girls:

1. Jessica
2. Jennifer
3. Amanda
4. Ashley
5. Sarah
6. Stephanie
7. Melissa
8. Nicole
9. Elizabeth
10. Heather

Top Ten Names of the 1990s

Boys:

1. Michael
2. Christopher
3. Matthew
4. Joshua
5. Jacob
6. Andrew
7. Daniel
8. Nicholas
9. Tyler
10. Joseph

Girls:

1. Ashley
2. Jessica
3. Emily
4. Sarah
5. Samantha
6. Brittany
7. Amanda
8. Elizabeth
9. Taylor
10. Megan

Top Ten Names of 2000

Boys:

1. Jacob
2. Michael
3. Matthew
4. Joshua
5. Christopher
6. Nicholas
7. Andrew
8. Joseph
9. Daniel
10. Tyler

Girls:

1. Emily
2. Hannah
3. Madison
4. Ashley
5. Sarah
6. Alexis
7. Samantha
8. Jessica
9. Taylor
10. Elizabeth

Top Ten Names of 2004

Boys:

1. Jacob
2. Michael
3. Joshua
4. Matthew
5. Ethan
6. Andrew
7. Daniel
8. William
9. Joseph
10. Christopher

Girls:

1. Emily
2. Emma
3. Madison
4. Olivia
5. Hannah
6. Abigail
7. Isabella
8. Ashley
9. Samantha
10. Elizabeth

Baby Names from Around the Globe

Popular Hawaiian Names

Boys:

- ✓ Aikane
- ✓ Ailani
- ✓ Kahoku
- ✓ Kai
- ✓ Kale
- ✓ Kane
- ✓ Keona
- ✓ Makani
- ✓ Meka
- ✓ Palani

Girls:

- ✓ Akela
- ✓ Alani
- ✓ Aloha
- ✓ Iolana
- ✓ Keilana
- ✓ Kiana
- ✓ Leilani
- ✓ Noelani
- ✓ Oliana
- ✓ Palila
- ✓ Roselani

Popular Names in Russia

Boys:

✓ Aleksei
✓ Arkadiy
✓ Feodor
✓ Ilya
✓ Kolya
✓ Misha
✓ Nikolai
✓ Pavel
✓ Sacha
✓ Sergei
✓ Vladilen
✓ Yakov

Girls:

✓ Dasha
✓ Galina
✓ Irina
✓ Lara
✓ Marina
✓ Natalia
✓ Natasha
✓ Oksana
✓ Olga
✓ Sofia
✓ Tatiana
✓ Yelena

Popular African-American Names

Boys:

✓ Deiondre
✓ Denzel
✓ Deshawn
✓ Dewayne
✓ Jamar
✓ Mykelti
✓ Roshaun
✓ Shaquille
✓ Taurean
✓ Tyrell

Girls:

✓ Ananda
✓ Beyonce
✓ Latanya
✓ Latisha
✓ Monisha
✓ Nichelle
✓ Shantell
✓ Talisha
✓ Tamira
✓ Taniel

Popular Korean Names

Boys:

- ✓ Chin
- ✓ Chul
- ✓ Chung-Ho
- ✓ Hyun-Ki
- ✓ Hyun-Su
- ✓ Jin-Ho
- ✓ Shin
- ✓ Soo
- ✓ Suk
- ✓ Yon

Girls:

- ✓ Cho
- ✓ Eun
- ✓ Hea
- ✓ Hei
- ✓ Hyun
- ✓ Min
- ✓ Sook
- ✓ Sun
- ✓ Young

Popular Names in Scotland

Boys:

- ✓ Lewis
- ✓ Jack
- ✓ Cameron
- ✓ James
- ✓ Kyle
- ✓ Ryan
- ✓ Ben
- ✓ Callum
- ✓ Matthew
- ✓ Jamie

Girls:

- ✓ Emma
- ✓ Ellie
- ✓ Amy
- ✓ Sophie
- ✓ Chloe
- ✓ Erin
- ✓ Rachel
- ✓ Lucy
- ✓ Lauren
- ✓ Katie

Popular Muslim Names
Boys:

- ✓ Abdul
- ✓ Ahmed
- ✓ Habib
- ✓ Hassan
- ✓ Hussein
- ✓ Jamal
- ✓ Khalil
- ✓ Omar
- ✓ Mohammed
- ✓ Salim
- ✓ Youssef
- ✓ Ziyad

Girls:

- ✓ Aliya
- ✓ Ayishah
- ✓ Farah
- ✓ Fatima
- ✓ Jamila
- ✓ Kalila
- ✓ Leila
- ✓ Malak
- ✓ Rana
- ✓ Samira
- ✓ Suha
- ✓ Yasmine

Popular Names in England
Boys:

- ✓ Jack
- ✓ Thomas
- ✓ James
- ✓ Joshua
- ✓ Daniel
- ✓ Harry
- ✓ Samuel
- ✓ Joseph
- ✓ Matthew
- ✓ Callum

Girls:

- ✓ Chloe
- ✓ Emily
- ✓ Megan
- ✓ Charlotte
- ✓ Jessica
- ✓ Lauren
- ✓ Sophie
- ✓ Olivia
- ✓ Hannah
- ✓ Lucy

Names from U.S. Locations

Boys:

- ✓ Arlington
- ✓ Austin
- ✓ Boston
- ✓ Dallas
- ✓ Denver
- ✓ Jackson
- ✓ Montgomery
- ✓ Orlando
- ✓ Reno
- ✓ Roswell
- ✓ Salem
- ✓ Sheridan

Girls:

- ✓ Alexandria
- ✓ Atlanta
- ✓ Augusta
- ✓ Charlotte
- ✓ Cheyenne
- ✓ Dakota
- ✓ Florida
- ✓ Georgia
- ✓ Helena
- ✓ Madison
- ✓ Montana
- ✓ Savannah

Popular Names in Ireland

Boys:

- ✓ Sean
- ✓ Jack
- ✓ Adam
- ✓ Conor
- ✓ James
- ✓ Daniel
- ✓ Michael
- ✓ Cian
- ✓ David
- ✓ Dylan

Girls:

- ✓ Emma
- ✓ Sarah
- ✓ Aoife
- ✓ Ciara
- ✓ Katie
- ✓ Sophie
- ✓ Rachel
- ✓ Chloe
- ✓ Amy
- ✓ Leah

THE EVERYTHING GET READY FOR BABY BOOK

Popular Names in Poland
Boys:

- ✓ Piotr
- ✓ Jan
- ✓ Andrzej
- ✓ Krzysztof
- ✓ Stanislaw
- ✓ Tomasz
- ✓ Pawel
- ✓ Jozef
- ✓ Marcin
- ✓ Marek

Girls:

- ✓ Anna
- ✓ Maria
- ✓ Katarzyna
- ✓ Malgorzata
- ✓ Agnieszka
- ✓ Krystyna
- ✓ Barbara
- ✓ Ewa
- ✓ Ellbieta
- ✓ Zofia

Popular Names in France
Boys:

- ✓ Théo
- ✓ Hugo
- ✓ Lucas
- ✓ Thomas
- ✓ Quentin
- ✓ Alexandre
- ✓ Antoine
- ✓ Maxime
- ✓ Valentin
- ✓ Clément

Girls:

- ✓ Léa
- ✓ Chloé
- ✓ Emma
- ✓ Camille
- ✓ Manon
- ✓ Sarah
- ✓ Océane
- ✓ Margaux
- ✓ Mathilde
- ✓ Laura

Popular Names in the Netherlands
Boys:

- ✓ Daan
- ✓ Sem
- ✓ Thomas
- ✓ Lars
- ✓ Milan
- ✓ Thijs
- ✓ Lucas
- ✓ Bram
- ✓ Jesse
- ✓ Tim

Girls:

- ✓ Emma
- ✓ Anna
- ✓ Sanne
- ✓ Iris
- ✓ Isa
- ✓ Maud
- ✓ Lotte
- ✓ Anouk
- ✓ Lisa
- ✓ Julia

Popular Names in Norway
Boys:

- ✓ Mathias
- ✓ Martin
- ✓ Andreas
- ✓ Jonas
- ✓ Tobias
- ✓ Daniel
- ✓ Sander
- ✓ Magnus
- ✓ Andrian
- ✓ Henrik

Girls:

- ✓ Emma
- ✓ Julie
- ✓ Ida
- ✓ Thea
- ✓ Nora
- ✓ Emilie
- ✓ Maria
- ✓ Ingrid
- ✓ Malin
- ✓ Tuva

Popular Names in Iceland

Boys:

- ✔ Sigurdur
- ✔ Gudmundur
- ✔ Jon
- ✔ Gunnar
- ✔ Olafur
- ✔ Magnus
- ✔ Einar
- ✔ Kristjan
- ✔ Bjorn
- ✔ Bjarni

Girls:

- ✔ Gudrun
- ✔ Sigrídur
- ✔ Kristín
- ✔ Margret
- ✔ Ingibjorg
- ✔ Sigrun
- ✔ Helga
- ✔ Johanna
- ✔ Anna
- ✔ Ragnheidur

Popular Names in Italy

Boys:

- ✔ Giuseppe
- ✔ Giovanni
- ✔ Antonio
- ✔ Mario
- ✔ Luigi
- ✔ Francesco
- ✔ Angelo
- ✔ Vincenzo
- ✔ Pietro
- ✔ Salvatore

Girls:

- ✔ Maria
- ✔ Anna
- ✔ Giuseppina
- ✔ Rosa
- ✔ Angela
- ✔ Giovanna
- ✔ Teresa
- ✔ Lucia
- ✔ Carmela
- ✔ Caterina

African Names

Boys:

- ✔ Adisa
- ✔ Amadi
- ✔ Imamu
- ✔ Jelani
- ✔ Kgosi
- ✔ Mfalme
- ✔ Obataiye
- ✔ Paki
- ✔ Sefu
- ✔ Thabo

Girls:

- ✔ Etana
- ✔ Imani
- ✔ Kamaria
- ✔ Malaika
- ✔ Morowa
- ✔ Nafisa
- ✔ Razina
- ✔ Sanura
- ✔ Thema
- ✔ Zuri

Popular Names in Chile

Boys:

- ✔ Jose
- ✔ Juan
- ✔ Luis
- ✔ Carlos
- ✔ Jorge
- ✔ Manuel
- ✔ Victor
- ✔ Francisco
- ✔ Cristian
- ✔ Pedro

Girls:

- ✔ Maria
- ✔ Ana
- ✔ Rosa
- ✔ Claudia
- ✔ Patricia
- ✔ Carolina
- ✔ Camila
- ✔ Daniela
- ✔ Margarita
- ✔ Juana

Popular Names in Germany

Boys:

✔ Maximilian
✔ Alexander
✔ Paul
✔ Leon
✔ Lukas
✔ Luca
✔ Felix
✔ Jonas
✔ Tim
✔ David

Girls:

✔ Marie
✔ Sophie
✔ Maria
✔ Anna
✔ Leonie
✔ Leah
✔ Laura
✔ Lena
✔ Katharina
✔ Johanna

Popular Greek Names

Boys:

✔ Alexander
✔ Aristotle
✔ Constantine
✔ Dimitri
✔ Demos
✔ Lucas
✔ Nikos
✔ Nicholas
✔ Stefanos
✔ Theo
✔ Vasilis

Girls:

✔ Ariadne
✔ Athena
✔ Calista
✔ Dimitria
✔ Helena
✔ Ionia
✔ Katrina
✔ Nia
✔ Olga
✔ Philana
✔ Theodora
✔ Zoe

Popular Chinese Names

Boys:

- An
- Cheng
- Ho
- Hu
- Jin
- Kong
- Li
- Liang
- Ning
- Po
- Qiang
- Shing
- Wen
- Wing
- Yong
- Yu

Girls:

- Ai
- Bao
- Chan
- Dai
- Hua
- Jiao
- Jun
- Li
- Lin
- Ling
- Mei
- Ping
- Qian
- Ting
- Xian
- Yan

Popular Hindu Names

Boys:

- Aditya
- Arjun
- Arnav
- Dalal
- Hardeep
- Nikhil
- Pranav
- Rishi
- Rahul
- Samir

Girls:

- Aditi
- Chandi
- Devi
- Garesa
- Maya
- Natesa
- Shreya
- Sita
- Tara
- Veda

Popular Names in Spain

Boys:

- ✔ Alejandro
- ✔ Daniel
- ✔ Pablo
- ✔ David
- ✔ Javier
- ✔ Adrian
- ✔ Alvaro
- ✔ Sergio
- ✔ Carlos
- ✔ Hugo

Girls:

- ✔ Lucia
- ✔ Maria
- ✔ Paula
- ✔ Laura
- ✔ Marta
- ✔ Andrea
- ✔ Alba
- ✔ Sara
- ✔ Claudia
- ✔ Ana

Popular Names in Sweden

Boys:

- ✔ William
- ✔ Filip
- ✔ Oscar
- ✔ Lucas
- ✔ Erik
- ✔ Emil
- ✔ Isak
- ✔ Alexander
- ✔ Viktor
- ✔ Anton

Girls:

- ✔ Emma
- ✔ Maja
- ✔ Ida
- ✔ Elin
- ✔ Julia
- ✔ Linnéa
- ✔ Hanna
- ✔ Alva
- ✔ Wilma
- ✔ Klara

Popular Names in Japan

Boys:

- ✔ Shun
- ✔ Takumi
- ✔ Shou
- ✔ Ren
- ✔ Shouta
- ✔ Souta
- ✔ Kaito
- ✔ Kenta
- ✔ Daiki
- ✔ Yuu

Girls:

- ✔ Misaki
- ✔ Aoi
- ✔ Nanami
- ✔ Miu
- ✔ Riko
- ✔ Miyu
- ✔ Moe
- ✔ Mitsuki
- ✔ Yuuka
- ✔ Rin

Popular Names in Australia

Boys:

- ✔ Jack
- ✔ Joshua
- ✔ Lachan
- ✔ Thomas
- ✔ William
- ✔ James
- ✔ Ethan
- ✔ Samuel
- ✔ Daniel
- ✔ Ryan

Girls:

- ✔ Emily
- ✔ Chloe
- ✔ Olivia
- ✔ Sophie
- ✔ Jessica
- ✔ Charlotte
- ✔ Ella
- ✔ Isabella
- ✔ Sarah
- ✔ Emma

Index

Notes

_____

_____

_____

_____

_____

_____

_____

_____

_____

_____

_____

_____

_____

_____

Notes

_____

_____

_____

_____

_____

_____

_____

_____

_____

_____

_____

_____

_____

_____

Notes

_____

_____

_____

_____

_____

_____

_____

_____

_____

_____

_____

_____

_____

_____

_____

_____

THE EVERYTHING SERIES!

BUSINESS & PERSONAL FINANCE

Everything® Accounting Book
Everything® Budgeting Book
Everything® Business Planning Book
Everything® Coaching and Mentoring Book
Everything® Fundraising Book
Everything® Get Out of Debt Book
Everything® Grant Writing Book
Everything® Guide to Personal Finance for Single Mothers
Everything® Home-Based Business Book, 2nd Ed.
Everything® Homebuying Book, 2nd Ed.
Everything® Homeselling Book, 2nd Ed.
Everything® Improve Your Credit Book
Everything® Investing Book, 2nd Ed.
Everything® Landlording Book
Everything® Leadership Book
Everything® Managing People Book, 2nd Ed.
Everything® Negotiating Book
Everything® Online Auctions Book
Everything® Online Business Book
Everything® Personal Finance Book
Everything® Personal Finance in Your 20s and 30s Book
Everything® Project Management Book
Everything® Real Estate Investing Book
Everything® Retirement Planning Book
Everything® Robert's Rules Book, $7.95
Everything® Selling Book
Everything® Start Your Own Business Book, 2nd Ed.
Everything® Wills & Estate Planning Book

COOKING

Everything® Barbecue Cookbook
Everything® Bartender's Book, $9.95
Everything® Cheese Book
Everything® Chinese Cookbook
Everything® Classic Recipes Book
Everything® Cocktail Parties and Drinks Book
Everything® College Cookbook
Everything® Cooking for Baby and Toddler Book
Everything® Cooking for Two Cookbook
Everything® Diabetes Cookbook
Everything® Easy Gourmet Cookbook
Everything® Fondue Cookbook
Everything® Fondue Party Book
Everything® Gluten-Free Cookbook
Everything® Glycemic Index Cookbook
Everything® Grilling Cookbook

Everything® Healthy Meals in Minutes Cookbook
Everything® Holiday Cookbook
Everything® Indian Cookbook
Everything® Italian Cookbook
Everything® Low-Carb Cookbook
Everything® Low-Fat High-Flavor Cookbook
Everything® Low-Salt Cookbook
Everything® Meals for a Month Cookbook
Everything® Mediterranean Cookbook
Everything® Mexican Cookbook
Everything® No Trans Fat Cookbook
Everything® One-Pot Cookbook
Everything® Pizza Cookbook
Everything® Quick and Easy 30-Minute, 5-Ingredient Cookbook
Everything® Quick Meals Cookbook
Everything® Slow Cooker Cookbook
Everything® Slow Cooking for a Crowd Cookbook
Everything® Soup Cookbook
Everything® Stir-Fry Cookbook
Everything® Tex-Mex Cookbook
Everything® Thai Cookbook
Everything® Vegetarian Cookbook
Everything® Wild Game Cookbook
Everything® Wine Book, 2nd Ed.

GAMES

Everything® 15-Minute Sudoku Book, $9.95
Everything® 30-Minute Sudoku Book, $9.95
Everything® Blackjack Strategy Book
Everything® Brain Strain Book, $9.95
Everything® Bridge Book
Everything® Card Games Book
Everything® Card Tricks Book, $9.95
Everything® Casino Gambling Book, 2nd Ed.
Everything® Chess Basics Book
Everything® Craps Strategy Book
Everything® Crossword and Puzzle Book
Everything® Crossword Challenge Book
Everything® Crosswords for the Beach Book, $9.95
Everything® Cryptograms Book, $9.95
Everything® Easy Crosswords Book
Everything® Easy Kakuro Book, $9.95
Everything® Easy Large Print Crosswords Book
Everything® Games Book, 2nd Ed.
Everything® Giant Sudoku Book, $9.95
Everything® Kakuro Challenge Book, $9.95
Everything® Large-Print Crossword Challenge Book

Everything® Large-Print Crosswords Book
Everything® Lateral Thinking Puzzles Book, $9.95
Everything® Mazes Book
Everything® Movie Crosswords Book, $9.95
Everything® Online Poker Book, $12.95
Everything® Pencil Puzzles Book, $9.95
Everything® Poker Strategy Book
Everything® Pool & Billiards Book
Everything® Sports Crosswords Book, $9.95
Everything® Test Your IQ Book, $9.95
Everything® Texas Hold 'Em Book, $9.95
Everything® Travel Crosswords Book, $9.95
Everything® Word Games Challenge Book
Everything® Word Scramble Book
Everything® Word Search Book

HEALTH

Everything® Alzheimer's Book
Everything® Diabetes Book
Everything® Health Guide to Adult Bipolar Disorder
Everything® Health Guide to Controlling Anxiety
Everything® Health Guide to Fibromyalgia
Everything® Health Guide to Postpartum Care
Everything® Health Guide to Thyroid Disease
Everything® Hypnosis Book
Everything® Low Cholesterol Book
Everything® Massage Book
Everything® Menopause Book
Everything® Nutrition Book
Everything® Reflexology Book
Everything® Stress Management Book

HISTORY

Everything® American Government Book
Everything® American History Book, 2nd Ed.
Everything® Civil War Book
Everything® Freemasons Book
Everything® Irish History & Heritage Book
Everything® Middle East Book

HOBBIES

Everything® Candlemaking Book
Everything® Cartooning Book
Everything® Coin Collecting Book
Everything® Drawing Book
Everything® Family Tree Book, 2nd Ed.
Everything® Knitting Book
Everything® Knots Book
Everything® Photography Book

Everything® Quilting Book
Everything® Scrapbooking Book
Everything® Sewing Book
Everything® Soapmaking Book, 2nd Ed.
Everything® Woodworking Book

HOME IMPROVEMENT

Everything® Feng Shui Book
Everything® Feng Shui Decluttering Book, $9.95
Everything® Fix-It Book
Everything® Home Decorating Book
Everything® Home Storage Solutions Book
Everything® Homebuilding Book
Everything® Organize Your Home Book

KIDS' BOOKS

All titles are $7.95

Everything® Kids' Animal Puzzle & Activity Book
Everything® Kids' Baseball Book, 4th Ed.
Everything® Kids' Bible Trivia Book
Everything® Kids' Bugs Book
Everything® Kids' Cars and Trucks Puzzle
    & Activity Book
Everything® Kids' Christmas Puzzle
    & Activity Book
Everything® Kids' Cookbook
Everything® Kids' Crazy Puzzles Book
Everything® Kids' Dinosaurs Book
Everything® Kids' First Spanish Puzzle and
    Activity Book
Everything® Kids' Gross Cookbook
Everything® Kids' Gross Hidden Pictures Book
Everything® Kids' Gross Jokes Book
Everything® Kids' Gross Mazes Book
Everything® Kids' Gross Puzzle and
    Activity Book
Everything® Kids' Halloween Puzzle
    & Activity Book
Everything® Kids' Hidden Pictures Book
Everything® Kids' Horses Book
Everything® Kids' Joke Book
Everything® Kids' Knock Knock Book
Everything® Kids' Learning Spanish Book
Everything® Kids' Math Puzzles Book
Everything® Kids' Mazes Book
Everything® Kids' Money Book
Everything® Kids' Nature Book
Everything® Kids' Pirates Puzzle and Activity Book
Everything® Kids' Presidents Book
Everything® Kids' Princess Puzzle and Activity Book
Everything® Kids' Puzzle Book
Everything® Kids' Riddles & Brain Teasers Book
Everything® Kids' Science Experiments Book
Everything® Kids' Sharks Book
Everything® Kids' Soccer Book
Everything® Kids' States Book
Everything® Kids' Travel Activity Book

KIDS' STORY BOOKS

Everything® Fairy Tales Book

LANGUAGE

Everything® Conversational Japanese Book with
    CD, $19.95
Everything® French Grammar Book
Everything® French Phrase Book, $9.95
Everything® French Verb Book, $9.95
Everything® German Practice Book with CD,
    $19.95
Everything® Inglés Book
**Everything® Intermediate Spanish Book with
    CD, $19.95**
**Everything® Learning Brazilian Portuguese
    Book with CD, $19.95**
Everything® Learning French Book
Everything® Learning German Book
Everything® Learning Italian Book
Everything® Learning Latin Book
**Everything® Learning Spanish Book with
    CD, 2nd Edition, $19.95**
Everything® Russian Practice Book with CD, $19.95
Everything® Sign Language Book
Everything® Spanish Grammar Book
Everything® Spanish Phrase Book, $9.95
Everything® Spanish Practice Book
    with CD, $19.95
Everything® Spanish Verb Book, $9.95
Everything® Speaking Mandarin Chinese Book
    with CD, $19.95

MUSIC

Everything® Drums Book with CD, $19.95
**Everything® Guitar Book with CD, 2nd
    Edition, $19.95**
Everything® Guitar Chords Book with CD, $19.95
Everything® Home Recording Book
Everything® Music Theory Book with CD, $19.95
Everything® Reading Music Book with CD, $19.95
Everything® Rock & Blues Guitar Book
    with CD, $19.95
**Everything® Rock and Blues Piano Book
    with CD, $19.95**
Everything® Songwriting Book

NEW AGE

Everything® Astrology Book, 2nd Ed.
Everything® Birthday Personology Book
Everything® Dreams Book, 2nd Ed.
Everything® Love Signs Book, $9.95
Everything® Numerology Book
Everything® Paganism Book
Everything® Palmistry Book
Everything® Psychic Book
Everything® Reiki Book

Everything® Sex Signs Book, $9.95
Everything® Tarot Book, 2nd Ed.
Everything® Toltec Wisdom Book
Everything® Wicca and Witchcraft Book

PARENTING

Everything® Baby Names Book, 2nd Ed.
Everything® Baby Shower Book
Everything® Baby's First Year Book
Everything® Birthing Book
Everything® Breastfeeding Book
Everything® Father-to-Be Book
Everything® Father's First Year Book
Everything® Get Ready for Baby Book
Everything® Get Your Baby to Sleep Book, $9.95
Everything® Getting Pregnant Book
Everything® Guide to Raising a One-Year-Old
Everything® Guide to Raising a Two-Year-Old
Everything® Homeschooling Book
Everything® Mother's First Year Book
**Everything® Parent's Guide to Childhood
    Illnesses**
Everything® Parent's Guide to Children
    and Divorce
Everything® Parent's Guide to Children
    with ADD/ADHD
Everything® Parent's Guide to Children
    with Asperger's Syndrome
Everything® Parent's Guide to Children
    with Autism
Everything® Parent's Guide to Children with
    Bipolar Disorder
**Everything® Parent's Guide to Children with
    Depression**
Everything® Parent's Guide to Children
    with Dyslexia
**Everything® Parent's Guide to Children with
    Juvenile Diabetes**
Everything® Parent's Guide to Positive Discipline
Everything® Parent's Guide to Raising a
    Successful Child
Everything® Parent's Guide to Raising Boys
Everything® Parent's Guide to Raising Girls
Everything® Parent's Guide to Raising Siblings
Everything® Parent's Guide to Sensory
    Integration Disorder
Everything® Parent's Guide to Tantrums
Everything® Parent's Guide to the Strong-Willed
    Child
Everything® Parenting a Teenager Book
Everything® Potty Training Book, $9.95
Everything® Pregnancy Book, 3rd Ed.
Everything® Pregnancy Fitness Book
Everything® Pregnancy Nutrition Book
Everything® Pregnancy Organizer, 2nd Ed., $16.95
Everything® Toddler Activities Book
Everything® Toddler Book

Everything® Tween Book
Everything® Twins, Triplets, and More Book

PETS

Everything® Aquarium Book
Everything® Boxer Book
Everything® Cat Book, 2nd Ed.
Everything® Chihuahua Book
Everything® Dachshund Book
Everything® Dog Book
Everything® Dog Health Book
Everything® Dog Obedience Book
Everything® Dog Owner's Organizer, $16.95
Everything® Dog Training and Tricks Book
Everything® German Shepherd Book
Everything® Golden Retriever Book
Everything® Horse Book
Everything® Horse Care Book
Everything® Horseback Riding Book
Everything® Labrador Retriever Book
Everything® Poodle Book
Everything® Pug Book
Everything® Puppy Book
Everything® Rottweiler Book
Everything® Small Dogs Book
Everything® Tropical Fish Book
Everything® Yorkshire Terrier Book

REFERENCE

Everything® American Presidents Book
Everything® Blogging Book
Everything® Build Your Vocabulary Book
Everything® Car Care Book
Everything® Classical Mythology Book
Everything® Da Vinci Book
Everything® Divorce Book
Everything® Einstein Book
Everything® Enneagram Book
Everything® Etiquette Book, 2nd Ed.
Everything® Inventions and Patents Book
Everything® Mafia Book
Everything® Philosophy Book
Everything® Pirates Book
Everything® Psychology Book

RELIGION

Everything® Angels Book
Everything® Bible Book
Everything® Buddhism Book
Everything® Catholicism Book
Everything® Christianity Book
Everything® Gnostic Gospels Book
Everything® History of the Bible Book
Everything® Jesus Book

Everything® Jewish History & Heritage Book
Everything® Judaism Book
Everything® Kabbalah Book
Everything® Koran Book
Everything® Mary Book
Everything® Mary Magdalene Book
Everything® Prayer Book
Everything® Saints Book, 2nd Ed.
Everything® Torah Book
Everything® Understanding Islam Book
Everything® World's Religions Book
Everything® Zen Book

SCHOOL & CAREERS

Everything® Alternative Careers Book
Everything® Career Tests Book
Everything® College Major Test Book
Everything® College Survival Book, 2nd Ed.
Everything® Cover Letter Book, 2nd Ed.
Everything® Filmmaking Book
Everything® Get-a-Job Book, 2nd Ed.
Everything® Guide to Being a Paralegal
**Everything® Guide to Being a Personal
    Trainer**
Everything® Guide to Being a Real Estate
    Agent
Everything® Guide to Being a Sales Rep
Everything® Guide to Careers in Health Care
Everything® Guide to Careers in Law
    Enforcement
Everything® Guide to Government Jobs
Everything® Guide to Starting and Running
    a Restaurant
Everything® Job Interview Book
Everything® New Nurse Book
Everything® New Teacher Book
Everything® Paying for College Book
Everything® Practice Interview Book
Everything® Resume Book, 2nd Ed.
Everything® Study Book

SELF-HELP

Everything® Dating Book, 2nd Ed.
Everything® Great Sex Book
Everything® Self-Esteem Book
Everything® Tantric Sex Book

SPORTS & FITNESS

Everything® Easy Fitness Book
Everything® Running Book
Everything® Weight Training Book

TRAVEL

Everything® Family Guide to Cruise Vacations
Everything® Family Guide to Hawaii
Everything® Family Guide to Las Vegas, 2nd Ed.
Everything® Family Guide to Mexico
Everything® Family Guide to New York City,
    2nd Ed.
Everything® Family Guide to RV Travel &
    Campgrounds
Everything® Family Guide to the Caribbean
Everything® Family Guide to the Walt Disney
    World Resort®, Universal Studios®,
    and Greater Orlando, 4th Ed.
Everything® Family Guide to Timeshares
**Everything® Family Guide to Washington
    D.C., 2nd Ed.**

WEDDINGS

Everything® Bachelorette Party Book, $9.95
Everything® Bridesmaid Book, $9.95
Everything® Destination Wedding Book
Everything® Elopement Book, $9.95
Everything® Father of the Bride Book, $9.95
Everything® Groom Book, $9.95
Everything® Mother of the Bride Book, $9.95
Everything® Outdoor Wedding Book
Everything® Wedding Book, 3rd Ed.
Everything® Wedding Checklist, $9.95
Everything® Wedding Etiquette Book, $9.95
Everything® Wedding Organizer, 2nd Ed., $16.95
Everything® Wedding Shower Book, $9.95
Everything® Wedding Vows Book, $9.95
Everything® Wedding Workout Book
Everything® Weddings on a Budget Book, $9.95

WRITING

Everything® Creative Writing Book
Everything® Get Published Book, 2nd Ed.
Everything® Grammar and Style Book
Everything® Guide to Magazine Writing
Everything® Guide to Writing a Book Proposal
Everything® Guide to Writing a Novel
Everything® Guide to Writing Children's Books
Everything® Guide to Writing Copy
Everything® Guide to Writing Research Papers
Everything® Screenwriting Book
Everything® Writing Poetry Book
Everything® Writing Well Book
